Contemporary Security Analysis and Copenhagen Peace Research

This volume brings together internationally prominent scholars who take stock of present-day peace research and security studies in an effort to explore their present challenges and future developments. It begins with a re-appraisal of the very identity of contemporary 'peace research', and then presents current research agendas and conceptual innovations in the European and global contexts. The volume pays particular attention to the significant contributions made by the Copenhagen Peace Research Institute and associated scholars.

The book addresses students and scholars in International Relations and members of the peace research community. Its deliberately concise chapters provide readers with an updated, accessible and broad coverage of modern peace and security studies.

Stefano Guzzini is a Senior Research Fellow at the Institute for International Studies, Copenhagen and Associate Professor of Government at Uppsala University. He previously held a position at the Central European University, Budapest. **Dietrich Jung** is a political scientist who also specialises in Islamic studies. He is currently a Senior Research Fellow at the Institute for International Studies, Copenhagen.

The New International Relations

Edited by Barry Buzan
London School of Economics

and

Richard Little
University of Bristol

The field of International Relations has changed dramatically in recent years. This new series will cover the major issues that have emerged and reflect the latest academic thinking in this particularly dynamic area.

Contemporary Security Analysis and Copenhagen Peace Research

Edited by Stefano Guzzini and Dietrich Jung

Routledge
Taylor & Francis Group

LONDON AND NEW YORK

First published 2004 by Routledge
11 New Fetter Lane, London EC4P 4EE

Simultaneously published in the USA and Canada
by Routledge
29 West 35th Street, New York, NY 10001

Routledge is an imprint of the Taylor & Francis Group

Typeset in Baskerville by Wearset Ltd, Boldon, Tyne and Wear
Printed and bound in Great Britain by MPG Books Ltd, Bodmin

British Library Cataloguing in Publication Data
A catalogue record for this book is available from the British Library

Library of Congress Cataloging in Publication Data
Contemporary security analysis and Copenhagen peace
research / edited by Stefano Guzzini and Dietrich Jung.
    p.cm.
Includes bibliographical references and index.
    1. Peace–Research. 2. Security, International. I. Guzzini, Stefano.
    II. Jung, Dietrich, 1959–
    JZ5534.C665 2004
    327.1′72–dc21

                                                        2003013605

ISBN 0-415-32410-6

Contents

Series editor's preface

In the depths of the Cold War, strategists and peace theorists established mirror images of each other and worked within what were often seen to be mutually antagonistic academic camps. Peace theorists, on the one hand, often believed that strategists were, wittingly or unwittingly, part of the defence establishment and that their strategic analysis of, and support for, deterrence theory, for example, simply served to fuel the arms race and perpetuate the hostile relations that existed between the United States and the Soviet Union. By the same token, strategists frequently viewed peace theorists as naïve, at best, or, more ominously, fellow travellers, who encouraged the West to lower its guard and, at the same time, helped to promote the fallacious image of a benign Soviet Union. Such stereotyped views not only inhibited a fruitful interchange, but they also masked the complexity and diversity of views that existed within the two schools of thought.

Once this complexity and diversity is taken into account, it becomes apparent that the research agendas of peace theorists and strategists have always had the potential to overlap, at least to some extent. So, in the Cold War era, at the centre of both of these research agendas lay the issues of war and peace. In contrast to the strategists, however, peace theorists were never prepared to accept, as permanent, the wisdom of the realist injunction that if you want peace, then you must be prepared for war. In a nuclear era, such an injunction was viewed as both reckless and defeatist in the extreme. But peace theorists have certainly acknowledged that if you want peace, then you must at least be prepared to study war.

Despite this common interest in peace and war, peace theorists and strategists were, unsurprisingly, often drawn to different accounts of the Cold War itself, with strategists tending to accept the orthodox explanation that placed the blame for the war at the Soviet Union's door, and peace theorists generally accepting more revisionist accounts that focused on mutual misperception and the implementation of self-defeating strategies. These competing assessments helped to consolidate the divisions between peace theorists and strategists.

During the era of détente, however, as tensions between the Soviet

Union and the United States diminished, the possibilities for identifying common ground between peace theorists and strategists began to emerge, but these were largely snuffed out at the end of the 1970s and the start of what is often termed the Second Cold War. With the demise of the Soviet Union, and the risk of a nuclear holocaust considerably reduced, however, there has been no alternative but for both schools to reposition themselves and, to some extent, redefine their research agendas. In the process, civil wars, ethnic conflict, terrorism and organised crime, all features of the Cold War, have now moved up their respective research agendas. As a consequence, strategists and peace researchers have found a growing area of common ground associated with a new conceptualisation of security that extends beyond the purely military dimension. Indeed, for peace theorists, security is now often seen to provide the central focus for their research agenda. At the same time, the preoccupation with East–West relations has given way to a growing interest in understanding and facilitating the peaceful enlargement of the European Union alongside the need to find ways of regulating endemic violence across the globe. It is now over a decade since the end of the Cold War and this is a good moment to re-assess what peace research now stands for. This important book is designed to do just that. It provides a vital stock-taking of the current concerns of contemporary peace researchers and the chapters here provide an excellent and representative sample of the most important issues and debates that are currently taking place.

A second aim of this book, however, is to celebrate the crucial role that was played by the Copenhagen Peace Research Institute, popularly known as COPRI, in the task of promoting peace research and, more specifically, to pay tribute to its Director, Håkan Wiberg. Peace research was very largely established in the Nordic countries, and the intellectual and political fights associated with this process as described in this book make fascinating reading. Although a relative latecomer on the Nordic peace research scene, COPRI quickly established a distinctive and authoritative voice. In particular, it provided an important bridge between peace research and strategic studies and helped to make dialogue possible.

Following a change in government in Denmark, COPRI was merged in 2003 with other institutes under the auspices of the Danish Foreign Ministry. Indeed, the institute would have been disbanded but for a vigorous international campaign by a large number of academics around the world who attested to the importance of the work that had gone on in the institute since its inception. So the book is a celebration, but it is also a valediction for an exceptionally vibrant institution that provided a home for a number of significant peace researchers, as well as the seedbed for some of the most interesting young scholars in the field.

Richard Little
University of Bristol

Acknowledgements
A cheer for Håkan Wiberg

When Håkan Wiberg celebrated his sixtieth birthday in 2002 at the Copenhagen Peace Research Institute (COPRI), a first version of this book, nicknamed the 'golden book', was presented to him. In this, former and present colleagues honoured him with a series of essays which both takes stock and moves forward in contemporary peace, conflict and security studies.

During the writing process, a change of government in Denmark suddenly threatened COPRI with closure. The firing of its staff was by and large avoided, also due to an international support campaign for which we want to thank all who signed the petition for COPRI's survival. Nevertheless in early 2002, the government decided that the institution itself was to be abolished by 1 January 2003 when it would merge with other Danish research institutes into the Danish Center of International Studies and Human Rights. In the new institute, the word 'peace research/studies' has been deleted so that it no longer appears in any of the department headings. An academic research culture is no longer assured and many people from COPRI preferred to leave.

As a result, the book got a further spin. By celebrating Håkan Wiberg's scholarly work, this book also testifies to a certain period of peace research in Denmark and a unique and successful research culture which developed under his directorship of COPRI between 1988 and 2001.

This book would not have been possible without the financial assistance of COPRI for the language editing and material production of the 'golden book'. We are also grateful for the willingness of all contributors to write in a short format (5,500 words), and for the support of the then COPRI director Tarja Cronberg and board director Bengt Sundelius. In addition we thank Catherine Schwerin for her careful and swift language correction. Finally, we would like to thank Anita Elleby for compiling Håkan's voluminous bibliography, and the team at Routledge for their very professional support.

And he's a jolly good fellow...

Stefano Guzzini, Dietrich Jung
Copenhagen, April 2003

The editors and publisher would like to thank Sage Publications Ltd for permission to reprint Mouritzen, H. 'Security Communities in the Baltic Sea Region: Real and Imagined', *Security Dialogue*, 32 (3), 2001.

Contributors

Barry Buzan is Professor of International Relations at the LSE. From 1988 to 2002 he was director of the project group on European Security at COPRI. His most recent books are *International Systems in World History* (Oxford University Press, 2000, with Richard Little) and *Regions and Powers* (Cambridge University Press, 2003, with Ole Wæver). His new book *From International to World Society?* will be published by Cambridge University Press in 2004.

Christopher S. Browning is Research Fellow in Security Studies, the Department of Political Science and International Studies, the University of Birmingham. Before his recent move, he was Research Fellow in the Baltic–Nordic Studies Programme at COPRI and then at the IIS. His research interests include Nordic/Baltic security and the construction of political space and identities in regional cooperation and European integration. He is currently working on a project analysing the role and power of margins in world politics. His most recent publications are 'The region-building approach revisited: the continued othering of Russia in discourses of region-building in the European north', *Geopolitics* 8/1 (2003); 'Complementarities and Differences in EU and US Policies in Northern Europe', *Journal of International Relations and Development* 6/1 (2003).

Thomas Diez is a senior lecturer in International Relations Theory at the University of Birmingham and co-ordinator of an EU-funded research project on the impact of European integration on the transformation of border conflicts. Before coming to Birmingham, he was a research fellow in the European Security programme of COPRI. He has published widely on discourse analysis and European governance, as well as on the Cyprus conflict. He is co-editor of *European Integration Theory* (Oxford University Press, 2004).

Nils Petter Gleditsch, Mag.art. in sociology (University of Oslo, 1968), has been affiliated with the International Peace Research Institute, Oslo (PRIO) since 1964, since 1988 as Research Professor. He has been editor of *Journal of Peace Research* since 1983 and Professor of Political Science at the Norwegian University of Science and Technology (NTNU) in Trondheim since 1993. He is head of the working group on environmental factors in civil war in PRIO's new Centre for the Study of Civil War.

Stefano Guzzini is Associate Professor of Government at Uppsala University and Senior Research Fellow at the Institute for International Studies, Copenhagen. Before joining COPRI in 2000, he taught for six years at the Central European University in Budapest. His main research interests include theories of International Relations and international political economy, concepts and theories of power, political sociology and foreign policy analysis. From 2004, he will be co-editor of the *Journal of International Relations and Development.*

Lene Hansen was a Research Fellow at the Copenhagen Peace Research Institute from 1997 to 2000, when she moved to become an Associate Professor of international politics in the Department of Political Science, the University of Copenhagen. She is the co-editor with Ole Wæver of *European Integration and National Identity: The Challenge of the Nordic States* (Routledge, 2002) and has published articles on the concept of security, poststructuralism, the Balkans and gender in *Millennium, Alternatives, Journal of Peace Research, International Feminist Journal of Politics* and *Cooperation and Conflict.*

Ulla Holm is Senior Research Fellow at the Institute for International Studies, Copenhagen, and external Associate Professor at the University of Copenhagen, Department of Political Science. Her main research interests are discourse theories, conceptual history and theory of French, European and Mediterranean security including the question of Islam, terrorism and immigration. She is a member of several Scandinavian boards. Among her recent publications are 'Religion, the idea of Europe and the European constitution' in Håkan Arvidsson (ed.), *Europæiske brytningspunkter* (*European Fault Lines,* Lund University Press, 2003).

Pertti Joenniemi, previously Senior Research Fellow and Programme Director for Baltic–Nordic studies at COPRI (1996–2002), now Senior Research Fellow at the Institute for International Studies, Copenhagen. His main research focuses on the unfolding of political space in Northern Europe. He is the co-editor of the *NEBI (North European and Baltic Integration) Yearbook* and his latest publications include *The Nordic Peace* (edited together with Clive Archer, Ashgate, 2003).

Dietrich Jung is Senior Research Fellow at the Institute for International Studies in Copenhagen. He has taught political science and Middle Eastern affairs at Aarhus University, Bilkent University (Ankara) and the Universities of Copenhagen, Hamburg and Southern Denmark. He has published on causes of war, theories of world society and on conflicts in the Middle East. His most recent books are *Turkey at the Crossroads. Ottoman Legacies and a Greater Middle East* (with Wolfango Piccoli, Zed Books, 2001), *Shadow Globalization, Ethnic Conflicts and New Wars. A Political Economy of Intra State Wars* (ed., Routledge, 2003) and *Kriege in der Weltgesellschaft. Strukturgeschichtliche Erklärung kriegerischer Gewalt, 1945–2000* (together with Klaus Schlichte und Jens Siegelberg, Westdeutscher Verlag, 2003).

Morten Kelstrup is Professor of International Relations at the Institute of Political Science, the University of Copenhagen. He was, from 2000–2 Senior Researcher at the Copenhagen Peace Research Institute and served there as Programme Director for the programme 'Global Governance and Peace'. He has authored, edited and co-edited several books and articles including (edited with Hans Branner) *Denmark's Policy Towards Europe after 1945: History, Theories and Options* (edited with Hans Branner, Odense Universitetsforlag, 2000) and *International Relations Theory and the Politics of European Integration* (edited with Michael Williams, Routledge, 2000).

Anna Leander joined COPRI in 2000 and is currently Associate Professor at the Department of Political Science, the University of Southern Denmark, Odense. She has published on international political economy, globalisation and security studies. Her current research focuses on the shifting boundaries between private and public authorities, and particularly on the authority to define the legitimate use of force.

Hans Mouritzen, Institute for International Studies, Copenhagen, is a Senior Research Fellow and has served as a Project Director for several research projects. He is the author of seventeen books, ten of which are edited volumes. His research covers fields such as small state adaptation, international organisation and administration, democracy and foreign policy, transnational relations, security communities, European integration, and the Baltic Sea area. His basic conception of international politics is formulated in *Theory and Reality of International Politics* (Ashgate, 1998). He is a co-editor of the *Danish Foreign Policy Yearbook* and until recently a member of Norway's Research Council.

Bjørn Møller is a Senior Research Fellow at the Institute for International Studies. He is external lecturer at the Institute of Political Studies and at the Centre for African Studies, the University of Copenhagen and was Secretary General of the International Peace Research Association (IPRA) in the period 1997–2000. Since 1985, he has been (senior) Research Fellow, subsequently Programme Director and board member at the Copenhagen Peace Research Institute (formerly Centre for Peace and Conflict Research). In addition to being the author of numerous articles and editor of six anthologies, he is the author of the following books: *Resolving the Security Dilemma in Europe. The German Debate on Non-Offensive Defence* (Brassey's Defence Publishers, 1991), *Common Security and Nonoffensive Defense. A Neorealist Perspective* (Lynne Rienner; UCL Press, 1992) and *Dictionary of Alternative Defense* (Adamantine Press; Lynne Rienner, 1995).

Sten Rynning, previously a Fulbright Scholar and NATO–EAPC Research Fellow, is Associate Professor at the Department of Political Science, the University of Southern Denmark, Odense. His main research areas are security and strategic studies and NATO, EU and transatlantic security relations. He is the author of *Changing Military Doctrine: Presidents and Military Power in Fifth Republic France, 1958–2000* (Praeger, 2001) as well as co-editor of *New Roles of Military Forces* (IIS, 2002), and has published articles in journals such as *Security Studies, Security Dialogue, Politique étrangère, European Security, Defense and Security Analysis* and *European Foreign Affairs Review.*

Jaap H. de Wilde is Senior Research Fellow in European Studies and International Relations Theory at the Centre for European Studies and the Department of Political Science at the University of Twente (the Netherlands), since 1995. Since 2001 he has held a chair in European Security Studies in the Department of Political Science at the Free University Amsterdam. He worked at the Copenhagen Peace Research Institute from 1992–5. He co-edited with Haaken Wiberg, *Organized Anarchy in Europe. The Role of States and IGOs* (I.B. Tauris, 1996). His recent publications focus on sovereignty, multilevel governance, and trans-Atlantic relations.

Raimo Väyrynen is Professor of Political Science and Senior Fellow of the Joan B. Kroc Institute for International Peace Studies at the University of Notre Dame, Indiana. He is now on leave from Notre Dame and serves as Director of the Helsinki Collegium for Advanced Studies at the University of Helsinki. He was also Director of the COPRI board. His publications focus on European security and arms control, international political economy and conflict research.

Ole Wæver is Professor of International Relations at the University of Copenhagen, Department of Political Science, and was a researcher at COPRI, Copenhagen Peace Research Institute, 1985–99. His main research interests are theories of International Relations (including the history and sociology of the discipline), conceptual history, concepts and theories of security and European security/integration. He is a member of the editorial committee of *European Journal of International Affairs* and several other international journals and book series. Among his recent publications, is *Regions and Powers: The Structure of International Security* (with Barry Buzan, Cambridge University Press, 2003).

1 Copenhagen peace research

Stefano Guzzini and Dietrich Jung

In recent decades, not only peace but also security has become a 'contested' concept. The military-focused and state-centred reading of traditional strategic studies has been put on the defence. The expansion of the research agenda by new security sectors – economic, environmental, cultural – and new security referents – societies, non-state actors, individuals – is challenging the 'realism' of the strategic gaze that has for so long dominated the field. This conceptual widening has led to an erosion of the walls that previously divided strategic studies and peace research. To some extent, the two fields have merged to become security studies, which covers a range from more traditional approaches (Walt 1991) to so-called 'critical security studies' (Krause and Williams 1997).

But this has not only been a conceptual development. There have also been major tendencies in world politics that have contributed to rendering this antagonism between strategic studies and peace research obsolete. On the one hand, the international system has faced a transformation regarding the forms of organised violence. A mixture of civil war, ethnic strife, organised crime and (trans)national terrorism could no longer be treated as purely local or domestic phenomena, but started to be linked with and, indeed, compete with the classical form of inter-state war. These forms of armed conflict, echoed by the ongoing talk about so-called 'new wars' (Kaldor 1999), made the former Third World the predominant theatre of war. Against the background of a rising global human rights discourse, the interventionist debate – under headings such as peace-enforcement/making/building – again blurred the demarcation lines between peace and security studies. Finally, the identity of the European Union as a 'security community' indicates a remarkable departure from the classical meaning of security according to which states challenge each other's sovereignty with military means. Thus, the process of European integration became the central empirical reference for some of the above-mentioned conceptual innovations in security studies.

In this context, the Copenhagen Peace Research Institute (COPRI) developed into one of the leading European institutes in the field, despite its precarious origins and small size. Founded in 1985, it achieved a certain stability from 1988 under its first official director, Håkan Wiberg, who oversaw a handful of people on limited tenure contracts. Wiberg had two main principles for building COPRI: basic research and internationalisation. For him, to develop independent thought and to make it flourish needed a defence against external demands for short-term policy-oriented studies. But concomitantly, in order to avoid the development of a dormant and detached research institute, Wiberg insisted from the start on the necessity of internationalising COPRI, opening it to international competition. This commitment was certainly reinforced by the parallel hiring of Barry Buzan. As the 'absentee landlord' of the programme on 'Non-Military Aspects of European Security' (later, 'European Security'), Buzan regularly flew in to chair a research seminar which socialised its members into a culture of peer-reviewed publication. At COPRI, we have all heard Håkan's disdain towards 'in-house publications'. Hence, COPRI's output was to be continuously exposed and tested on the international 'front', where it eventually achieved a notoriety far beyond its national one, and this with, at most, a dozen full-time researchers.

In this book, scholars who have been either former researcher staff members or former board directors of the late Copenhagen Peace Research Institute use the opportunity of a *Festschrift* for Håkan Wiberg to take stock of the development of peace research and to explore *some* of its present challenges. For there is an irony of sorts showing up on COPRI's CV. At the end of the Cold War, when it was finally established, it met a historical juncture when it seemed least needed. Now, at a time when Cold War rhetoric – of the early 'roll-back', not of the containment type – is again on the rise and multilateralism in decline, a governmental change in Denmark threatened to close it, and eventually merged it with other institutes under the auspices of the Danish Foreign Ministry. As the contributions to this volume testify, however, there are good reasons for scholars and practitioners in International Relations not to forget the lessons of 'security studies', which had come to include the insights of peace research.

Conceptual innovations of a latecomer

COPRI emerged at a particular historical and intellectual juncture. It arrived as a latecomer in the peace research community, when the antagonism with the establishment had to some extent receded, and it joined the theoretical debates in International Relations, which witnessed a major broadening and sophistication in the 1980s, further spurred by the end of the Cold War.

COPRI arrived on stage when both academic peace research and the Helsinki process had already seen their heyday. Peace research had emerged as a critique of both Cold War politics and the way security studies used to be conducted. Indeed, in the understanding of peace research, the two phenomena were linked (Senghaas 1972). On the one hand, classical security studies, with their focus on parameters of rational action as exemplified by deterrence theories, underplayed the role of structural factors, which might systematically favour an international arms race. On the other hand, peace research claimed that the Cold War was partly a result of the very mindset of scholarly observers and politicians alike: by assuming a permanent state of war, they were compelled to produce it in the first place.

With the turn towards détente policies, peace research increasingly lost this role of being a mere critique of practitioners and observers. It influenced politics when the social–democratic triad – Olof Palme/Willy Brandt/Bruno Kreisky – headed their respective governments in the 1970s. In particular, the German *Ostpolitik* and the Helsinki-process resulting from this had redefined the parameters of security in Europe. Furthermore, the process of European integration and the establishment of a European 'security community' anchored a different meaning of security, applied again in the enlargements of the EU.

Hence, in seeing some of its concepts and strategies appropriated, European peace research has been at least partly integrated into the professional reality of both academia and politics. Although they had certainly not lost all their antagonism, security studies and peace research have been affecting each other, at least in many parts of Europe. Whereas the first generation of European peace researchers fought to get on the agenda and to establish a presentable pedigree, the second generation was perhaps less radical – at least when compared with their northern neighbours (yet more comparable to German peace research). The younger generation could take some of the intellectual and political successes for granted and seek a forward-looking exchange with academic research. As a latecomer, COPRI had the typical features of a second generation, which, building on the old, was looking for new challenges.

At the same time, the discipline of International Relations was undergoing rather profound changes. After neorealism's unsuccessful last-ditch attempt to contain the agenda of International Relations theory, IR's theoretical debates opened up to the developments in social theory and the philosophy of knowledge. It developed an unprecedented richness and scope, from IR gender studies to international political economy. As a result, some of the classical ideas about, and issues of, war and peace shifted in their importance or meaning (cf. Senghaas and Zürn 1992). In particular, the sudden end of the Cold War begged a re-thinking of the dominant theories in International Relations (Lebow and Risse-Kappen 1995).

Hence, starting from the vantage point of a second generation during times of theoretical turmoil, COPRI had the opportunity for conceptual innovation by confronting European détente politics in the 1970s with academic debates, not of the early Cold War, but of the 1980s. Luckily for the development of COPRI, the initial research centre turned out not to be driven by short-term political concerns, but by more long-term and theory-informed research interests, which were to prove the stock from which innovative research developed. Rather than reacting to a political agenda already given, it was free to develop themes and confront them with international politics and academic discourse from the 1980s onwards.

This happened in both of the two original research programmes which got the early *Center for Freds- og Konfliktforskning*[1] going: 'Non-Offensive Defence' and 'Non-Military Aspects of European Security'. 'Non-Offensive Defence' was initially headed by the late Anders Boserup, who had been not only a long-standing advocate of non-military as well as defensive defence (Boserup and Mack 1974; Boserup and Neild 1990), but also a theorist of war and conflict (Boserup 1990). Leading the same programme, and being the only scholar to be at the centre for its entire existence, Bjørn Møller worked on German security debates and other attempts to devise a different type of non-offensive military posture – an analysis which he later connected to neorealist theorising (Møller 1991, 1992, 1995).[2] The early days of the programme on 'Non-Military Aspects of European Security', initially headed by Egbert Jahn, also had a clear theoretical problematique (Jahn *et al.* 1987), which provided the fundament for the first 'book' published by the centre (Wæver *et al.* 1989). When Buzan took over, his reconceptualisation of security (Buzan 1983) met with the ideas of Ole Wæver (1989b, 1989c, 1995). Wæver, inspired by speech act theory, analysed the logic of *Ostpolitik* where political room for manoeuvre and possible change in the European theatre was achieved by successfully moving some items out of the national security agenda ('desecuritisation').

Contemporary security analysis: a short survey of COPRI's research

COPRI always hosted a variety of scholarly directions and interests. It did not have only one single soul, even if it was the cradle of a 'Copenhagen School' of security studies and operated under the continuity of a benign patriarch, as Håkan Wiberg was often described.[3] Although all researchers would relate themselves to security studies in a wider sense, some came from policy debates, some from IR theory, some emphasised conceptual and theoretical research, some analysed security in particular regions. And most did more than one of these at different points in time.

Yet, a short survey of COPRI research should probably start with the so-called 'Copenhagen School' of security studies (Buzan 1991; Buzan *et al.* 1998; Buzan and Wæver 2003; Wæver *et al.* 1993), since many researchers worked in or around it (for a discussion of the 'school', see *inter alia* Hansen 2000a, Huysmans 1998 and the exchange between McSweeney 1996, 1998 and Buzan and Wæver 1997). The school epitomises this scholarly equivalent of the 'march through the institutions' typical for a second generation. The main aim was not to establish a parallel analysis, but to influence the mainstream without making undue concessions to it. The central concept of security would be analysed, developed and re-inserted into the usual analyses – thus affecting them since this concept no longer fitted.

True, with 'strategic studies', now often re-baptised as 'security studies', moving to a less military understanding of the subject, peace research found an easier interlocutor. Yet, by and large, the mainstream still kept the basic objectivist logic of the previous studies. It made little difference whether the threat was new weaponry, rising immigration or water shortage. It was still a given threat out there, waiting to be detected by an ever-bigger cohort of security experts and answered by suddenly alarmed politicians.

In contrast, the Copenhagen School more decisively broke with this objectivist logic, and not just the sectors of strategic studies. This resulted in a series of conceptual innovations. First, building on Wolfers' (1962) analysis of national security as an 'ambiguous symbol', it does not understand security as an 'objective' phenomenon, which could be deduced from some power calculus. At the same time, it avoids the pitfall of reducing security to an arbitrary 'subjective' phenomenon. It does so by not concentrating on what 'security' means and is exactly, but rather on what 'security' does. It argues that whenever security (or the national interest/security) is invoked, particular issues are taken out of regular politics and made part of a special agenda with special decision-making procedures and justifications attached to it. 'Security' mobilises intersubjectively shared dispositions of understanding and political action. In other words, it needs to be understood as an intersubjective phenomenon, not an objective or subjective one. The study must understand when 'securitisation' functions as much as when it fails. Second, in the analysis of 'societal security', parallel to state security, the reference object of security is no longer the state, but 'society', who securitises not its sovereignty, but its identity.

The research on non-offensive defence (NOD) was based on realism, in the sense that it was exploring alternative means of national defence against military threats which would allow for circumventing or transcending the security dilemma. The working assumption of the NOD project was thus – in line with Robert Jervis (1978) and others – that distinctions could be made between offensive and defensive, albeit not in terms of weapons as such but of military strategies and postures. The ambition was to enhance international stability through a strengthening of defence over offence. Ideally, two opponents should be able to defend themselves against each other, but neither one should be in a position to prevail with aggression, thereby removing incentives for pre-emptive strikes or preventive wars. As it had to be acknowledged that some wars are premeditated wars of aggression, this had to be ensured without weakening traditional defensive strength.

As this very short presentation shows, COPRI always had a strong linkage to a variety of theoretical discussions in IR. Although US neorealism has been further developed (Buzan *et al.* 1993; Mouritzen 1998), there has always been an equal sensitivity to classical realists, for which the continuous interest in the English School is good proof (Buzan 1993, 2001; Wæver 1992, 1998). At the same time, gender studies (Hansen 2000a), poststructuralist approaches and discourse analysis (Hansen and Wæver 2002; Wæver 1989a) have been developed. Later members of COPRI have shared similarly wide concerns (Diez 2001; Guzzini 1993, 1998; Rynning and Guzzini 2002), but also introduced more sociological approaches into the institute (Guzzini 2000; Jung 2001b; Leander 2000).

Indeed, more recent COPRI research programmes on 'Intra-State Conflicts' and 'Global Governance and Peace' also reflected those processes in the post-Cold War system which further undermined the distinctions between peace research, security and development studies. The classical form of inter-state war has receded (Joenniemi 2002), while a mixture of civil war, ethnic strife, organised crime and (trans)national terrorism has been on the rise (Jung 2003; Wiberg and Scherrer 1999). These transformations are also part of COPRI research on globalisation (Leander 2001) and the privatisation of organised violence (Leander 2002; Møller 2001b).

On the more empirical side, COPRI's research agenda has been mainly, but not exclusively, focused on Europe, its Nordic dimension (which had an independent research programme), the process of European integration and its conflict-prone periphery on the Balkans and around the Mediterranean rim. On the Northern rim, several studies have concentrated on the features of the Nordic security community (Mouritzen 1988), as well as its developments after the Cold War (Browning 2002; Joenniemi 1993), including the peculiar situation around the Russian exclave of Kaliningrad (Joenniemi 2000). Other research has focused on the process of European integration (Diez 2001; Diez *et al.* 1998; Kelstrup 1998, 2000; Kelstrup and Williams 2000), and on individual country studies (Holm 1993, 2000; Rynning 2001, 2001/2). Finally, COPRI members have researched the Balkan Wars (Hansen 2000b; Wiberg 1996) and, whether before or during their stay in Copenhagen, investigated the various security issues around the Mediterranean rim and in the Middle East (Buzan and Diez 1999; Diez 2002; Holm 1998; Holm and Olsen 1997; Jung 2001a; Leander 1995; Møller 1998a, 2001a) and East Asia (Buzan 1996; Buzan and Segal 1994; Møller 1998b).

Looking forward: essays in honour of Håkan Wiberg

The above-mentioned components also structure this book. The chapters move from an assessment of the role and state of peace research and IR theory via analyses of the changing nature of organised violence and authority in international affairs towards more focused empirical security analyses.

Characteristic for the tradition of peace research in Copenhagen, the first part includes a re-appraisal of the very identity of contemporary 'peace research' in the first place. This analysis, made by the two former Directors of COPRI's international board, Nils Petter Gleditsch and Raimo Väyrynen, provides the background for the development of peace research in general and in Scandinavia in particular. In taking up the battle between peace research and IR in Scandinavia, Nils Petter Gleditsch's chapter presents methodological disputes and personal struggles in the rise of peace research as a distinct field of analysis. Raimo Väyrynen's chapter deals with the relationship between peace research and national policy-makers in Finland, in which Väyrynen can observe a significant change since the 1960s. Stefano Guzzini then analyses the linkage between classical peace research as it developed during the Cold War and the theoretical and empirical research agenda of contructivism in IR today. The first part of the book ends with Ole Wæver's chapter on the relationship between the contested concepts of peace and security. Wæver places the history of peace research in the larger context of the dual conceptual history of peace and security, investigating the complexities that have characterised the relationship between the two concepts.

Following these chapters about the development of peace research as a field of analysis, the volume attempts to take stock of present research agendas and conceptual innovations, some of which having originated at COPRI. This part of the book has its particular focus on the various transformations in the field of peace and security studies that are commonly linked to the buzzword of the 1990s: globalisation. In her chapter on warmaking and state-making, Anna Leander puts Charles Tilly's model of European state-building into perspective. She argues that international finance, in particular, has severed the positive link between war and statemaking, if not reversed the mechanism of Tilly's model. Bjørn Møller looks at the mere concept of war that is still linked to the classical paradigm of 'Trinitarian Warfare'. In order to regulate large-scale violence in contemporary wars, he concludes, an expanded concept of 'war' is required. In applying the lenses of the English school in IR, Barry Buzan analyses the idea of global civil society. He argues that the debate about global civil society started by opening a divide between economic and social liberals, but with the rise of concern about terrorism it may return to a much older and deeper division between liberal and conservative views of the relationship between state and society.

Morten Kelstrup, then, takes up the question of the globalisation of societal insecurity. With reference to the concept of societal security as the 'Copenhagen School' has framed it, Kelstrup discusses various forms of societal insecurity, the role of the state and the role of the UN in managing the legitimate control of violence. In addressing the relationship between security and surveillance, Lene Hansen's chapter looks at the increased use and heightened institutionalisation of surveillance in the post-September 11 world. She argues that the conceptualisation of security as military security has an inherent instability with regard to measures of surveillance, in particular if surveillance is seen as an objective mechanism to achieve security. The second part ends with Thomas Diez posing the question of whether borders make good neighbours or, rather, engender conflict. Based on some work of the 'Copenhagen School', he uses the concept of securitisation in order to make the case for a transformation of boarder. Diez comes to a conclusion that runs against the conceived wisdom of many parties involved in current border conflicts.

The last part of the book gives a focused discussion on security analysis in the larger European context, on which the majority of research at COPRI has been conducted. Pertti Joenniemi and Hans Mouritzen utilise the concept of 'security communities' in addressing security issues in northern Europe. Joenniemi's chapter analyses the case of 'Norden' as a region that is characterised by its nature of being a non-war community. He revises the Nordic case of a security community along the lines of the 'Copenhagen School' in order to show that the Nordic non-war community is of cognitive or semiotic rather than sociological construction. In posing the question of whether Baltic–Russian relations should be modelled according to the Nordic 'bottom-up' or the EU 'top-down' paradigm for a security community, Hans Mouritzen argues that the EU 'top-down' example seems to be the most fruitful model to extend peaceful relations all around the Baltic Sea area. With Europe's north as a case study, Christopher Browning analyses some of the paradoxes that the EU exposes in its process of identity building, in particular the question about how much inclusion and how much exclusion the EU should attach to its borders. Jaap de Wilde addresses questions about Europe's future in drawing on some insights from the development of northern Europe into a security community. In particular he analyses European security in terms of three spheres of power politics: a geopolitical setting, the realm of international organisations and the impact of globalisation.

The remaining three chapters present more typical case studies. Sten Rynning investigates the relationship between NATO and the EU's Common Security and Defence Policy. Thereby he examines two contrasting dynamics of European integration: first, the EU's tendency of policy expansion, driving the EU increasingly into the field of defence; and, second, the impact of the EU's external security environment, whose diffuse and largely non-military threats channel the attention of Brussels in directions other than defence. Related to EU policies, Dietrich Jung discusses the particular strategy of some nationalist circles in Turkey that have tried to facilitate the EU accession of the country by exploiting its geostrategic assets. Against the background of the historical development of Turkey's relationship with the EU, the chapter claims that these circles do not understand the dynamics of Europe as a security community and that, without fundamental political reforms, Turkey could turn into an insecurity provider instead of playing the role of a security partner from the perspective of EU policies. Ulla Holm, finally, takes up the case of

Algeria, showing how the relationships between state, regime, nation and religion have frequently been securitised by the different sides involved. In order to overcome the violent political stalemate in the country, Holm points at the need for a process of de-securitisation in which the fusion of state, regime, nation and Islam must be reversed.

The book ends with a selected bibliography of Håkan Wiberg's work, which in itself reflects a good part of the history of, and debates in, European peace research.

Notes

1 The Danish name was the only official name of the centre. The English translation was a contested issue before Copenhagen Peace Research Institute eventually came into use.
2 Moreover, COPRI has used its research findings and experience on non-offensive defence in areas other than the pacified portion of Europe, such as Southern Africa, the Middle East and East Asia, for instance (see, respectively, Buzan *et al.* 2003; Cawthra and Møller 1997; Møller 1998a, 1998b, 2001a).
3 For Håkan Wiberg's scholarly work, see the selected bibliography at the end of the book.

References

Boserup, Anders (1990) 'Krieg, Staat und Frieden. Eine Weiterführung der Gedanken von Clausewitz', in Carl-Friedrich von Weizsäcker (ed.), *Die Zukunft des Friedens in Europa. Politische und militärische Voraussetzungen*, München: Hanser: 244–63.

Boserup, Anders and Andrew Mack (1974) *War Without Weapons: Non-violence in National Defence*, London: Frances Pinter.

Boserup, Anders and Robert Neild (eds) (1990) *The Foundations of Defensive Defence*, London: Macmillan.

Browning, Christopher (2002) 'Coming home or moving home? "Westernising" narratives in Finnish foreign policy and the re-interpretation of past identities', *Cooperation and Conflict* 37 (1): 47–72.

Buzan, Barry (1983) *People, States and Fear: National Security Problem in International Relations*, first edn, New York, NY: Harvester Wheatsheaf.

—— (1991) *People, States and Fear: An Agenda for International Security Studies in the Post-Cold War Era*, second edn, New York, NY: Wheatsheaf.

—— (1993) 'From international system to international society: structural realism and regime theory meet the English school', *International Organization* 47 (3): 327–52.

—— (1996) 'International security in East-Asia in the 21st century: options for Japan', *Dokkyo International Review* 9: 281–314.

—— (2001) 'The English School: an underexploited resource in IR', *Review of International Studies* 27 (3): 471–88.

—— and Thomas Diez (1999) 'Turkey and the European Union', *Survival* 41 (1): 41–57.

——, Katsuya Kodama, Bjørn Møller and Håkan Wiberg (2003) *Nippon no hichoo hatsuteki booei (Japan and Non-Offensive Defence)*, Okayama: Daigakukyoiku Shuppan.

——, Richard Little and Charles Jones (1993) *The Logic of Anarchy: From Neorealism to Structural Realism*, New York, NY: Columbia University Press.

—— and Gerald Segal (1994) 'Rethinking East Asian security', *Survival* 36 (2): 3–21.

—— and Ole Wæver (1997) 'Slippery, contradictory, sociologically untenable? The Copenhagen School replies', *Review of International Studies* 23 (2): 241–50.

—— (2003) *Regions and Powers*, Cambridge: Cambridge University Press.

—— —— and Jaap de Wilde (1998) *Security: A Framework for Analysis*, Boulder: Lynne Rienner.

Cawthra, Gavin and Bjørn Møller (eds) (1997) *Defensive Restructuring of the Armed Forces in Southern Africa*, Aldershot: Dartmouth.

Diez, Thomas (2001) 'Europe as a discursive battleground: European integration studies and discourse analysis', *Cooperation and Conflict* 36 (1): 5–38.

—— (ed.) (2002) *The European Union and the Cyprus Conflict: Modern Conflict, Post-modern Union*, Manchester: Manchester University Press.

——, Marcus Jachtenfuchs and Sabine Jung (1998) 'Which Europe? Conflicting models of a legitimate European order', *European Journal of International Relations* 4 (4): 409–45.

Guzzini, Stefano (1993) 'Structural power: the limits of neorealist power analysis', *International Organization* 47 (3): 443–78.

—— (1998) *Realism in International Relations and International Political Economy: the Continuing Story of a Death Foretold*, London, New York, NY: Routledge.

—— (2000) 'A reconstruction of constructivism in International Relations', *European Journal of International Relations* 6 (2): 147–82.

Hansen, Lene (2000a) 'The Little Mermaid's silent security dilemma and the absence of gender in the Copenhagen School', *Millennium* 29 (2): 285–306.

—— (2000b) 'Past as preface: civilizations and the politics of the "Third" Balkan War', *Journal of Peace Research* 37 (3): 345–62.

—— and Ole Wæver (eds) (2002) *European Integration and National Identity: Challenge of Nordic States*, London, New York, NY: Routledge.

Holm, Ulla (1993) *Det franske Europa* (*The French Europe*), Århus: Århus Universitetsforlag.

—— (1998) 'Algeria: France's untenable engagement', *Mediterranean Politics* 3 (2): 104–14.

—— (2000) 'France: A European civilizational power', in J. Peter Burgess and Ola Tunander (eds), *European Security Identities. Contested Understandings of EU and NATO*, Olso: PRIO Report 2/2000: 173–91.

—— and G.R. Olsen (1997) *Vandring mod Europa: Algeriet–Frankrig* (*Migration Towards Europe: Algeria–France*), København: Geofocus.

Huysmans, Jef (1998) 'Revisiting Copenhagen, or: on the creative development of a security studies agenda in Europe', *European Journal of International Relations* 4 (4): 479–505.

Jahn, Egbert, Pierre Lemaitre and Ole Wæver (1987) 'European security – problems of research on non-military aspects', *Copenhagen Papers 1*, Copenhagen: Centre of Peace and Conflict Research, University of Copenhagen.

Jervis, Robert (1978) 'Cooperation under the security dilemma', *World Politics* 30 (2): 167–214.

Joenniemi, Pertti (1993) 'Neutrality beyond the Cold War', *Review of International Studies* 19 (3): 289–304.

—— (2000) 'Kaliningrad, borders and the figure of Europe', in James Baxendale, Stephen Dewar and David Gowan (eds), *The EU and Kaliningrad*, London: Federal Trust: 157–76.

—— (2002) 'Kosovo and the end of war', in Peter van Ham and Sergei Medvedev (eds), *Mapping European Security after Kosovo*, Manchester: Manchester University Press.

Jung, Dietrich (with Wolfgang Piccoli) (2001a) *Turkey at the Crossroads: Ottoman Legacies and a Greater Middle East*, London: Zed Books.

Jung, Dietrich (2001b) 'The political sociology of world society', *European Journal of International Relations* 7 (4): 443–74.

—— (ed.) (2003) *Shadow Globalization, Ethnic Conflicts and New Wars: A Political Economy of Intra-State War*, London, New York, NY: Routledge.

Kaldor, Mary (1999) *New & Old Wars: Organized Violence in a Global Era*, Cambridge: Polity Press.

Kelstrup, Morten (1998) 'Integration theories: history, competing approaches and new perspectives', in Anders Wivel (ed.), *Explaining European Integration*, Copenhagen: Copenhagen Political Studies Press: 15–55.

—— (2000) 'Integration policy: between foreign policy and diffusion', in Hans Branner and Morten Kelstrup (eds), *Denmark's Policy Towards Europe After 1945: History, Theory and Options*, Odense: Odense Universitetsforlag: 100–38.

—— and Michael Williams (eds) (2000) *International Relations Theory and the Politics of European Integration: Power, Security, and Community*, London, New York, NY: Routledge.

Krause, Keith and Michael C. Williams (eds) (1997) *Critical Security Studies: Concepts and Cases*, London: UCL Press.

Leander, Anna (1995) 'Turkish businessmen and the Middle East peace process: more of the same – maybe', in Louis Blin and Philippe Fargues (eds), *L'économie de la paix au Proche-Orient*, Paris: Maisonneuve et Larose/CEDEJ: 353–75.

—— (2000) 'A "nebbish presence": the neglect of sociological institutionalism in international political economy', in Ronen Palan (ed.), *Global Political Economy: Contemporary Theories*, London, New York, NY: Routledge: 184–96.

—— (2001) 'The globalisation debate: dead-ends and tensions to explore', *Journal of International Relations and Development* 4 (3): 274–85.

—— (2002) 'Conditional legitimacy, reinterpreted monopolies: globalisation and the evolving state monopoly on legitimate violence', COPRI Working Papers 10/2002.

Lebow, Richard Ned and Thomas Risse-Kappen (eds) (1995) *International Relations Theory and the End of the Cold War*, New York, NY: Columbia University Press.

McSweeney, Bill (1996) 'Identity and security: Buzan and the Copenhagen School', *Review of International Studies* 22 (1): 81–93.

—— (1998) 'Durkheim and the Copenhagen School: a response to Buzan and Wæver', *Review of International Studies* 24 (1): 137–40.

Møller, Bjørn (1991) *Resolving the Security Dilemma in Europe: The German Debate on Non-Offensive Defence*, London: Brassey's Defence Publishers.

—— (1992) *Common Security and Nonoffensive Defense: A Neorealist Perspective*, Boulder, CO: Lynne Rienner; London: UCL Press.

—— (1995) *Dictionary of Alternative Defense*, London: Adamantine Press; Boulder, CO: Lynne Rienner.

—— (1998a) 'Non-offensive defence in the Middle East', in Bjørn Møller, Gustav Däniker, Shmuel Limione and Ioannis A. Stivachtis (eds), *Non-Offensive Defense in the Middle East*, Geneva: UNIDIR: 3–90.

—— (1998b) *Security, Arms Control and Defence Restructuring in East Asia*, Aldershot: Ashgate.

—— (ed.) (2001a) *Oil and Water: Cooperative Security in the Persian Gulf*, London: I.B. Tauris.

—— (2001b) 'Private militære virksomheder og fredsoperationer i Afrika' ('Private military companies and peace operations in Africa'), *Militært Tidsskrift* 130 (3): 175–99.

Mourtizen, H. (1988) *Finnlandization: Towards a General Theory of Adaptive Politics*, Aldershot: Gower.

—— (1998) *Theory and Reality of International Politics*, Aldershot: Ashgate.

Rynning, Sten (2001) *Changing Military Doctrine: Presidents and Military Power in Fifth Republic France, 1958–2000*. New York, NY: Praeger.

—— (2001/2) 'Shaping military doctrine in France: decisionmakers between international power and domestic interests', *Security Studies* 11 (2): 85–116.

—— and Stefano Guzzini (2002) 'Réalisme et analyse de la politique étrangère', in Frédéric Charillon (ed.), *Politique étrangère: nouveaux regards*, Paris: Presses de la Fondation Nationale des Sciences Politiques: 33–63.

Senghaas, Dieter (1972) *Rüstung und Militarismus*, Frankfurt am Main: Suhrkamp.

—— and Michael Zürn (1992) 'Kernfragen für die Friedensforschung der neunziger Jahre', *Politische Vierteljahresschrift* 33 (3): 455–62.

Wæver, Ole (1989a) 'Beyond the "beyond" of critical international theory', Copenhagen Peace Research Institute, Working Paper 1/1989.

—— (1989b) 'Security the Speech Act: Analysing the Politics of a Word', Copenhagen Peace Research Institute, Working Paper 19/1989.

—— (1989c) 'Conceptions of détente and change: some non-military aspects of security thinking in the FRG', in Ole Wæver, Pierre Lemaitre, Elzbieta Tromer (eds), *European Poliphony: Perspectives Beyond East–West Confrontation*, Houndmills: Macmillan: 186–224.

—— (1992) 'International society – theoretical promises unfulfilled?', *Cooperation Conflict* 27 (1): 97–128.

—— (1995) 'Securitization and desecuritization', in Ronnie Lipschutz (ed.), *On Security*, New York, NY: Columbia University Press: 46–86.

—— (1998) 'Four meanings of international society: a trans-atlantic dialogue', in Barbara Allen Roberson (ed.), *International Society and the Development of International Relations*, London: Pinter: 80–144.

——, Barry Buzan, Morten Kelstrup and Pierre Lemaitre (1993) *Identity, Migration and the New Security Agenda in Europe*, London: Pinter.

——, Pierre Lemaitre and E. Tromer (eds) (1989) *European Poliphony: Perspectives Beyond East-West Confrontation*, Houndmills: Macmillan.

Walt, Stephen M. (1991) 'The renaissance of security studies', *International Studies Quarterly* 35 (2): 211–39.

Wiberg, Håkan (1996) 'Third party intervention in Yugoslavia: problems and lessons', in Jaap de Wilde and Håkan Wiberg (eds), *States, IGOs and Peace in Europe: An Introduction to the Institutionalization of European Security*, London: I.B. Tauris: 203–26.

—— and Christian P. Scherrer (eds) (1999) *Ethnicity and Intra-State Conflict: Types, Causes and Peace Strategies*, Aldershot: Ashgate.

Wolfers, Arnold (1962) *Discord and Collaboration: Essays on International Politics*, Baltimore, CO: the Johns Hopkins University Press.

Part I

Peace research and IR theory

2 Peace Research and International Relations in Scandinavia

From enduring rivalry to stable peace?[1]

Nils Petter Gleditsch

Peace research in Scandinavia – a mini-history

Peace research in Norway emerged in the late 1950s and the early 1960s from a cross-disciplinary research environment with a focal point in sociology. Although first trained as a mathematician, Johan Galtung held a second graduate degree in sociology, had taught sociology at Columbia University and was primarily identified as a sociologist. This was also true for most of his close associates at PRIO and his first Norwegian students, although right from the start, he aimed at building a cross-disciplinary research environment. In Sweden, too, Galtung attracted several talented sociology students, one of the most visible – in several ways – being Håkan Wiberg.

In the pioneer days, Scandinavian peace researchers tended to look down on political science as being state-centred, essayistic, politically conservative and methodologically backward. Peace research was part of the behavioural revolution in sociology, whereas political science was one part history, one part law and one part power politics. The study of political behaviour was advancing rapidly, but was frequently classified as 'political sociology'. To people inspired by non-violence as much as by quantitative methods, the teaching of International Relations seemed an unhealthy combination of anecdotes and deterrence theory.

Both peace research and International Relations had its spokespeople in the political arena. One of the early initiatives was to set up a Nordic committee to fund research in this area. The name reflected the bureaucratic battle, including who won the first round: 'Nordic Cooperation Committee for International Politics, including Conflict and Peace Research.' Although International Relations held the upper hand in the naming, the committee (in its later life known as NORDSAM) published a useful newsletter *(International Studies in the Nordic Countries)* that balanced nicely between the two camps. NORDSAM became an important source of funding for smaller peace research projects over the years, until it was abolished in a large Nordic bureaucratic housecleaning effort in the early 1990s. Its successor is a membership organisation, Nordic International

Studies Association, which has taken over responsibility for the Nordic International Relations journal, *Cooperation and Conflict.*

Although some sociologists saw the conflict perspective as so central to sociology that they would have liked peace research to stay within sociology,[2] the founding father had greater ambitions. He had been instrumental in starting up a Section for Peace and Conflict Research at the Institute for Social Research in 1959, headed it from its foundation, and had it upgraded to a fully independent institute, International Peace Research Institute, Oslo (PRIO), in 1966.[3] He had launched the *Journal of Peace Research* in 1964. When the second chair in sociology was advertised at the University of Oslo in 1965, Galtung was widely expected to apply, but he eventually dismissed the idea.[4] Instead, he kept pushing the idea of a separate chair in peace research at the University of Oslo, with considerable academic and political support. The fall of the labour government in the autumn of 1965 was a setback, but eventually Parliament provided funding for a chair in peace research. Galtung competed with a political scientist and a diplomat with a background in international law. Both later became professors at the University of Oslo, but proved no match for Galtung on this occasion.[5]

When Galtung was appointed in the summer of 1969, he initially shared his time between PRIO and the university. However, this dual operation – on top of an increasingly busy schedule of international conference participation and guest lecturing – became increasingly difficult to maintain. Asbjørn Eide took over as Director of PRIO in 1970, soon followed by a long line of rotating Directors, chosen among the research staff.[6] Galtung increasingly devoted his time (at least the portion of it that he spent in Norway) to his university position. Initially his lectures were listed under the Department of Sociology, but later he succeeded in having 'the Chair', as it increasingly came to be called, placed directly under the Faculty of Social Sciences, borrowing a model from a recently established chair in administrative science.

This move was not an unqualified success. Galtung's office at the university was located in the old physics building, a good distance away from the social sciences. Much sought after as a guest professor and consultant, Galtung spent an increasing amount of time abroad. He generated considerable activity around the Chair, and generated a long series of research reports, but he was unable (or unwilling) to recruit a new group of students and staff with a long-term dedication to peace research. Had he put his mind to it, he could probably have repeated his success as an entrepreneur, but both in a personal and academic sense he was already on his way out of Norway by the time he got the position at the University of Oslo. The links between 'the Chair' and PRIO also became more tenuous. In 1976, after two years of co-editorship, Galtung relinquished the position of editor of the *Journal of Peace Research*. The string of top articles in the *JPR* with which Galtung had won international fame for the journal (and, deservedly, for himself) had ended with 'A Structural Theory of Imperialism' in 1971.[7]

When Galtung obtained his position at the University of Oslo in 1969, the student revolt was in full swing. Whereas behaviourism had been linked to radicalism just a few years earlier, it now became a symbol of imperialism and US dominance. What started out as 'critical research' was followed by neo-Marxism and eventually, for some, rather uncritical application of Marxist–Leninist dogma. Peace research became an early target of attack by the radicals. The goal set for committed social scientists was not to make peace between the oppressors and the oppressed, but to fight for liberation. Many young peace researchers joined the critics of peace research, one of the most vociferous being Håkan Wiberg's close associate in Lund, Herman Schmid.[8] Galtung let him have space in the *JPR* for his views in a special issue prepared by the Swedish Peace and Conflict Research Groups (Schmid 1968). He responded in the same journal (although he noted that his article was inspired by Schmid's argument rather than a systematic answer to it) with what became his most-cited work (Galtung 1969) until his imperialism article appeared two years later. In the 1969 article, Galtung launched the concept of 'structural violence' and attempted to incorporate the radical view of the North–South conflict into the same conceptual framework as his view of the East–West conflict, which had originally inspired peace research.

Another influence of the student revolution on peace research was Galtung's public statement, soon after he had been appointed, that no one should be a professor for more than ten years.[9] To most people's surprise he was as good as his word. In 1977 he wrote his resignation to the University of Oslo.

The succession

When Galtung left the peace research chair, there was no obvious successor. Several from his first generation of Nordic students might be qualified, but no one was an obvious choice. Galtung wrote a memo to the university about the future of the Chair, focusing on organisational aspects rather than people, but the university did not respond.

His departure coincided with a period of increasing strain on the university budgets in the social sciences, following a long period of strong growth. This period had created many ambitious young men (and a few women), but left relatively few university positions open for them. The situation invited rivalry between the fields.

Since the 1960s, political science at the University of Oslo had straightened out its act. The field now had a much clearer identity, stronger methodology,[10] and a clearer recruitment strategy. Sociology, on the other hand, had entered a period of political correctness and academic decline. The time when sociology students were ahead of political science students in methodology training was long past. The demise of sociology was not, of course, a peculiar Norwegian phenomenon.

The Dean of the Faculty of Social Sciences at the time, Henry Valen, was a political scientist. He wrote a memo to the Faculty Assembly, its governing body, where he proposed that the Chair be assigned to the department where the successful applicant naturally belonged by virtue of his or her academic background.[11] He also suggested that development theory and the study of nation-building should play a central role in peace research. Valen was a key figure in Norwegian election studies, and had a strong empirical orientation in his own work. He had been supportive of peace research as part of the behavioural revolution, but he was no friend of the student revolt or the radicalisation of the social sciences. His entrepreneurial spirit and enthusiasm were similar to Galtung's. But his forthright and populist North Norwegian manner provided quite a contrast to the aristocratic style of Johan Galtung, a descendant of one of the few families that could trace its origins back to Norwegian nobility.

Upon learning of Valen's position, many peace researchers thought they smelled a rat, but took their time to figure out where it was hiding. There was speculation about several candidates, but after a while the word began to spread that Valen had been preparing the ground for Øyvind Østerud.[12] Østerud was a former Rokkan student who had written on planning, agriculture and development theory – but with few contributions to International Relations, not to speak of peace research.[13]

At PRIO, discussion initially centred on the possibility of applying for a 'collective chair', i.e. a position of shared responsibility between several researchers. In the egalitarian spirit of the times, this did not seem as odd as it may sound today. Galtung supported the idea, but none of PRIO's traditional supporters at the university did. As a backup option, the idea was aired that no one from PRIO should apply, but that we should throw our weight behind a good candidate from outside Norway. Håkan Wiberg was one of the names mentioned most frequently. Both ideas died when a couple of senior researchers at PRIO made it clear that they would apply individually. Eventually, three of PRIO's researchers applied, as did Håkan Wiberg. As a result, it became difficult for PRIO to get involved in the lobbying about the composition of the evaluation committee.

At the university, Vilhelm Aubert played an important role in modifying Valen's suggestions for the terms of reference for the chair. The evaluation committee came out relatively balanced, consisting of Kjell Goldmann (political science), Erik Allardt (sociology) and Stein Rokkan (who defies classification, but is probably most accurately considered as having belonged equally to both disciplines).

The committee reported in the fall of 1979. A few weeks earlier, Rokkan – one of the best-known Norwegian social scientist at the international level (if not the most-frequently cited) – had died. He had participated in the committee's single meeting and appeared as a signatory to the report, even though he did not participate in the final polishing. In fact, the report became a sort of academic final will by Rokkan, which did not detract from its status.

The committee applied a high standard and found only three of the applicants qualified for a full professorship. (Two of the five rejected candidates lodged formal complaints.) The committee agreed that Østerud and Wiberg were ahead of the field. In ranking the two, the committee split along somewhat unexpected lines. Predictably, Stein Rokkan supported Østerud. Less predictably, Kjell Goldmann went for Håkan Wiberg. Allardt placed them at the same level, each stronger than the other on certain criteria. He wanted the Faculty of Social Sciences to make the choice. In the event that this was inconsistent with his role as evaluator, he said he would put Østerud a little ahead of Wiberg. Thus the committee vote was hardly 2–1, but more like 1.6–1.4 in Østerud's favour.

Although one of the PRIO researchers had been found competent for the position, it was clear that the choice was now between the two top-ranked candidates, neither of whom had a PRIO affiliation. So several PRIO staff members felt free to engage in lobbying, as did many others. The campaign became quite heated. The pro-Østerud forces in the Faculty Assembly were headed by Olav Knudsen, a political scientist, and the pro-Wiberg forces by Vilhelm Aubert. On 8 November 1979 the Assembly voted 20 to 17 to recommend hiring Øyvind Østerud. The Faculty Assembly also gave the evaluation committee a slight slap on the wrist in awarding (by 18 to 15 votes) professorial competence to Malvern Lumsden, a decision that however had no direct bearing on the main issue.

This should ordinarily have been the end of the matter. From the Faculty of Social Sciences the matter went to the Academic Senate of the University of Oslo, which more or less automatically approved the decision of the Faculty. But at that time, Norwegian professors were still civil servants and had to be appointed by the King (i.e. by the Cabinet). The Minister of Education in the Labour cabinet, Einar Førde, was a former left-winger with some sympathy for peace research. When prompted, he was willing to take a fresh look at the case, given that there was a split at the university. Eventually, however, Førde did not find sufficient support within the university for action that might be construed as a violation of the university's autonomy, and on 4 July 1980, Øyvind Østerud was appointed professor of peace research. After a decent interval, he applied to have the designation changed to 'professor of international conflict studies', and this was granted by the university.

The battle moves East

In Sweden, peace research had enjoyed greater political support in the 1960s, partly because of the country's non-aligned status, and partly because of the unchallenged primacy of the social democrats. While behind the scenes the social democratic establishment maintained close liaison with the West in military and intelligence matters, and at one time seriously considered acquiring nuclear weapons for Sweden, it also maintained a political profile of neutrality and peace. In 1966, the Swedish government had set up the Stockholm International Peace Research Institute (SIPRI) in commemoration of the country's 150 years of unbroken peace. SIPRI quickly established itself with a high international profile, but had limited contact with the social sciences in Swedish universities.

In the 1960s peace research working groups had emerged at several Swedish universities. In 1971, three universities, with support from the government, set up departments for peace and conflict research. Before long, they were headed by three junior figures who would become major actors in Scandinavian peace research, Peter Wallensteen (a political scientist) in Uppsala, Björn Hettne (an economic historian) in Gothenburg and Håkan Wiberg in Lund. By the late 1970s, the climate was right for taking the next step and establishing chairs in conflict and peace research at one or two of these universities. A mild tug-of-war ensued between the three, eventually won by Uppsala. The attitude to the idea of a separate chair in peace research met with considerable scepticism in the political science establishment. Peter Wallensteen, who had been teaching at the University of Michigan, seriously considered seeking permanent employment in the USA. In 1981, the Uppsala chair was advertised. The university appointed a committee with two political scientists (Knut Midgaard from Oslo and H.F. Peterson from Lund) and one sociologist (Erik Allardt). Håkan Wiberg and Björn Hettne withdrew their applications because no peace research professors had been asked to serve on the committee, and only Peter Wallensteen was left to fight the battle for the self-designated peace researchers.

When the committee reported, the recommendation was once again a split one. Erik Allardt reported in favour of Peter Wallensteen, while the two political scientists went for Kjell Goldmann, who was already professor of political science at Stockholm University. None of the other applicants could give these two serious competition.

Once again, in addition to the routine appeals from applicants who felt unfairly treated, a political campaign ensued. For the second time, it seemed to self-designated peace researchers, a university position in peace research would be taken away from the peace research community and given to a political scientist and an outsider. Goldmann's scholarship was not questioned and, unlike Østerud, his main field of specialisation was indeed International Relations. But he had not participated in the peace research community and was widely perceived in that community as sceptical or even hostile to organised peace research. Why, many peace researchers asked, should he now become professor of peace research, and what would happen to the department that Peter Wallensteen and his associates had built in Uppsala? Goldmann and his supporters, on the other hand, interpreted this scepticism as a desire to give the peace research movement higher priority than the academic study of war and peace.

The university nominated Goldmann for the position, based on the conclusion of the majority of the evaluation committee. But the government found a 'solution' that conceded a point to the peace research community while not running too directly counter to the autonomy of the university: it cancelled the original position in Uppsala and reverted to the idea of having two positions in peace research, one in Uppsala (with an orientation towards war and disarmament) and one in Gothenburg (with an orientation towards development and environment). Kjell Goldmann refused to apply and the field was open for two of the original three Swedish peace research entrepreneurs. In 1985 Peter Wallensteen and Björn Hettne assumed the chairs in Uppsala and Gothenburg respectively.

That left Lund without a professor of peace research and Håkan Wiberg in limbo. Wiberg had meanwhile become professor of sociology in Lund, while continuing as the senior person in the Department of Peace and Conflict Research, which eventually became Lund Peace Research Institute (LuPRI). He had written the leading Scandinavian textbook in peace research (Wiberg 1976), but the prospects of a peace research chair in Lund seemed dim.

In 1983, the so-called security-policy majority in the Danish Parliament (a left–liberal alliance) had granted funds for the establishment of an independent peace research centre to be located at Copenhagen University. This decision was taken against the wish of the non-socialist cabinet (in which the liberals also participated).[14] In the worst tradition of Danish peace research, the Centre was a hotbed of factionalism. Eventually, the Board decided that it needed a Director – prior to this, the Centre had been organised around two projects with autonomous project directors. One of the applicants for the position of Director was Håkan Wiberg. He was the unanimous choice of the evaluation committee, but liberal Danish procedures with regard to complaints permitted another candidate to hold up his appointment for a year. He eventually assumed the position in August 1988 and quickly steered COPRI (as it came to be called) into smoother waters.

Aftermath

The controversies over the filling of the chairs in Oslo and Uppsala were not trivial academic squabbles. They were fuelled by strong and legitimate disagreements about matters academic, methodological and political. Yet they also became personal, and the decisions left vestiges of bitterness. When the first pure conservative government in over fifty years assumed power in Oslo in the autumn of 1981, there was some fear that PRIO would pay a price. Indeed, the government soon appointed a committee to look into the organisation of peace research and International Relations, largely manned by political scientists from the University of Oslo. However, the committee produced a balanced and thoughtful report (NOU 1985). While critical of some practices in PRIO's past, there were few specific recommendations that affected the institute's current operations. When the leadership of PRIO was reorganised in 1986, with a stronger Director and more power to the Board, and its equal-salary scheme abolished, this was due more to a general retreat away from 1960s idealism and 1970s radicalism inside the institute than as a response to outside pressure. Although Østerud wrote a few articles that were seen as critical of organised peace research, the principal actors on both sides generally adopted a non-confrontational style. In 1991 Øyvind Østerud joined the editorial committee of the *Journal of Peace Research,* and in 1997 he became an Associate Editor. A factor that few if any foresaw in the early 1980s, of course, was that within a decade of the university battles, the Cold War would end. The political overtones of the debate about peace research largely evaporated.

By that time, too, political science had become a much more important recruiting ground for peace research than sociology or any other discipline. While peace research has retained some of its cross-disciplinary character, its main disciplinary foundation is now firmly in political science and International Relations. In the *JPR,* 40 per cent of the space in the first five volumes (1964–8) was taken up by sociologists and only 27 per cent by political scientists; in the next five-year period, political science was ahead of sociology, and soon it became dominant (Gleditsch 1989). In the eleven-year period, 1991–2001, nearly two-thirds of the articles were written by political scientists. The journal's current editor and its founder, both sociologists with not even a minor degree in political science, had now become professors of political science.

In Sweden the wounds took a little longer to heal. But by the early 1990s, peace research had gained respectability within Uppsala University and had generally friendly relations with the political science department. When a second chair of conflict and peace research was advertised in Uppsala at the end of 2001, revanchism was not on the agenda.

The organised peace researchers were correct in assuming that it *did* make a difference in organisational terms who was going to fill the positions of professor of peace research. Øyvind Østerud became a high-profile professor of political science, author of a remarkable textbook (Østerud 1991) and head of a major public commission to study power and democracy in Norway. Today, hardly anyone would think of him as professor of anything but political science. As a separate entity, the University of Oslo chair in peace research has vanished. On the other hand, in 2000, Øyvind Østerud served on the committee to evaluate the academic merits of the applicants for the position as the new Director of PRIO, and in 2002 he collaborated with the new Director, Stein Tønnesson, among others, on a committee to establish an MA degree in peace and conflict studies at Oslo University.

In Uppsala, Peter Wallensteen has built a strong department, with an extensive teaching program, from introductory courses to PhD training.[15] In Copenhagen, the Centre was transformed into COPRI and, under Håkan Wiberg's leadership, went from strength to strength, gaining repeated high marks from evaluation committees. In Uppsala, Håkan played an important role as a guest lecturer and member of doctoral committees. Kjell Goldmann, still a respected scholar in International Relations, remained in Stockholm.

Remarkably, during the long period of strife, a few people seemed to rise above the battle and stay on speaking terms with both sides. Håkan Wiberg was one of these. While he was one of the chief contestants for the peace research chair in Oslo, he retained the respect of both sides in the struggle. While he led LuPRI, he was able to assemble a pluralistic and highly competent set of associates, including Wilhelm Agrell and Jan Øberg. Håkan had retired from the formal leadership of LuPRI when he became professor of sociology. When he moved to Copenhagen, Agrell and Øberg soon drifted apart.

The old divisions have now largely been overcome. It may be too early to speak of stable peace between peace researchers and International Relations scholars. But the risk of the enduring rivalry erupting into another hot dispute seems remote. As a sociologist directing an institute dominated by political scientists, Håkan Wiberg played an important part in the peaceful transition.

Today, two new fault lines are appearing in peace research. Critiques of positivism are once again in vogue, with opponents ranging from social constructivism to postmodernism. In this debate, Øyvind Østerud has emerged as a leading spokesman for some of the ideals that inspired peace research in the pioneer days, dismissing the moderate version of dissident thought as trivial and the radical postmodernism as self-defeating and contradictory (Østerud 1996). In this role as champion of traditional academic values, he has been attacked in language reminiscent of the charges levelled against 'liberal' peace researchers in the late 1960s.

A second fault line has emerged between liberal and radical peace researchers, again to some extent reminiscent of the late 1960s. The idea of a democratic peace was born within peace research, but has been embraced by a much wider community of scholars and practitioners. It has also gathered substantial opposition from a loose coalition of realists and radicals. The idea of a wider liberal peace, built on democracy, international trade and international organisation, has brought some peace researchers into an alliance with market liberals. Radical peace researchers have raised the spectre of globalisation as promoting democratic decay, inequality and violence. Liberal peace researchers see globalisation as generally promoting democracy, prosperity and peace. The political overtones are strong. The activist segment that has always been close to the peace research movement feels betrayed by the liberals embracing ideologies that are associated with the world's number one hegemonic power.[16] Many articles in recent volumes of *JPR* have been sympathetic to the liberal position; the journal's founder is very critical of it.

On the first issue, there is little question that Håkan Wiberg largely shares Østerud's academic orientation. Yet, remarkably, he has served as Director of an institute that has been the host of one of the strongest milieus of critical security studies, directed by Barry Buzan and Ole Wæver and emerging under the demanding name of the 'Copenhagen School'. One can only speculate whether there would have been an Oslo School, a Lund School or an Uppsala School had Håkan Wiberg been given the opportunity for leadership elsewhere. But for COPRI, his Danish exile proved to be a blessing.[17] Paradoxically, after COPRI had gained an international standing, it was rewarded with a threat to close it down by a hostile new government in Denmark. This outcome was averted, but at the time of writing, it remains uncertain how much of COPRI's identity will remain in the new Institute for International Studies operating under the auspices of the Danish Foreign Ministry.

On the second issue, the jury is still out. My sense is that Håkan, while critical of some of the liberal positions, is more anxious than most of the critics to understand them and to engage them on their merits. He holds strong political views on the former Yugoslavia and other matters, but he does not let such views totally dominate his agenda. He brought to COPRI the secretariat of the International Peace Research Association, an organisation with a strong activist orientation, in the hope of strengthening its academic orientation. With his great intellectual capacity and in continuation of his traditional role as a respected figure rising somehow above the fray, Håkan could make an important contribution to bringing the academic and activist objections to the liberal model into the mainstream research agenda. That would certainly be my hope now that he is free of the tremendous administrative burden that he carried for over a dozen years.

Notes

1 This account is based in part on notes made in the aftermath of the struggle over the Oslo and Uppsala peace research chairs in the early 1980s, on *JPR's* archive and database, on PRIO's archive of newspaper clippings, as well as information and comments – some complimentary, some critical – from most of the major actors discussed in this chapter. I have also received comments from several colleagues. I am grateful to all those who took the time to read the manuscript. Because of the personal nature of some of my remarks, I strongly emphasise that no one else is responsible for my selection of informa-

tion or my judgements. For other histories of the early years of peace research, see Wallensteen (1988, 2001) and Wiberg (1988).

2 The most prominent example being Vilhelm Aubert, who himself contributed to the literature on conflict.

3 In an intermediate stage, PRIO was named an institute in 1964 (Peace Research Institute, Oslo), got its abbreviation (PRIO), and its own premises, and obtained its own public funding, but remained a section of ISR. In 1966 it became a fully independent institute, with its own board, and with 'International' added to the name, initiating lasting confusion about the abbreviation.

4 Most Norwegian university departments had only one professor and the availability of a second chair in sociology was not an opportunity to be easily dismissed. Eventually, Sverre Lysgaard won this appointment.

5 An engagingly subjective account of this period can be found in Galtung (2000).

6 A system that lasted until 1986.

7 By 1980, Galtung was by a wide margin the most frequently cited Norwegian social scientist according to the data in *Social Sciences Citation Index* (Gleditsch *et al.* 1980). At that time, his imperialism article made up about 25 per cent of his citations, and was probably one of the most widely-cited articles in peace research. Until 1993, Galtung remained in the top position (but was overtaken a few years later by Jon Elster) and his *JPR* articles in the period 1964–71 remained his most widely cited works. Cf. Gleditsch (1993a, b).

8 Frequent visitors to Oslo in the late 1960s, the two became known as 'Laurel and Hardy'. The joke is more comprehensible when recalling that the Norwegian names of these two characters are Helan ('the whole') and Halvan ('the half'). Schmid later moved towards the traditional (more or less pro-Moscow) communist party, while many of the other rebels went to the Maoists.

9 Interview in *Dagbladet*, 2 June 1969.

10 Its leading methodologist, Ottar Hellevik, was a Galtung student with a graduate degree in sociology.

11 *Notat til Fakultetsrådet* 8 December 1977.

12 Henry Valen denies that he had Østerud in mind at this early stage (pers. comm., May 2002).

13 His major work at the time was Østerud (1978), a masterful synthesis of development theory.

14 A more famous (or infamous, if you like) example of the schizophrenic character of Danish politics during this period, with the liberals supporting the Government on most domestic issues, but voting with the opposition on security policy, was the string of Danish footnotes to NATO communiqués about the double-track decision and other aspects of nuclear policy.

15 Cf. the Department's webpage at www.pcr.uu.se.

16 For a survey of the academic debate on these issues, see Schneider *et al.* (2003).

17 For a history of COPRI, see COPRI (2002).

References

COPRI (2002) *Final report 1985–2002*. Working papers (40). Copenhagen: Copenhagen Peace Research Institute.

Galtung, Johan (1969) 'Violence, peace and peace research', *Journal of Peace Research* 6 (3): 167–91.

—— (1971) 'A structural theory of imperialism', *Journal of Peace Research* 8 (2): 81–117.

—— (2000) *Johan uten land. På fredsveien gjennom verden*, Oslo: Aschehoug.

Gleditsch, Nils Petter (1980) *Johan Galtung. A Bibliography of his Scholarly and Popular Writings 1951–1980*, Oslo: PRIO.

—— (1989) 'Bibliography of the *Journal of Peace Research* 1964–88. With tables on authorship, circulation, and citations', *PRIO Report* (1).

—— (1993a) 'Gründerens rolle' ('The Role of the Founder'), *Forskningspolitikk* 16 (2): 10–11.

—— (1993b) 'The most-cited articles in *JPR*', *Journal of Peace Research* 30 (4): 445–9.

NOU (1985) *Forskning om sikkerhets- og fredsspørsmål og internasjonale forhold. Innstilling fra et utvalg oppnevnt ved kongelig resolusjon av 17. september 1982, avgitt til Kultur- og vitenskapsdepartementet 25. april 1985*, Norges offentlige utredninger, 1985/17, Oslo: Norwegian University Press.

Østerud, Øyrind (1978) *Utviklingsteori og historisk endring*, Oslo: Gyldendal.

—— (1991) *Statsvitenskap: Innføring i politisk analyse*, Oslo: Norwegian University Press, second edition, 1996.

—— (1996) 'Antinomies of post-modernism in international studies', *Journal of Peace Research* 33 (4): 385–90 (see also debate in *JPR* 34(3).

Schmid, Herman (1968) 'Politics and peace research', *Journal of Peace Research* 5 (3): 217–32.

Schneider, Gerald, Katherine Barbieri and Nils Petter Gleditsch (eds) (2003) *Globalization and Armed Conflict*, Boulder, CO: Rowman & Littlefield.

Wallensteen, Peter (1988) 'The origins of peace research', in Peter Wallensteen (ed.), *Peace Research: Achievements and Challenges*, Boulder, CO: Westview: 7–29.

—— (2001) 'The growing peace research agenda', Occasional Paper 24: 4, Joan B. Kroc Institute for International Peace Studies, University of Notre Dame, www.nd.edu/~krocinst/ocpapers/index.html.

Wiberg, Håkan (1976) *Konfliktteori och fredsforskning*, Stockholm: Scandinavian University Books, [Second edition 1990.]

—— (1988) 'The peace research movement', in Peter Wallensteen (ed.), *Peace Research: Achievements and Challenges*, Boulder, CO: Westview: 30–53.

3 Peace research between idealism and realism

Fragments of a Finnish debate[1]

Raimo Väyrynen

Norman Davies argues that the great divide in Polish intellectual life has been between the 'romantic–insurrectionary–idealist camp' on the one side and the 'positivist–conciliatory–realist camp' on the other. Polish positivism, following the ideas of Comte and Spencer, was concerned with ways to make Poland stronger and, over time, ready for an independent statehood. For romantics, this approach was too fainthearted and conciliatory, prompting them to demand immediate action. This omnipresent intellectual divide also reflected, as so often happens, generational differences; in Poland, the Romantics dominated roughly between 1830–64 and again after 1905, while the positivist generation was ascendant between 1864–1905 (Davies 2001: 179–86).

A similar bifurcation into two camps also existed in Finnish politics prior to the First World War; the realists wanted to accommodate Russian demands and defend the status quo by legal arguments, while the 'insurrectionaries' called for political and even military action to liberate the country. In Finland, however, historical realists, such as Danielson-Kalmari and Paasikivi, always had an upper hand, while the 'insurrectionaries' never had, except for very brief periods, major intellectual or ideological influence.

It is in this context of an attack on established realism that the clashes around peace research in Finland have usually been perceived, also among its protagonists. Yet peace research fits neither the 'romantic–insurrectionary' idealism of nineteenth-century Poland nor the status-quo idealism of the inter-war period (Carr 1946). As the following will show, peace research in Finland included both idealist and realist insights and relied on a positivist understanding of science. This chapter will therefore argue that the clashes which peace research prompted in Finland in the past are not reducible to such theoretical divides. Rather, they happened for political and generational reasons, since peace research was perceived by established foreign and security policy circles as a kind of fifth column of the left in academia with which to compete for President Kekkonen's soul. By the 1990s, however, such clashes faded out.

Finnish peace research and the theoretical realism–idealism divide

The institutionalisation of peace research happened in the 1960s. Although there were peace research groups in Turku and Helsinki, most practitioners of the field, then in their twenties and early thirties, were active in Tampere. They were organised first as the Tampere Peace Research Group, established in 1968, with its own office in the city centre, and then in the Tampere Peace Research Institute (TAPRI). The Institute was set up in 1970 under the auspices of the Finnish Ministry of Education (for a history of Finnish peace research, see Vesa 1980, 1984).

The stereotype view on the clash between peace researchers and security analysts more generally is that it simply replays the classical idealism–realism divide. And indeed, this often was the self-perception of the protagonists. But, as this section will show, the story is not that simple. Applying the categories of Polish intellectual history, it will claim that Finnish peace research has been both 'romantic–idealist' and 'positivist–conciliatory', a fact overlooked due to a simplistic reception of the realist–idealist debate in Finland.

A stereotyped debate

Realism in Finland had different roots and orientations. The leading Finnish realists in IR were Risto Hyvärinen, Kullervo Killinen and Keijo Korhonen. They had all studied in the United States, but only Korhonen held, for a while, a permanent professorship at the University of Helsinki. Hyvärinen and Killinen had a military background. Hyvärinen and Korhonen were employed by the Finnish Foreign Ministry – and Korhonen was briefly a Foreign Minister in the 1970s – while Killinen was active in private business. Hyvärinen's realism had theoretical roots, while Korhonen was inclined to historical realism and Killinen to geopolitical doctrines (Killinen 1964).[2]

Yet Finnish realists did tend to agree on their critique of peace researchers who were accused of having rose-coloured glasses. According to the critics, peace researchers were too fainthearted or ideologically distorted to face the 'real' reality, which is nasty and brutish due to the rivalries among the great powers. As the historical calamities experienced by small powers show, they are at the mercy of these rivalries unless they pursue a kind of small-power realism.

Undoubtedly, Finnish peace research had some idealistic elements, if by that we mean a normative orientation to international troubles and a belief that they can be mitigated by appropriate ideas and policies. The key objectives in early Finnish peace research were nuclear disarmament, the East–West détente and a greater equity in North–South relations.

Yet, if we apply the categories of Polish intellectual history, these were by no means 'insurrectionary' goals and did not foster any 'revolutionary peace research', with which some Swedish researchers briefly flirted. In fact, these rather conventional values reflected the fact that many Finnish peace researchers became members of the Social Democratic Party at the turn of the 1970s. This left-leaning image of peace research was reinforced by the fact that some of its other key figures were close to the non-Communist People's Democrats. Conservatives were reluctant to shed that image even if there were several prominent Swedish-speaking liberal academics among the supporters of peace research (including Erik Allardt, Göran von Bonsdorff, and Jan-Magnus Jansson).

As much as peace research was never really 'insurrectionary' in Finland, realism was also traditionally divided into two wings. Osmo Apunen and Helena Rytövuori have argued that one can find in Finnish scholarly debates both emancipatory and repressive concepts of power which are also reflected in the specific modes of action recommended to assure the survival of the country. In other words, they have shown that, in traditional historical and political scholarship in Finland, one can find realism divided, to an extent, into two wings. However, there has not been any kind of an alignment between the 'progressive' traditionalists and peace researchers; rather, these two approaches have tended to keep a distinct cognitive distance (Apunen and Rytövuori 1982).

Consequently, the Finnish case is interesting because, while the realism–idealism debate had formative influences, peace research as practised cannot be neatly placed in either of the standard intellectual camps. It has cut across the simple ideological divisions and combined elements that, in some respects, seem to be antithetical to each other.

The simplistic reception of the debate

This section challenges the stereotypical differentiation between idealism and realism that was so common in the debates between early peace researchers and its conservative opponents. It claims that this resulted from an overly simplistic reception of the realism–idealism debate.

The concepts of realism and idealism were not, of course, brewed in Finland, but imported from international sources. With hindsight, though, it looks as if the Finnish usage of concepts was rather vulgar; they were often used as labels showing that the other side was not quite sane. There were few interventions in the public debate that would have convinced the audience that the speaker had read more than the first chapter of Morgenthau's *Politics Among Nations* (1973). For instance, Risto Hyvärinen's dissertation focuses most of his discussion of Morgenthau on that very first chapter (Hyvärinen 1960: 105–7, 109–10).

Yet Morgenthau's intellectual position in Finland was fairly well established. He had some connections with Finland; in the 1930s, Morgenthau had corresponded with Yrjö Ruutu, the first holder of an IR chair in Finland.

In 1973, he participated in Helsinki in a Pugwash symposium on nuclear weapons.[3] *Politics among Nations* was used in the late 1960s and the early 1970s as a required textbook at both the Universities of Helsinki and Tampere. Some contemporary students regarded it, though, more as an introduction to the *Weltanschauung* of the Foreign Ministry than a scientific work.

It is interesting that, among the Finnish realists, there seems to have been only a limited familiarity with E.H. Carr, who had initiated the entire debate about realism and idealism with his *The Twenty Years' Crisis*. One reason for this relative inattention may have been British parochialism and limited interaction between Continental and British scholarship in the 1950s and the 1960s; there was 'fog in the Channel' (Brown 2001). Another reason for the relative neglect of Carr might have been that his quasi-Marxist philosophy of history and science did not match the simplified power-security versions of realism that many of its defenders held. For instance, the brief discussion of Carr by Hyvärinen (1960: 104–5) refers only to his realist convictions without exploring at all their philosophical underpinnings. Be that as it may, a closer look at Carr would have revealed a much less homogeneous vision of realism than the one that became predominant in the Finnish reception.

Carr's idea of realism has deep roots in positivism; it has to be anchored in the facts of a historical process by recognising that there is no reality outside this particular process. For him, realism

> places its emphasis on the acceptance of facts and on the analysis of their causes and consequences. It tends to depreciate the role of purpose and to maintain . . . that the function of thinking is to study a sequence of events which it is powerless to influence or to alter.
>
> (Carr 1946: 10)

For realism, 'there can be no reality outside the historical process'. Therefore, 'history cannot be judged except by historical standards' (Carr 1946: 67). In making this point, realism in Carr subscribes to a deterministic interpretation of history, which is opposed to the idea of free will in utopianism. As succinctly put by Nicholson (1998: 65), 'realists stress the constraints in life; the utopians stress the opportunities'.

Quotations like these, however, too easily caricature Carr, whose philosophical and moral take on issues is much more complex than is recognised by many advocates of brute realism. Carr himself did not make things easier, as he used to resort to 'rhetorical tricks' (Jones 1998: 12) and to defend the policy of appeasement. Behind Carr's realism was a methodological approach that he had derived from Karl Mannheim's sociology of knowledge, in which theory and facts were mutually constitutive. A practical consequence of this stance was that Carr rejected empiricism as too crude a way of dealing with history and came to favour a more dialectical approach.

By a rhetorical twist, utilising Mannheim's concept of ideology, Carr developed a reading of utopianism whose supporters, in his view, advocated hypocritically the harmony of interests in order to defend their privileged position. In his view, realism also provided a rationalisation of power, but it did so in plain words, without hypocrisy (Jones 1998: 121–43). Carr applied, as did Morgenthau (1973: 89), the Mannheimian term of 'particular ideology' to unmask the deceptive uses of concepts such as common interest.

Carr's methodology may not have been the only reason why he was not favoured by Finnish realists, except for borrowing loosely his twin concepts of utopianism and realism and labelling their opponents with them. A more fundamental reason may have been Carr's ultimate denunciation of realism as yet another conditioned mode of thinking that is unable to provide for effective political thinking and purposive action (see also Guzzini 1998: 21–3). Instead, Carr felt that there is a need to 'build a new utopia of our own ... based on elements of both utopia and reality'. Making things yet more complicated, Carr says that utopia and reality belong to 'two different planes which can never meet'. While the 'human will will continue to seek an escape from the logical consequences of realism in the vision of an international order', the sad situation is that when this new order is accomplished, it 'crystallizes itself into concrete political form [and] becomes tainted with self-interest and hypocrisy' (Carr 1946: 93).[4]

Finnish peace research and positivism

The standard realist is supposed to stick to positivist guns by which the 'true' nature of politics can be observed. This perhaps only applies to Waltzian structural realism, born in the 1970s; as already mentioned, the practitioners of Finnish realism of the time can hardly be placed in a single methodological category.

Therefore, one should not characterise the Finnish realists by the Polish criteria of positivism and conciliatoriness. Indeed, these traits seem to fit better to Finnish 'idealist' peace researchers. The empirical method was considered by young Finnish peace researchers a superior instrument in the effort to know the world better compared with the 'pre-modern' tools of description and interpretation that the realist scholars favoured. It was a 'modern' way to uncover the invariances in arms races, warfare, dependency relations and other ills plaguing the world, which was, in turn, a precondition for the ability to 'break invariances'.

In fact, positivism was characteristic of early Finnish peace researchers, most of whom worked in IR, where the quantitative revolution had started in the middle of the 1960s. Much of that influence came from the United States and made IR even more an 'American social science', as Stanley Hoffmann (1977) has described it. It is almost paradoxical that the

American academic landscape became familiar to many young Finnish IR scholars long before they had ever visited the country. Names like Chadwick Alger, Hayward Alker, Rudolph Rummel and Bruce Russett (who visited Tampere for the first time in 1970) became well known early on. Rosenau (1961), Schelling (1960) and Singer (1968) were obligatory reading for IR undergraduates. It was also realised that Karl Deutsch was a key figure behind this new movement. For instance, his theory of security communities and works on transaction flows were studied widely (and in 1982 he was invited for a special visit to Finland, which he had toured with his wife in the late 1930s).

The empirical method also came to Finland by other routes. Finnish sociology had, by the late 1960s, made a partial switch to analysing statistical data, which the development of computing technology now permitted. In peace research, this was reflected in the Finnish participation in an international project, conducted under UNESCO's auspices, to gauge the attitudes of young people to international issues. With three collaborators, Håkan Wiberg co-directed this project revealing thus both his organisational skills and commitment to empirical social science (Ornauer *et al.* 1976). The rationalist element can also be seen in Wiberg's fondness for game theory, of which he was, in the 1960s and the 1970s, one of the very few Nordic social scientists mastering the method (Wiberg 1976).

In Finland, as in other Nordic countries, the influence of Johan Galtung was pervasive during that era. Familiarity with his structural theories of conflict, imperialism and integration was a must. These theories had an empirical foundation and it has even been said that Galtung's early production was driven more by empirical than theoretical interests. This reflected his effort to unseat unscientific traditionalism, which was found not only in conservative realism, but also in popular peace thinking. For peace researchers, values such as non-violence and equity were, of course, relevant, but they were often either taken for granted, converted to testable hypotheses, or integrated loosely in theoretical constructs.[5] Against this backdrop it does not seem to be unfair to characterise Galtungian 'peace research as science' (Lawler 1995).

Galtung's penchant for structural theories and empirical methods also provided the core idea for Finnish peace research. In fact, the bulk of Nordic peace research was structured as an epistemic community around the Galtungian core. This is also reflected in the tendency to speak of a 'peace research movement' (Wiberg 1988). The methodological tenets of early Galtungian peace research were formulated in the first volume of his *Theory and Methods of Social Research* (1967). The vantage point of this book, the data matrix and its manipulation, was followed in the method courses that the University of Tampere offered in the late 1960s for undergraduate students. Each and every student had to take, in addition to an introduction to statistics, a course either in empirical content analysis or the analysis of survey data.[6]

Now, the old contenders have, to some degree, traded places. With the constructivist turn in peace research and IR, the old realist classics are being reinterpreted and new methodological elements being found in their writings. This is, to some extent, a countermove against the dominance of the Waltzian structural realism and its policy advice (such as the spread of nuclear weapons). On the other side, it has been argued that political realism and peace research are not fundamentally opposed to each other, but there are opportunities for theoretical cross-fertilisation (Väyrynen 1986). Moreover, a major part of peace research has remained predominantly empirical and rationalist in nature. This is attested, for instance, by the editorial policy consistently pursued by both the *Journal of Conflict Resolution* and the *Journal of Peace Research.*

Beyond stereotypes: political reasons for the clash

Having disposed of the facile theoretical answer, namely that the clash around peace research was merely due to a rehearsal of the classical realist–idealist debate, this leads us back to our initial question: why did the Finnish realists feel a need to attack, sometimes fiercely, this rather harmless group of young scholars? The best explanation I am able to come up with is that it was a clash of generational and political values, which was amplified by the competition on the ideology and agenda of Finnish foreign and security policy.

Academic competition

To my mind, the main reasons were political in nature. Peace research rode to Finland with the general leftward shift in European and Finnish politics. The Social Democrats had a landslide win in the parliamentary elections in 1966, and, together with the People's Democrats, they had a majority in Parliament. The critics – who mostly supported the agrarian Centre Party and the conservative Coalition Party – perceived peace research as a fifth column of the Finnish left which was feared to undermine the *status quo* of the established academic community. This fear was not entirely unfounded; most professors of International Relations in Finnish universities have been, in their time, active peace researchers, and some still recognise this epithet.

This perception was probably reinforced by the fact that Finnish peace researchers were a rather tight-knit group who did not have any significant theoretical and political differences of opinion among themselves. In fact, it has been argued that early Finnish peace research, with its own distinct political culture, meets all the features of an epistemic community. It was also a part of the like-minded community of young Nordic scholars with close ties especially with PRIO and Uppsala (Vesa 1996). Regular Nordic peace research conferences, such as the one held in Finland in 1970, were an important forum for creating this community.

Perhaps one additional reason for the tensions between the realists and peace researchers was that their topical interests overlapped. Had peace researchers been content to study only the problems of global economic relations, socio-economic development, or remote local conflicts, the critics could probably have easily neglected them. Some realists sneered at these issues and refused to attribute any formative influence to them.

Apunen and Rytövuori conclude that, in the 1970s, the Finnish 'peace research community, in turn, is intellectually preoccupied with global issues and has clearly a world community point of view'. In contrast to the traditionalist scholars whose work has been close to the policy establishment, peace researchers have suffered from a 'persuasive handicap'. This means that they have not developed specific arguments or policies to tell how Finland should alter global conditions. On that basis, they conclude that the two communities 'do not meet or confront each other intellectually in any substantial manner' (Apunen and Rytövuori 1982: 80).

This observation has it right to the extent that there were, indeed, many traditional historians who were not interested in peace research and engaged with scholars in this field. On the other hand, the article suffers from a selection bias. It leaves out practically all the works written by peace researchers on Finnish foreign, defence and integration policies, regional security issues, and great-power relations. When this is done and the choice of material falls mostly on studies dealing with global issues, it is not difficult to find a penchant for globalism in contrast to the traditionalists' concern with Finland's position.

Foreign policy advice

Thus much of the writing on peace research dealt directly with the foreign policy agenda; nuclear arms control, détente and Finnish foreign and defence policy. What exacerbated the debate was that both more established scholars and peace researchers competed to give policy advice. In fact, peace researchers tended to regard President Urho Kekkonen as their patron saint whose policies they almost uncritically supported.[7] As at least some of the realists were his close collaborators; the debate was, to a degree, about Kekkonen's soul.[8]

In this competitive context, it is almost ironic that, on most of the big issues, the views of realists and peace researchers were not that far from each other. They both supported the so-called Paasikivi–Kekkonen line in Finnish foreign policy, friendly relations with the Soviet Union, the Nordic nuclear-free zone, the organisation of the CSCE and the United Nations.

There were differences, however. Realists feared that peace researchers were too soft towards the Soviet Union and did not appreciate enough the value of political toughness and military capacity that had, after all, saved Finland's independence in the Second World War. Obviously, the critical attitude of peace researchers towards the United States, due to its war in Vietnam, added fuel to the fire. The official policy was that Finland should not blame the USA for its policies, as long as they did not harm Finland directly, as it was unable to balance that criticism with an equally critical attitude towards the USSR. In that sense, official Finnish policy differed in a major way from that of Sweden. Moreover, realists considered bipolarity, nuclear deterrence and great-power bilateralism in general to be a source of stability in Europe. This argument was, for peace researchers, who favoured disarmament and the lowering of bloc barriers, somewhat difficult to swallow.

In this regard, there may have been an internal tension in Finnish peace research. On the one hand, there was almost unqualified support for the policies of détente and arms control, alongside resistance to greatpower dominance and bipolarity in International Relations. On the other hand, it has been shown that there has been an emancipatory streak in Nordic peace research in which there was a strong feeling that the repressive and unequal global structures constrained political choices (Rytövuori-Apunen 1990: 140–53, 180–91). The 'utopianism' of peace research was reflected in support for policies by which these structural straitjackets could be removed. These policies included a greater selfreliance for developing countries in the context of a New International Economic Order (NIEO), as well as progress in nuclear arms control and disarmament.

A Nordic perspective

How unique is the Finnish case? It may have its *Eigenart*, as it seems that the debate between realism and peace research did not play out in the same way in Denmark, Norway and Sweden. True, there were realists – such as Erling Bjøl in Denmark and Nils Ørvik in Norway – who were opposed to theoretical and political commitments of peace researchers and also said so. In these two countries the dispute seemed to be, however, more about politics than scholarship.

Danish and Norwegian peace researchers were either opposed to the NATO membership of their countries or felt that they were too deeply integrated in the military and even nuclear strategies of NATO. They advocated more cooperative, pan-European or global approaches to International Relations, which was not always well received by the most ardent defenders of NATO. Peace researchers wanted to pursue alternative opportunities that the relaxation of the Cold War from the late 1960s on seemed to have opened up.

As said, there were no doubt political and generational differences of opinion between Danish and Norwegian peace researchers, but they do not seem to have been as divisive as they were for a period of time in Finland, where the entire existence of Nordic-style peace research was challenged. In other countries, conflicts were often more personal in nature. In Denmark, Erling Bjøl and Anders Boserup were frequently at odds. Both of them participated, first, in the Seidenfaden Committee in 1968–70 exploring Denmark's security policy options and, then, ten years later, in the board of the Committee of Security and Disarmament (SNU). Representing the security policy establishment, Bjøl seems to have had difficulties to personally tolerate Boserup, who had good political and media connections (Bjøl 1994: 122).

In Norway, PRIO and NUPI may have viewed each other as competitors, but it appears that different organisational cultures rather than divisive political and methodological commitments separated the two institutes. Again, personality issues seem to have shaped some of the interactions. Thus, J. David Singer, who spent a year in Oslo in 1963–4, tells that he had difficulties getting along with Johan Galtung; although they had professional and social interaction, serious intellectual issues were seldom addressed. On the other hand, Singer found Nils Ørvik, the arch-realist of Norway, 'not only very intelligent, but also lively, a good conversationalist, and a man who knew something about practical politics' (pers. comm.). This reflected, of course, Ørvik's primary interest in security policy and Norwegian foreign policy.

In Sweden, it is difficult to identify any coherent realist school that would have turned against peace research, although individual efforts were made. Rather, the counterpart was, by Nordic standards, the vast establishment of defence and strategic studies. Its members swore in the name of neutrality and strong conventional defence, but also advocated nuclear disarmament and were even interested in non-violent defence if it suited Swedish national interests. Defence researchers and peace researchers obviously had different views on, for instance, how much of the nation's resources should be spent on the military.

This was not an issue that would inflame controversies, though, partly because the peace research community was not strong enough to take on the defence establishment and both were characterised by typical Swedish moderation. The high degree of consensus can be seen, for instance, in the general support of the establishment of SIPRI in 1967. In hindsight, it seems that peace research faced bigger difficulties within universities than in its relations with the representatives of strategic interests. The main struggle in Sweden, especially in Uppsala, was between political science and peace research concerning the right to define the nature of the latter field.

Thus, in sum, it seems that, compared with other Nordic countries, the Finnish situation had at least some Polish features. Various ideological schools were more deeply rooted in the Finnish historical and political consciousness than in other Nordic countries and also shaped debates in IR and peace research. The Finnish schools, however, did not follow any strict line, but there were also crossovers which created a mismatch between political commitments and methodological orientations. Finnish peace researchers have had their feet in realist and idealist traditions, their methodology was, until the late 1980s at least, predominantly positivist and they recognised external constraints on political action, while trying to promote progress and emancipation. On the other hand, Finnish realists remained loyal members of their own policy-oriented camps. By the 1990s, at the latest, the clash between realism and peace research had faded to history.

Notes

1 I am grateful to several colleagues for the information they shared with me in the course of preparing this chapter. I would like to thank, in particular, Nils Petter Gleditsch, Raimo Lintonen, Nikolaj Petersen, J. David Singer, Unto Vesa and Peter Wallensteen for their insights and helpful comments. The responsibility remains, of course, solely mine.

2 On the other hand, of the older generation of Finnish IR scholars, Göran von Bonsdorff was close to peace research, although his main scholarly works had dealt with the Finnish party system and a broad history of technology and political systems (von Bonsdorff 1964). Klaus Törnudd specialised in regional integration and international organisations (and also served in distinguished positions in the Foreign Ministry).

3 Information on contacts between Morgenthau and Ruutu are derived from Korhonen (1983), which is an excellent study on Morgenthau's intellectual background in Europe, but has unfortunately appeared only in Finnish.

4 These kinds of views, which can easily be considered inconsistent, have enamoured Carr to social constructionists, who, in the 1990s, discovered him as a fellow traveller *avant la lettre*. Thus, Jones (1998: 154) characterises Carr as 'both a post-positivist and critical social scientist and a post-modern statesman'.

5 Although early peace research was essentially non-normative and had difficulties in dealing with value questions, it never went as far as the Peace Science Society (International), which actively rejected values in favour of the scientific method. Rytövuori-Apunen (1990: 255–72) has explored the problem of value in Nordic peace research.

6 Against this backdrop, it is appropriate that when the University of Tampere gave an honorary doctorate to Galtung in May 1975, the reasons mentioned were his merits in the development of social science methodology and peace research, in that order.

7 This attitude is reflected in a small event in 1977 when the Tampere Peace Research Institute and IMEMO in Moscow co-published a book on 'International Détente and Disarmament' (see Kalyadin and Vesa 1977). As the Director of TAPRI, I went to the residence of President Kekkonen with Unto Vesa and a Soviet contributor, who later turned out to be a KGB colonel. Kekkonen received the book and talked with us for about half an hour.

8 For instance, the Finnish Peace Research Association invited President Kekkonen as its first honorary member, an invitation he accepted immediately.

References

Apunen, Osmo and Helena Rytövuori (1982) 'Ideas of "survival" and "progress" in the Finnish foreign policy tradition', *Journal of Peace Research* 19 (1): 61–82.

Bjøl, Erling (1994) *Fra magtens korridorer*, Copenhagen: Politikens Forlag.

Bonsdorff, Göran von (1964) *Världspolitiken i teknikens tidsåldern*, Borgå: Söderströms.

Brown, Chris (2001) 'Fog in the Channel: continental International Relations theory isolated', in Robert Crawford and Darryl Jarvis (eds), *International Relations – Still an American Social Science?* Albany, NY: State University of New York Press: 203–19.

Carr, E.H. (1946) *The Twenty Years' Crisis 1919–1939. An Introduction to the Study of International Relations*, second rev. edn, London: Macmillan.

Davies, Norman (2001 [1984]) *Heart of Europe: The Past in Poland's Present*, Oxford: Oxford University Press.

Galtung, Johan (1967) *Theories and Methods of Social Research*, Oslo: Universitetsforlaget.

Guzzini, Stefano (1998) *Realism in International Relations and International Political Economy: the Continuing Story of a Death Foretold*, London: Routledge.

Hoffmann, Stanley (1977) 'An American social science: International Relations', *Daedalus* 106 (3): 41–60.

Hyvärinen, Risto (1960) 'Monistic and pluralistic interpretations in the study of international politics', in *Commentationes Humanarum Litterarum, tomus XXIV*, Helsinki: Societas Scientiarum Fennica.

Jones, Charles (1998) *E.H. Carr and International Relations*, Cambridge: Cambridge University Press.

Kalyadin, Alexander and Unto Vesa (eds) (1977) *International Détente and Disarmament*, Tampere: Tampere Peace Research Institute.

Killinen, Kullervo (1964) *Kansainvälinen politiikka, I: Politiikan ja strategian maantieteelliset perusteet; II: Voimapolitiikan kansainvälisen turvallisuuden peruskysymykset*, second edn, Porvoo: WSOY.

Korhonen, Pekka (1983) *Hans Morgenthau. Intellektuaalinen historia*, Jyväskylä: University of Jyväskylä, Department of Political Science.

Lawler, Peter (1995) *A Question of Values. Johan Galtung's Peace Research*, Boulder, CO: Lynne Rienner.

Morgenthau, Hans J. (1973 [1948]) *Politics Among Nations. The Struggle for Power and Politics*, fifth edn, New York, NY: Alfred A. Knopf.

Nicholson, Michael (1998) 'Realism and Utopianism revisited', in Tim Dunne, Michael Cox and Ken Booth (eds), *The Eighty Years Crisis. International Relations 1919–1999*, Cambridge: Cambridge University Press: 65–82.

Ornauer, Helmut, Håkan Wiberg, Andrej Sicinski and Johan Galtung (eds) (1976) *Images of the World in 2000. A Comparative Ten Nations Study*, The Hague: Mouton.

Rosenau, James (ed.) (1961) *International Politics and Foreign Policy: A Reader in Research and Theory*, New York, NY: Free Press.

Rytövuori-Apunen, Helena (1990) *Barefoot Research and Tribune of Reason. An Analysis of the Textual Corpus of Peace Research in Scandinavia, 1959–1986*, Studia Politica Tamperensis, University of Tampere: Department of Political Science and International Relations.

Schelling, Thomas (1960) *Strategies of Conflict*, Cambridge, MA: Harvard University Press.

Singer, J. David (ed.) (1968) *Quantitative International Politics: Insights and Evidence*, New York, NY: Free Press.

Vesa, Unto (1980) 'Miten rauhantutkimus tuli Suomeen?' *Rauhaan tutkien* no. 3.

—— (1984) 'Rauhantutkimuksen tulo Suomeen: tieteenhistoriallinen ja – sosiologinen näkökulma', *Rauhantutkimus* no. 1–2.

—— (1996) 'Suomalaisen rauhantutkimuksen alkuvalinnat', in Unto Vesa (ed.), *Rauhantutkimuksesta ja rauhanajattelusta. Rauhan- ja konfliktintutkimuskeskus,* Tutkimustiedote no. 71: 5–17.

Väyrynen, Raimo (1986) 'Anarki, magt og moral: om forholdet mellem politisk realisme og fredsforskning', *Politica (Aarhus)* 18 (3): 243–51.

Wiberg, Håkan (1976) *Konfliktteori och fredsforskning,* Stockholm: Esselte studium.

—— (1988) 'The peace research movement', in Peter Wallensteen (ed.), *Peace Research: Achievements and Challenges,* Boulder, CO: Westview: 30–53.

4 'The Cold War is what we make of it'

When peace research meets constructivism in International Relations[1]

Stefano Guzzini

This chapter argues that one of the lineages of present-day 'constructivist' research in International Relations is peace research. Indeed, the ease with which constructivism-inspired research has swept over Western and Northern Europe cannot be understood otherwise. Constructivism provides the meta-theoretical support and furthered the classical peace research criticism that the Cold War was no necessity, but politically 'constructed'.

Peace research, as well as constructivism, insists that international 'anarchy' does not exclude the existence of an international society. In its view, anarchy has no unbreakable logic: its effects are a construct of that international society. It does not exclude that agents can learn in international society, that its rules can be amended and that these are, in turn, related to the constitution of the roles these very agents can play in that society. In other words, International Relations are the effect of political processes, not structural or historical necessities. Peace research/constructivism does not deny that 'power politics' can exist. This power politics is, however, not the result of invariable laws of politics, but is the compounded effect of agents who believe in such pessimistic invariable laws of politics caught in structures reflecting these beliefs. In terms of research, this meant that the Cold War lock was at least partly a 'self-fulfilling prophecy' whose extent needed to be empirically established and not axiomatically excluded from research. In political terms, the potential for détente policies was to be sorted out step-by-step, with controlled confidence-building measures and arms control, not excluded through a policy which mistook the sometimes necessary *means* of containment and deterrence with the *ends* of foreign policy.

Arguing for this point of encounter, even if central, comes with a series of caveats, however. First, it should not be mistaken to mean that everything there was and is to peace research can be subsumed under constructivism, or vice versa. Rather, it wants to remind constructivists that some of their political argument creates a sense of 'déjà vu' for peace researchers, and that they might be well advised to also look at the rest of peace research, in particular its emancipatory tradition (Alker 1996). Inversely, peace research would gain from taking some of the particular constructivist or indeed post-structuralist insights seriously. For constructivism has been inspired by a series of developments in the philosophy of social sciences which have undermined the faith in 'data'. Since the recourse to the 'real world' to question the validity of realism was *alone* not enough, it needed to provide an ontological base for the claim of a self-fulfilling prophecy; it needed to provide a general approach which could conceptualise learning and process in a more coherent manner. If constructivists should be more aware of the analytical, practical and normative agenda of peace research, peace research, in turn, should not take the 'déjà vu' as an excuse to neglect the theoretical and meta-theoretical turn in the social sciences which is necessary to their own defence.

The second caveat has to do with the presentist presentation of the main claim. I will try to address mainly IR scholars, which means, as a result, that peace research is primarily seen through the lenses of the discourse in IR, of 'realism and its critics'. Although this makes the lineage around self-fulfilling prophecies more visible, it also does some violence to the very self-conception of much peace research. I hope that this shortcoming is at least partly offset by the advantage of opening up for this encounter, and by Heikki Patomäki's (2001) article, which, written from within peace research, can be read parallel to much of the following.

The early critique of the logic of anarchy and the realist opening for process

Realists insisted that whereas politics in a domestic setting was able to show instances of progress, international affairs could not (Wight 1966; for the most forceful critique of this dichotomy, see Walker 1993). There, history was bound to return. For all his own scepticism about science, Morgenthau was read as a protagonist of a determinist realism insisting, as he was, on the balance of power, the 'self-regulatory mechanism of the social forces which manifests itself in the struggle for power on the international scene', which was there out 'of necessity' (Morgenthau 1948: 9, 125).

The first important step in reclaiming ground from realism consisted in showing that politics can make a difference, that realpolitik was no necessity. Two conceptual critiques have been particularly important. Inis Claude's (1962, and again 1989) and Ernst Haas' (1953) analyses of the balance of power had to conclude that, far from being a 'necessity' as in Morgenthau's treatment, it was void because tautological, and hence rather a normative appeal for its implementation, a 'prescription' or 'ideology'. Similarly, Morgenthau's concept of the national interest was scrutinised – with much the same result, as the young Robert Tucker's (1952) sober and all the more cruel dissection of Morgenthau's self-contradictions shows. Later, and on a more theoretical level, Raymond Aron (1962: 97–102) tried to show that a utilitarian theory of politics cannot hold where the national interest (security) in terms of power would be analogous to utility (wealth) expressed in terms of money in neo-classical economics. For power is not analogous to money. Hence, national interest assessments are intrinsically indeterminate.

The implications of this indeterminacy did not escape all 'realists': they had to open up for the understanding of process and not just necessity. Wolfers (1962) proposed an approach which was not saying outright that realism was (always) wrong, but that realism was simply *a special case* which applies at one pole of the international continuum between power and indifference. Crucially, one had to find out what makes some systems drive towards the pole of power and some towards the pole of indifference. And with all but the name, Wolfers analysed the risk of power politics as a self-fulfilling prophecy. For there were situations in which power politics was the right strategy and some where strategies of re-assurance, as we would call them now, would be the correct ones. Power politics/escalation before the First World War was as fatal as appeasement before the Second World War. In some cases, it is the effect of worst case thinking which only produces the very worst case it is supposedly trying to avoid.

Peace research as the study of process pathologies

Starting with a section on realism exemplifies the IR lenses of the present chapter. Although presenting realism as peace research's 'other' is not uncommon in the literature (Vasquez 1983), it is more correct to say that, for early peace researchers, the 'other' was war, not realism.[2] Yet there is a crucial link between war and realism which is also central for the argument about 'self-fulfilling prophecies'. For early peace research was interested in finding out the systematic reasons for being locked in the Cold War posture. In doing this, it focused on material impediments to change, such as the imperialist structures of the international system (Galtung 1971) or the military–industrial complexes in both superpowers (for a critique of the Western model, see Galbraith 1978, especially chapter XXIX). More consequential for the link to present-day constructivism was, however, the focus on the role of realpolitik ideas in reproducing Cold War politics and the 'worst case'. As put by Herbert Kelman (1978: 166), one of the founders of peace research in the USA (and the *Journal of Conflict Resolution*), '[i]n the search of a settlement, however, the dangers to be avoided are self-fulfilling prophecies that a satisfactory settlement is unattainable. . . .'

When détente seemed possible, enemy-images and systematically biased understandings of world politics were perceived to blind high politics. Yet, in contrast to classical deterrence analysis, early peace researchers tended to see this blindness not as a kind of collective action problem, i.e. as the irrational outcome of strategic interaction due to the adverse condition of anarchy. Instead, they relied heavily on insights from social psychology (Kelman 1958) and studied what appeared to be *systematic learning patholo-gies* and irrationalities.

For the economy of this short reconstruction, Karl W. Deutsch will play a doubly pivotal role (for the lineage of Deutsch, and Ernst Haas, to con-structivism, see also Adler 2002). On the one hand, Deutsch and his asso-ciates (1957) launched a research agenda on amalgamated or pluralistic 'security communities'. Rather than being fixed on the bipolar divide and the conditions for a simple Concert, they looked back at the conditions under which former zones of war have become zones of peace. For their focus on process, it is not fortuitous that such studies were then related to the analysis of international organisation (Claude 1956) and integration (Haas 1964). Since much of this experience is based on the lessons of European integration, and in particular the 'anomalous' Scandinavian/ Nordic peace (Wiberg 1993, 2000), accordingly much of the security community model was ingrained in European peace research, indeed providing an important part of its identity.

Deutsch, the scholar of cybernetics, that is the science of information, plays a second pivotal role. For systems theory and more particularly cybernetics was to provide peace research with one crucial theoretical underpinning. Indeed, it allowed peace research to systematically analyse learning pathologies in terms of perverse effects of self-referentiality. Cybernetics allowed the connection of two crucial research agendas, namely the self-referentiality of military build-up/deterrence on the one hand, and of psychological processes on the other. It looked at the system-atic effects of political economy on foreign policies, as well as at the possi-bility of *systematic* misperception, either because of the systematic bias in decoding information (coherence versus cognitive dissonance) or because of the functional needs for upholding *Feindbilder* (enemy-images), for example, to rally domestic support and national/group identity.

It is in particular this *Feindbild* literature (the concept stems from Dieter Senghaas), very prominent in Europe, which is a forerunner of present constructivism-inspired scholarship in IR, and in its insistence on self/other politics also of post-structuralist IR. Similar to those studies of 'belief systems', which focus more explicitly on social components (Little 1988), this literature is more encompassing than the literature on sheer misperception (Jervis 1976), which tends to be more cognitively oriented (see also Frei 1985). Yet, by focusing on the ideational components of social constructions, it has a less materialist ontology than Marxism-inspired peace research approaches.

'Autism' and the social learning pathology of deterrence practices

Deutsch's communicative approach starts from the self-referential characteristics of systems and looks for the way information is processed within a system to respond to disturbances (Deutsch 1966). As such, the approach, although not being 'functionalist' in an IR sense, has a theoretical functionalism to it.

When applied to international politics during the Cold War, this way of looking at politics in terms of complex information management has important consequences. The usual way of presenting the Cold War consisted in an action–reaction scheme. Whether intended or not, the security dilemma pushed international 'powers' to be on their guard and react to any advance of the other side. Whether intended or not, such relentless 'being on guard' produces a spiral in the arms race. It is a process which is basically outside-in driven.

Instead, basing politics on the structure of communication process produces a different result. Dieter Senghaas, a student of Deutsch, called an extreme closure 'autism' (Senghaas 1972: 38–62), i.e. a pattern of communication which is not only self-referential, as practices generally are, but has an inbuilt logic which makes adaptation to the environment extremely difficult. Expressed the other way round, when dispositions, both institutional and perceptual, clash with the context of their application, it is not the dispositions, but the processing of reality that is adapted. In cybernetics, this would be considered a learning pathology.

Deterrence theory survives only via the expectation of the worst-case. Deterrence policies *predispose* to a particular stereotyped understanding of the world which reproduces autonomously the perceptions of threats. Thus, the arms race is not an action–reaction between perceptions/actions of agents, but the product of self-generated moments of inertia and autonomously produced threat-perceptions. Escalation is less a collective action problem of individually rational agents and more an inertial effect of two autistic systems. Super-power relations were decreasingly the product of their interaction and increasingly the result of the juxtaposition of their internal dynamics. In other words, deterrence thinking is connected to a process pathology which risks locking the international system into a self-fulfilling prophecy of a worst-case perception relentlessly reproduced.

Feindbilder *and individual learning pathologies*

This pathological self-referentiality was also understood at a more individual level which concentrated on social groups linked with and dependent of the practices of deterrence, such as some politicians, academics and military lobbyists.

Feindbilder provide the analytical link between the social and the individual level. From the literature, Weller (2000: 87–93) has distilled five basic approaches to the understanding of 'enemy-images' in peace research, which are not mutually exclusive: (1) stereotypisation, (2) selective perception, (3) dichotomisation of the social world (reduction to friend–foe relations), (4) an effect of psychological projections from oneself onto others, and (5) socially functional in so far as they allow, for example, the strengthening of unity of a population to legitimate government, arms race and diversionary warfare.

All five enemy-image approaches link up with the study of social pathologies, the first three methodologically, the last two in terms of the collective level of action. The first three derive their explanation from the cognitive economy of mental processes usually understood in cybernetic terms (Steinbruner 1974) just as much as Deutsch and Senghaas used it on the social level. The last two refer to social psychology and a functional theory of society, respectively. Hence, whereas enemy images refer to both the individual and the social level of explanation, they share an interest in a functional/system analysis of mental and social processes respectively.

This link of peace research to social psychology and the study of prejudice and stereotypes has also been very important in shaping its normative component (for the following, see also Weller 2001). For it allowed perceptions to be criticised as 'distorted' and not 'reality-suitable' (*realitäts-un-an-ge-messen*), inertial to change or cognitively dissonant with 'real' politics.

Finally, assuming the interrelationship of the material and ideal world, it hence allowed the more forceful and open criticism of the tendency to create self-fulfilling prophecies of such enemy-images, as done in the programmatic statement of the project at the *Hessische Stiftung für Friedens- und Konfliktforschung* (Nicklas and Gantzel 1975).

Constructivism and reflexivity on process

As this last section will show, many of the constructivist empirical insights come as little surprise to peace researchers (and many liberal writers in IR). Yet constructivism provides for the first time a meta-theoretical and social theoretical anchorage. It can show how self-fulfilling prophecies are something always present in the social world, not the villain result of intentional conspiracies. Because for its reflexivity, all social actions and processes tend towards self-fulfilling prophecies (McSweeney 1999: 140ff. and passim). In this way, constructivism provides the basis for theoretically more varied and, arguably, more refined explanations.

The paradoxical success of peace research-cum-constructivism

There is a certain paradox in this sweet, if silent, success of peace research through its new constructivist host. For its quantitative wing dominant in the USA had been put on the defensive, and appears at odds with present-day constructivism. Yet the less quantitative traditions, such as much of Galtung's writings and the German tradition, could argue that the end of the Cold War confirmed both peace research approaches and the détente policies they inspired (Wiberg 1992).

Some peace research faced a series of critiques. The quantitative nature of much peace research in the USA, like the famous 'Correlates of War' research project, and its imitators came under scrutiny again in the 'methodological turn' (Little 1991) of the 1980s. Although quantitative peace researchers have been much less simplistic than often decried (for a balanced defence, see Vasquez 1987), the very assumptions underlying huge cross-historical comparisons met with increasing incredulity in some parts of the scientific community (Suganami 1996). In parallel, the early peace research tradition, also including part of Galtung's writing, was relying on behaviouralist assumptions – the diminution of violence through social justice based on objective human needs (see in particular Burton 1985, 1986) – which were being increasingly challenged (Patomäki and Wæver 1995), albeit perhaps not the idea of a utopia itself. Finally, the normative peace research tradition, so strong in Europe, seemed to rely on a clear picture of what 'reality is really like', as compared to distorted perceptions others have, and how a more peaceful history could evolve if only we followed certain recipes – all of which belied a certain empiricism and West(Euro)-centrism. Hence, the varieties of peace research came under combined attack for their positivism, their empiricism and their unreflected normative character.

Yet the end of the Cold War worked as a catalyst. It seemed to give an immediate plausibility to the critiques of realism: peaceful change was possible. The starting point for understanding the meeting of peace research and constructivism in an IR perspective lies in the critique that neorealism was actually unable to even conceive of this type of peaceful change (Koslowski and Kratochwil 1994; Kratochwil 1993; Patomäki 1992). This critique relied on the rehearsal of the 1980s by writers who would be called post-structuralists today. Ashley (1986) and Walker (1987) had started the critique by showing the biases of neorealist theorising, Ashley (1987) later arguing that realism itself has been the (status quo) culture of an international society of diplomats.

Such a critique explicitly connected the level of observation with the level of action and hence comes to one of the crucial parameters of constructivism. For, in my understanding (Guzzini 2000), constructivism is a meta-theory that can be characterised as:

1   being particularly sensitive to the distinction between the level of action (proper), the level of observation and the relationship between the two (usually theorised in terms of power);
2   having an epistemological position which stresses the social construction of meaning (and hence knowledge);
3   having an ontological position which stresses the construction of social reality.

Such a position emphasises two major inspirations of recent theorising, namely the interpretivist and the sociological turns in the social sciences. Taking the interpretivist turn seriously means starting from the idea of meaningful action and hence from the difference between social sciences, which need to interpret an already interpreted world, and natural sciences, which need not (Schutz 1962). Theorising must therefore conceptualise the level of common-sense action apart from second-order action (or observation). Most importantly, it must analyse their relationship. Again setting the social world apart from the natural, our understandings of people and their action can make a real difference to the latter. For instance, being identified as an opportunist state representative influences options in future negotiations. Moreover, human beings – but not natural phenomena – can become reflexively aware of such attributions and influence their action in interaction with them. This 'looping effect' (Hacking 1999: 34) is one of the reasons for the importance of 'identity' in constructivist writings, theoretically and empirically – and for the study of self-fulfilling prophecies (McSweeney 1999).

Taking the sociological turn seriously implies that meaningful action (and hence also the knowledge of both agent and observer) is a social or intersubjective phenomenon. It cannot be reduced to cognitive psychology or to choice based on interests. Instead, the sociological turn emphasises the role of the social context within which identities and interests of both actor and acting observer are formed in the first place. It also focuses on language as the model case of intersubjectivity, both on the epistemological level and in its practical performative function (Kratochwil 1989; Onuf 1989; for a discussion, see Zehfuß 1998). Finally, it means that the relationship between the two has in itself to be problematised, i.e. the relationship between the social world and the social construction of meaning (including knowledge).

Hence, when Alexander Wendt (1992) published his 'Anarchy is what states make of it', he dressed up a basic peace research idea in new and arguably more coherent theoretical and meta-theoretical clothes (Wendt chose Giddens' social theory for this). Wendt provided a predominantly, but not pure, idealist ontology to base the 'social construction of reality' on, something not done in earlier peace research (for an assessment of his approach, see Guzzini and Leander 2001). It comes as no surprise that he then conceived of the international system as a society with different 'cultures of anarchy', including Hobbesian Realpolitik, which have a tendency of a self-fulfilling prophecy (Wendt 1999). Again, the realist case was special in a wider approach, and again research was to centre on questions of process, such as moving from the least to the most peaceful cultures (on change and process in Wendt, see Drulák 2001; Sárváry 2001), identified, again, in security communities.

Sketching the variety of IR research inspired by constructivism and peace research

Taking the interpretivist and the sociological turn seriously opened up many more paths for IR research than just Wendt's, some of them constructivist and close to peace research themes and claims. What follows cannot be an exhaustive list. The underlying theme of all approaches is how to create the conditions for a de-escalation or de-militarisation of conflicts, removing the inertial obstacles of predominant constructions of social reality.

Emanuel Adler's constructivism (Adler 1997) has had two interconnected research interests which, almost textbook-like, link up the emphasis on the social construction of knowledge with the construction of social reality. In his earlier work (Adler 1987), he studied the influence of political entrepreneurs and their ideas in shaping the policy process and initiating change (see also Checkel 1997). This theme was picked up in a study together with Peter Haas on epistemic communities, more resolutely asking questions about the power of ideas-entrepreneurs, reflexively applied to all knowledge producers (Adler and Haas 1992). To complete the picture, Adler together with Michael Barnett (1998, Chapter 1–2) explored the concept and the policies around 'security communities', trying to get it out of its originally objectivist and Euro-centric formulation.

Related to the last item, some constructivists have been concerned with the role of language in the process of change. Coming from a critique of instrumental rationality, Harald Müller (1994, 1995) has emphasised the role of communicative rationality in negotiation processes (see also Risse 2000). Such an approach can also be connected to questions of rhetorical action (Schimmelfennig 2001) and their potential for entrapment, which might force actors to change policies, as part of more general studies on norm-diffusion and socialisation (representatively, see Klotz 1995).

In a related manner, the 'Copenhagen School' of security studies has concentrated on the performative function of language for understanding processes of 'de/securitisation'. It does not understand security as an 'objective' phenomenon which could be deduced from some power calculus, nor as an arbitrary 'subjective' phenomenon. By concentrating not on what exactly 'security' means and is, but rather on what invoking 'security' does (Buzan *et al.* 1998; Wæver 1995), it argues that whenever security (or the national interest) is invoked, i.e. when issues are 'securitised', particular issues are taken out of regular politics and made part of a special agenda with special decision-making procedures and justifications attached to it. '(National) Security' mobilises intersubjectively shared dispositions of understanding, political action and legitimation. In reverse, and this shows the initial puzzle which prompted the conceptualisation, if issues are taken out of national security, if they are 'de-securitised', then politics can return to its place. Wæver's initial case study was German *Ostpolitik* as a conscious de-securitisation strategy. It accepted the post-45 border for changing their political meaning. Several issues were actively 'de-securitised' by being taken out of high politics, to allow more exchange between the two German states and to allow a possible change in the GDR.

Finally, the symbolic construction of social reality, which peace researchers had handled with the analysis of enemy images, has been picked up by another type of constructivism-inspired discourse analysis. The latter focuses on the construction of collective identities, be it national identities and 'other'-identities (Neumann 1995, 1999), or on the role of 'security imaginaries' in the construction of the national interest (Weldes 1999). It does not look as much at whether or not enemy images fit reality, nor whether they are reducible to lacking empathy, but on how they get inscribed into existing discourses/scripts and hence into patterns of understanding and legitimation. Campbell's (1992) earlier study, although self-avowedly not constructivist, seems related, exploring the relationship between foreign policy and identity construction, reversing the idea that foreign policy follows an already constituted identity.

Notes

1 An earlier version of this chapter was presented at the joined CEEISA/NISA/RISA convention in June 2002, Moscow and at COPRI, Malmö and Uppsala Universities. For helpful suggestions and criticisms, I am indebted to Emanuel Adler, Alexander Astrov, Chris Browning, Barry Buzan, Tarja Cronberg, Olya Gayazova, Mats Hammarström, Pertti Joenniemi, Dietrich Jung, Peter Katzenstein, Anna Leander, Sonia Lucarelli, Bill McSweeney, Andrey Makarychev, Heikki Patomäki, Alexander Sergounin, John Vasquez, Christoph Weller and Ole Wæver. The usual disclaimers apply.
2 I am indebted to Emanuel Adler for this idea and formulation.

References

Adler, Emanuel (1987) *The Power of Ideology: The Quest for Technological Autonomy in Argentina and Brazil*, Berkeley, CA: University of California Press.
—— (1997) 'Seizing the middle ground: constructivism in world politics', *European Journal of International Relations* 3 (3): 319–63.
—— (2002) 'Constructivism and International Relations', in Walter Carlsnaes, Thomas Risse and Beth A. Simmons (eds), *Handbook of International Relations*, London: Sage: 95–118.
—— and Michael Barnett (eds) (1998) *Security Communities*, Cambridge: Cambridge University Press.
—— and M. Peter Haas (1992) 'Conclusion: epistemic communities, world order, and the creation of a reflective research program', *International Organization* 46 (1): 369–90.
Alker, Hayward R. (1996) *Rediscoveries and Reformulations: Humanistic Methodologies for International Studies*, Cambridge: Cambridge University Press.
Aron, Raymond (1962) *Paix et guerre entre les nations*, Paris: Calmann-Lévy.

Ashley, Richard K. (1986 [1984]) 'The poverty of neorealism', in Robert O. Keohane (ed.), *Neorealism and its Critics*, New York, NY: Columbia University Press: 255–300.
—— (1987) 'The geopolitics of geopolitical space: toward a critical social theory of international politics', *Alternatives* XII (4): 403–34.
Burton, John W. (1985) 'World society and human needs', in Margot Light and A.J.R. Groom (eds), *International Relations: A Handbook of Current Theory*, London: Frances Pinter: 46–59.
—— (1986) *Global Conflict: The Domestic Sources of International Crisis*, Brighton: Harvester Press.
Buzan, Barry, Ole Wæver and Jaap de Wilde (1998) *Security: A New Framework for Analysis*, Boulder, CO: Lynne Rienner.
Campbell, David (1992) *Writing Security: United States Foreign Policy and the Politics of Identity*, Minneapolis, MN: University of Minnesota Press.
Checkel, Jeffrey T. (1997) *Ideas and International Political Change: Soviet/Russian Behaviour and the End of the Cold War*, New Haven, CT, London: Yale University Press.
Claude, Inis L. Jr. (1956) *Swords into Plowshares: The Problems and Progress of International Organization*, New York, NY: Random House.
—— (1962) *Power and International Relations*, New York, NY: Random House.
—— (1989) 'The balance of power revisited', *Review of International Studies* 15 (2): 77–85.
Deutsch, Karl W. (1966) *The Nerves of Government: Models of Political Communication and Control*, New York, NY: The Free Press.
Deutsch, Karl W. *et al.* (1957) *Political Community in the North Atlantic Area: International Organization in the Light of Historical Experience*, Princeton, NJ: Princeton University Press.
Drulák, Petr (2001) 'The problem of structural change in Alexander Wendt's *Social Theory of International Politics*', *Journal of International Relations and Development* 4 (4): 363–79.
Frei, Daniel (1985) *Feindbilder und Abrüstung: Die gegenseitige Einschätzung der UdSSR und der USA*, München: Beck.
Galbraith, John Kenneth (1978 [1967]) *The New Industrial State*, Boston, MA: Houghton Mifflin.
Galtung, Johan (1971) 'A structural theory of imperialism', *Journal of Peace Research* 8 (1): 81–117.
Guzzini, Stefano (2000) 'A reconstruction of constructivism in International Relations', *European Journal of International Relations* 6 (2): 147–82.
—— and Anna Leander (2001) 'A social theory for International Relations: an appraisal of Alexander Wendt's disciplinary and theoretical synthesis', *Journal of International Relations and Development* 4 (4): 316–38.
Hacking, Ian (1999) *The Social Construction of What?*, Cambridge, MA: Harvard University Press.
Haas, Ernst B. (1953) 'The balance of power: prescription, concept or propaganda?', *World Politics* V (3): 442–77.
—— (1964) *Beyond the Nation-State: Functionalism and International Organization*, Stanford, CA: Stanford University Press.
Jervis, Robert (1976) *Perception and Misperception in International Politics*, Princeton, NJ: Princeton University Press.
Kelman, Herbert C. (1958) 'Introduction', *The Journal of Conflict Resolution* II (1): 1–7.
—— (1978) 'Israelis and Palestinians: psychological prerequisites for mutual acceptance', *International Security* 3 (1): 162–86.

Klotz, Audie (1995) *Norms in International Relations: The Struggle Against Apartheid,* Ithaca, NY: Cornell University Press.

Koslowski, Roy and Friedrich Kratochwil (1994) 'Understanding change in international politics: the Soviet empire's demise and the international system', *International Organization* 48 (2): 215–47.

Kratochwil, Friedrich (1989) *Rules, Norms and Decisions: On the Conditions of Practical and Legal Reasoning in International Relations and Domestic Affairs,* Cambridge: Cambridge University Press.

—— (1993) 'The embarrassment of changes: neo-realism and the science of Realpolitik without politics', *Review of International Studies* 19 (1): 63–80.

Little, Richard (1988) 'Belief systems in the social sciences', in Richard Little and Steve Smith (eds), *Belief Systems and International Relations,* Oxford: Basil Blackwell: 37–56.

—— (1991) 'International Relations and the methodological turn', *Political Studies* XXXIX (3): 463–78.

McSweeney, Bill (1999) *Security, Identity and Interests: A Sociology of International Relations,* Cambridge: Cambridge University Press.

Morgenthau, Hans J. (1948) *Politics Among Nations: The Struggle for Power and Peace,* New York, NY: Knopf.

Müller, Harald (1994) 'Internationale Beziehungen als kommunikatives Handeln. Zur Kritik der utilitaristischen Handlungstheorien', *Zeitschrift für Internationale Beziehungen* 1 (1): 15–44.

—— (1995) 'Spielen hilft nicht immer. Die Grenzen des Rational-Choice-Ansatzes und der Platz der Theorie kommunikativen Handelns in der Analyse internationaler Beziehungen', *Zeitschrift für Internationale Beziehungen* 2 (2): 379–99.

Neumann, Iver B. (1995) *Russia and the Idea of Europe: A Study in Identity and International Relations,* London, New York, NY: Routledge.

—— (1999) *Uses of the Other: The 'East' in European Identity Formation,* Minneapolis, MN: University of Minnesota Press.

Nicklas, Hans and Klaus-Jürgen Gantzel (1975) 'Außenpolitische Freund-Feind-bilder in der Bundesrepublik 1949–1971', in Vorstand der DGFK (ed.), *Forschung für den Frieden. Fünf Jahre Deutsche Gesellschaft für Friedens- und Konfliktforschung. Eine Zwischenbilanz,* Boppard am Rhein: Harald Boldt: 231–44.

Onuf, Nicholas Greenwood (1989) *World of our Making: Rules and Rule in Social Theory and International Relations,* Columbia, SC: University of South Carolina Press.

Patomäki, Heikki (1992) 'What is it that changed with the end of the Cold War? An analysis of the problem of identifying and explaining change', in Pierre Allan and Kjell Goldmann (eds), *The End of the Cold War: Evaluating Theories of International Relations,* Dordrecht: Martinus Nijhoff: 179–225.

—— (2001) 'The challenge of critical theories: peace research at the start of the new century', *Journal of Peace Research* 38 (6): 723–37.

—— and Ole Wæver (1995) 'Introducing peaceful changes', in Heikki Patomäki (ed.), *Peaceful Changes in World Politics,* Tampere: Tampere Peace Research Institute, Research Report No. 71: 3–27.

Risse, Thomas (2000) '"Let's argue!": communicative action in world politics', *International Organization* 54 (1): 1–39.

Sárváry, Katalin (2001) 'Devaluing diplomacy? A critique of Alexander Wendt's conception of progress and politics', *Journal of International Relations and Development* 4 (4): 380–402.

Schimmelfennig, Frank (2001) 'The community trap: liberal norms, rhetorical action, and the eastern enlargement of the European Union', *International Organization* 55 (1): 47–80.

Schutz, Alfred (1962 [1953]) 'On the methodology of the social sciences', in Alfred Schutz (ed.), *The Problem of Social Reality*, The Hague, Boston, MA, London: Martinus Nijhoff Publishers: 3–47.

Senghaas, Dieter (1972) *Rüstung und Militarismus*, Frankfurt am Main: Suhrkamp.

Steinbruner, John D. Jr. (1974) *The Cybernetic Theory of Decision: New Dimensions of Political Analysis*, Princeton, NJ: Princeton University Press.

Suganami, Hidemi (1996) *On the Causes of War*, Oxford: Clarendon Press.

Tucker, Robert W. (1952) 'Professor Morgenthau's theory of "Realism"', *American Political Science Review* XLVI: 214–24.

Vasquez, John A. (1983) *The Power of Power Politics: A Critique*, London: Frances Pinter.

—— (1987) 'The steps to war: toward a scientific explanation of correlates of war findings', *World Politics* 40 (1): 108–45.

Wæver, Ole (1995) 'Securitization and desecuritization', in Ronnie Lipschutz (ed.), *On Security*, New York, NY: Columbia University Press: 46–86.

Walker, R.B.J. (1987) 'Realism, change and international political theory', *International Studies Quarterly* 31 (1): 65–86.

—— (1993) *Inside/Outside: International Relations as Political Theory*, Cambridge: Cambridge University Press.

Weldes, Jutta (1999) *Constructing National Interests: The United States and the Cuban Missile Crisis*, Minneapolis, MN: University of Minnesota Press.

Weller, Christoph (2000) *Die öffentliche Meinung in der Außenpolitik. Eine konstruktivistische Perspektive*, Wiesbaden: Westdeutscher Verlag.

—— (2001) 'Feindbilder. Ansätze und Probleme ihrer Erforschung', Universität Bremen: Institut für Interkulturelle und Internationale Studien (InIIS): InIIS-Arbeitspapier Nr. 22, 2001.

Wendt, Alexander (1992) 'Anarchy is what states make of it: the social construction of power politics', *International Organization* 46 (2): 391–425.

—— (1999) *Social Theory of International Politics*, Cambridge: Cambridge University Press.

Wiberg, Håkan (1992) 'Peace research and Eastern Europe', in Pierre Allan and Kjell Goldmann (eds), *The End of the Cold War: Evaluating Theories of International Relations*, Dordrecht: Martinus Nijhoff: 147–78.

—— (1993) 'Scandinavia', in Richard D. Burns (ed.), *Encyclopedia of Arms Control and Disarmament, Vol. 1*, New York, NY: Scribner: 209–26.

—— (2000) 'Security communities: Emanuel Adler, Michael Barnett and anomalous northerners', *Cooperation and Conflict* 35 (3): 289–98.

Wight, Martin (1966) 'Why is there no international theory?', in Herbert Butterfield and Martin Wight (eds), *Diplomatic Investigations*, Cambridge: Cambridge University Press: 17–34.

Wolfers, Arnold (1962) *Discord and Collaboration: Essays on International Politics*, Baltimore, MA, London: the Johns Hopkins University Press.

Zehfuß, Maja (1998) 'Sprachlosigkeit schränkt ein. Zur Bedeutung von Sprache in konstruktivistischen Theorien', *Zeitschrift für Internationale Beziehungen* 5, (1): 109–37.

5   Peace and security

Two concepts and their relationship

Ole Wæver

At least one thing about security seems to be agreed on by most authors –
it is something good. In other words, the very term 'security' is positively
value-loaded. And precisely for this reason much less agreement exists on
what clear meaning to attach to that word.

(Håkan Wiberg 1987: 340)

[P]eace researchers and security researchers are relatively close to each
other, sharing important dimensions in their analysis or the whole language of the analysis for that matter, only disagreeing on some basic points
right at the beginning. There is mutual understanding, but also a feeling
that the other party is simply wrong when it comes to those basic assumptions.

(Johan Galtung 1988: 61)

For when they shall say, peace and safety; then sudden destruction cometh
upon them, as travail upon a woman with child; and they shall not escape.

(I Thessalonians 5:3)

'Peace' and 'security' are closely related concepts. Yet there is strikingly
systematic variation in the usage of one or the other. One chapter in this
story is also a major element in the history of 'peace research'. During the
Cold War, it was widely assumed that mainstream policy research was
guided by the concepts of power and security. It was crucial to the self-
conception of peace research to take 'peace' as the aim in contrast to that
traditional interest. Similarly, there were 'peace movements' in the street,
rarely 'security movements', while governments worried about 'security
problems', not 'peace problems'. During the 1980s, the re-orientation of
much peace research, especially in Europe, was largely a move towards
'security' and a rapprochement with strategic studies under this guiding
theme. Similarly, strategic studies became re-labelled security studies in
many places.

The present chapter places this history of peace research in the larger
context of a dual conceptual history of peace and security. Peace has a

long conceptual history (as explored by several peace researchers), but what has been the particular meaning of 'peace' in different phases of the twentieth century? When could it be invoked, and for what purposes? Similarly, and much less studied: what has been the historical meaning of 'security' and how should we understand the particular twentieth century centrality of this concept? Finally: how did the two concepts relate to each other in different periods and contexts? For example, why is it that the magic formula of the UN Security Council, with which it can turn an issue into a Chapter 7 matter (and thereby grab extraordinary powers), is to label it a matter of 'international peace and security'? Many hear this as a typical UN pleonasm, but in the light of the continuous and complex relationship between the two concepts, it is more likely that sense could be made out of this. Most importantly, such a stereophonic conceptual history can alert us to post-Cold War conceptual shifts and emerging patterns.

History of the concept of security until 1945

Security seems to be a straightforward concept, and therefore most of the discussion claiming to problematise it has assumed that the critical part resided in its specifications such as 'national security' vs. 'common security' or 'human security'. Simultaneously, the 'uncritical' (mainstream, establishment, traditional) literature argued that there is no need to dissect the concept of security as used in international affairs, because it is a concept we know from our everyday experience, where we value it and accordingly should do so internationally (as a state) too. However, security as idea, concept or aspiration is far from stable or simple.

Enter conceptual history. It is often surprisingly revealing to look back at the history of seemingly familiar concepts because they have changed more often and more radically than usually assumed, and at a minimum this should alert us to the specificity, contingency and political content of contemporary usage. Potentially, it can in addition offer some clues to imprints and linkages still present in current concepts. The history of 'security' has been written a number of times – mostly in other contexts than International Relations, but always of relevance to it (Conze 1984; Delumeau 1986; Kaufman 1970; Osiander 1998; Rotschild 1995; Schrimm-Heins 1991–2; Wæver 2002; Winkler 1939).

The words used in English and the Romanic languages derive from Roman 'securus', 'se' meaning 'without' and 'cura' meaning 'worry'. When introduced in the first century BC, probably by Epicureans and Stoics, it was primarily *a state of mind*, 'the absence of distress upon which happy life depends' (Cicero 1971: V. 14, 42/466–7). It was visibly a negation. Today we tend to think of security as 'something' (and its absence: insecurity), but to Romans, a word for insecurity would be a meaningless double negative (Instinsky 1952).

Since then, the concept has gone through a number of changes and mutations. Some of the most important are outlined in the following (for a chronological survey, see Wæver 2002).

Security has not always been a clearly positive term. Especially to Christians, it was highly ambiguous – only God knows with certainty about your salvation, and for you, human, to be 'secure' is presumptuous. Already in ancient Rome, it was more common to find *securitas* on non-Christian than Christian tombstones. The potentially negative meaning was present throughout medieval theological discourse, only to break into the open with Luther and Calvin (Delumeau 1986; Schrimm-Heins 1991–2). Mostly, however, this negative meaning did not get attached to *securitas* as such, but to related concepts which made for a complex story of mutual delineation and shifting boundaries of security and its family of concepts. The concept of *certitudo* in particular became a vehicle for gradually developing a modern, unashamedly positive attitude to security.

Another important dimension of change relates to subjective and objective senses of security. Today, we tend to interpret this through a perceptional model, i.e. subjective means perception of the objective. Objective security is how threatened you actually are, and subjective is how you perceive (and misperceive) this. However, the original Roman concept of security does not fit this at all because, especially in Stoic thinking, the state of mind is the crucial level of reality not reductively derivative of something more real. Throughout its conceptual history, security has changed on this axis several times. For two centuries, the concept split into two separate concepts (*sûreté* vs. *sécurité*; safety vs. surety/security; Delumeau 1986: 11–14) only to merge again. This strange 'episode' introduced objective security, and the subjective/objective complexity led the way to probabilism. A conception of security as future-oriented and defined in terms of probability has been central to the concept ever since.

A final dimension to draw attention to is what we today call the 'levels of analysis' question, or 'security for whom?'. Many would grant that security in pre-modern times meant different (and irrelevant) things – with the birth of the modern state, security started to appear in ways that we can assimilate to twentieth-century ideas of 'national security'. Seemingly so. Yes, the state becomes the centre of security thinking (in the political realm) – but far from the way it is commonly assumed! To Hobbes and other key early modern thinkers, including notably the early liberals, the state is at the centre all right, but security – also to the state – is ultimately *individual* security (Rotschild 1995; Wæver 2002). The right of the individual to self-preservation is the starting point of Hobbes' Leviathan argument. The ultimate meaning and measure of security is individual security, but it is procured through vesting authority in the state.

Before the twentieth century, security was not at all a key concept or the organising centre of international thought. A first step in this direction came with collective security of the inter-war period. The status quo powers used 'security' as their 'watchword' (Carr 1981: 105) exactly because it blurred the distinction between national and international. It served to proclaim 'an identity of interest between the dominant group and the world as a whole in the maintenance of peace' (Carr 1981: 82). Thus, the rhetoric of security in Britain, and especially France, used security both at the collective level, where it meant status quo, peace and anti-revisionism, and at the national level, where it meant no compromising with national interests. No wonder that the first (and critical) conceptual history of security was written in the 1930s and by a German (Winkler 1939).

Today the general image is that one always had a policy in the name of national security, and at some point it was argued 'the national approach is deficient, let's have collective security.' It is rather the other way round: '(in)security' in some vague sense was a general concern, one word among many to use together with fear, danger, safety, etc. 'Collective security' became a slogan and approach; 'national security' was established, drawing meaning from the then already established 'collective security'.

In the 1940s, the concept of 'national security' made a spectacular entrance in the USA and gained surprising centrality (Yergin 1977). Among the reasons for this swift terminological change were the difficulties of civil–military co-ordination during the Second World War, partly reflecting the difficulty of mobilising the USA for enduring militarised efforts given that country's suspicion of 'standing armies'. To handle a long-term geo-political rivalry with the Soviet Union, the USA needed a concept to express an effort with both military and non-military components and justify a policy above normal political vacillations.

The concept entrenched itself in the USA and spread globally – very soon it seemed to have been always with us, probably because it 'borrowed' content from another concept, which had been undermined. The traditional idea that the state in extreme situations had a right to call on necessity and *raison d'état* (Meinecke 1976; Schnur 1975) had become less and less viable in modern democracies. 'Security' took over much of this idea of radical challenges justifying extreme measures.

In the post-war period, security has a particular international-affairs meaning distinct from its everyday sense (and certainly not the product of simply combining 'national' with a trans-contextual 'security'). This is the core of the theory of 'securitisation' (Buzan *et al.* 1998; Wæver 1995). Internationally (and increasingly in other contexts), the meaning of 'security' is what it does: someone (a securitising actor) points to a development or potentiality claiming that something or somebody (the referent object) with an inherent right to survive is existentially threatened, and therefore extraordinary measures (most likely to be wielded by the securitising actor himself) are justified. By this move, an issue is lifted above normal politics and attains urgency and precedence. This facilitates easier action but also de-politicisation domestically and an increased risk of vicious circles (security dilemmas) internationally, because the actor freed from constraints becomes more threatening to others, not least to the one that is assigned the quality of threat.

History of the concept of peace until 1945

If we follow the same trajectory as for 'security', i.e. from Rome through West and Central European history to include North America and eventually a westernised world, we again have to focus on first the interplay between Roman and Christian ideas and then the impact of the modern state. The Roman *pax* was a concept of absence of violence through order and unity based on the power of the centre (Galtung 1981: 187). *Pax Romana* included no *accommodation* with others; it was based on acceptance of hegemony (Osiander 1998).

In the Middle Ages, most developments took the form of modifications of a set of Augustinian differentiations within peace. True 'peace and justice' entailed an orderly world with everything in its proper place – and after the Fall this was not possible on Earth. Here we could only aspire for *pax temporalis* in distinction to *pax aeterna* in the hereafter (Janssen 1975: 548ff.). (In one of the later moves, *pax temporalis* would be contrasted primarily to *pax spiritualis* as two worldly forms representing roughly political and church matters and thereby shifting attention increasingly to inter-human affairs; Janssen 1975: 551.) Among earthly peaces, one should distinguish between *pax vera* and *pax falsa*, because *Christians* after all would and should aspire for a better peace than the heathens – a just peace.

For the remaining part of the period until 1945, I will mention only the two most important shifts.

First, internal peace was 'assured' with the Hobbesian Leviathan. Civil war had been the dominant peace question for centuries, and when this concern retreated, peace became a domestic reality in terms of 'public quiet and security'. The core meaning of peace accordingly moved towards external security during the eighteenth century (Janssen 1975: 564f., 586).

Second, the enlightenment introduced a systematic hope for peace in the sense of ruling out war from the social order. Michael Howard's *The Invention of Peace* (2000) starts off with a mid-nineteenth century quotation from Sir Henry Maine: 'War appears to be as old as mankind, but peace is a modern invention' (2000: 1). Howard argues:

> The peace invented by the thinkers of the Enlightenment, an international order in which war plays no part, had been a common enough aspiration for visionaries throughout history, but it has been regarded by political leaders as a practicable or indeed desirable goal only during the past two hundred years.
>
> (Howard 2000: 2)

Reason both demanded peace and promised the means for its realisation. A realm of law and reason would exclude its antithesis, war. In most peace plans, it was not enough to ask gradualistically for increasingly sensible policies: a once-and-for-all switch had to be found if peace should be credible and stable. A correctable error in human society had to be located. The political order was a prime candidate, with the expectations that republics (later, democracies) would produce peace, and some would emphasise the economic order where a shift from mercantilism to free trade would ensure peace. Peace through perfection became an aspiration for centuries to follow.

The 'ceasefire' of negative peace could not be the central object of the thinkers of the enlightenment and liberalism. Although valuable as such, an unstable vacillation between war and peace was still an affront to reason. With their optimism about progress, they naturally set 'perpetual peace' as the important – and realisable – aim (Janssen 1975: 586f.).

This vision of *pax aeterna* on earth became possible only when secularisation had freed political thought from the remaining constraints of the Augustinian categories. Yet, in another sense, secularisation far from implied a departure from these ideas, but rather their re-articulation as categories internal not external to this world (Janssen 1975: 544f., 567ff.).

The French Revolution showed how possession of the key to peace naturally leads to a thinking in terms of just war and interventionism along transnational political lines (oppressed vs. oppressor) (Herz 1950; Janssen 1975: 573–5). Self-righteous ideas about 'our side' having or being the key to peace while the opponent is inherently incompatible with peace leads straight into the 'nationalistic universalisms' which Morgenthau (1948) deemed a main cause of conflicts and diplomatic inflexibility.

Both negative and positive peace can de-politicise in a similar way to the securitisation act. Negative peace did so when war (with technological developments) became defined as absolute evil. Positive peace did so when it was tied to a model of the perfect society (democracy, free market or socialism) fixed through extra-political (scientific?) means. In practice, peace discourse often worked to politicise because of the intricate multiplicity of meanings and the affinity between the establishment and war.

Interim conclusion: interplay of security and peace prior to 1945

- Security and peace have usually been linked positively but often distantly, and their hierarchy has changed several times. Only with the modern state did they become closely tied together in one coherent package (Osiander 1998).
- During the Middle Ages, security was not a key concept, and when it slowly emerged as a political concept, this happened under the ascendancy of the concepts of peace and justice.

- With the modern state, however, the realisation of domestic peace – often conceptualised as security – transformed the concept of peace towards an international problematique. To some extent 'security' (although not in our mid-twentieth century meaning) came to define peace.
- Both peace and security hold histories far richer than what became tied into the modern package. Each had connections to other spheres and meanings, but when they met, they were usually seen as constructively connected. The Cold War was different, because peace and security were played *against* each other to an unusual extent.

'Peace' and 'security' during the Cold War

The Cold War section will focus on three elements: understanding the formula of 'peace and security' and its prominence in the UN system (and consequently in international law), looking at the East–West configuration in relation to peace versus security and, finally, understanding what happened in the 1980s (which has a special self-reflexive meaning to COPRI, this chapter and its author).

The Cold War constellation is confusing because, on the one hand, a formula of 'peace and security' is prominent in international law and the UN and, on the other hand, the concepts of peace and security politically were far from interchangeable because only peace *or* security would be meaningful in the political language of one Cold War party.

The charter of the UN uses the term 'international peace and security' frequently – probably adopted from the pre-amble of the Covenant of the League of Nations. 'Nowhere in the Charter is the term "international security" used alone, whereas the terms "peace" or "universal peace" can be found separately' (Wolfrum 1995: 50). 'Negative peace' is central because the main aim of the UN is to avoid (international) war. However, the broader aims of human rights, friendly relations among states and economic development can be seen as a broad-based view of the causes of war or as 'positive peace'. 'Security' in turn is not used in terms of 'national security' but as 'international security'. International security does not negate national security; rather, it contains the assumption that true national security can only be realised as international security, while international security aims not at securing something international but at providing national security in a healthy way. This is a usage of 'security' largely in the inter-war meaning.

In one important respect, the UN construct does draw on the Cold War meaning of security, its speech act function, even if not its national focus. The central operational mechanism of the collective security system is the ability of the Security Council to transform issues by enunciating the magic formula of 'a threat to international peace and security' (Art. 24; Art 39 speaks of the obligation of the SC to 'determine the existence of any threat to the peace, breach of the peace, or act of aggression'). The SC is openly given extraordinary powers here. First because most legal scholars agree that the formulation 'threat to international peace' is open to a dynamic interpretation, i.e. to include civil wars or even grave violations of human rights, even though traditionally it was quite clear that the notion presupposed 'the objective existence of a threat of aggression by one state against another or a real risk of international armed conflict in some other form' (DUPI 2000: 62). Second, the exercise of this labelling power by the SC is not to be scrutinised by any other organ. Legal scholars have contemplated whether the International Court of Justice should have some kind of overseer's function of gauging the 'constitutionality' of such acts by the SC – usually concluding that this is not a viable road (Fassbender 2000). Because the capacity is self-referential, widening security implies strengthening of the SC (Koskenniemi 1995).

In conclusion, the anomalies of the UN compared to other discourses stem partly from importing inter-war language, partly from establishing security in parallel to the dominant function for the states, but centred on the Security Council.

Otherwise, the concepts of peace and security were increasingly torn apart by the East–West split. A pre-condition for this was probably a weakening of the, until then, seemingly simple concept of negative peace. The Cold War blurred the concepts of war and peace as famously captured by Raymond Aron: 'peace impossible, war unlikely' (Hassner 1997: 14; Stephanson 1996).

Increasingly, security came to take the place of peace in the traditional sense of war prevention (Jahn *et al.* 1987: 39). Security settled in between peace and peace, between negative and positive peace (Jahn *et al.* 1987: 43f.).

However, as the Cold War unfolded, a split emerged between the terminology of 'East' (and Western critics) and 'West'. The East was more inclined than the West to use the concept of peace, which consequently got a 'communist' ring. The Eastern side was both comparatively less inclined to use 'security', which had no foundation in the theories of Marxism–Leninism (e.g. the authoritative *Reference Index to V.I. Lenin, Collected Works* contained several pages of references to 'war' and 'peace' but none for 'security'; Jahn *et al.* 1987: note 63, p. 71)[1] and more inclined to use 'peace', paradoxically both positive and negative peace. Positive peace came naturally to the East, which had, more openly, a philosophy of history and thus a basis for a vision about long-term full peace. At the same time, the East was diplomatically more conservative and thus inclined to support negative peace. In relation to the political situation in Europe, the East aimed at a stabilisation of the status quo to sanctify the outcome of the Second World War, especially the division of Germany and the re-drawing of borders around Poland and the Soviet Union.

The West was much more inclined to talk 'security', because of problems with both positive and negative peace. Positive peace was difficult because the West during the Cold War toned-down its philosophy of history and its evolutionism and thus removed the basis for a concept of eternal peace. As we see now after the end of the Cold War (cf. the next section, pp. 62–3), the West certainly *has* a theory of positive peace (primarily democratic peace, but also other strands of liberal and enlightenment thought), but so-called 'Cold War liberalism' stressed that in opposition to the dogmatism of totalitarianism, liberalism was without ideology, ultimate meaning of history and excessive societal voluntarism based on scientific certainty (Arblaster 1984: 299–332). Such scepticist liberalism was not well equipped to embrace an idea of ultimate, complete peace. The West also had problems with negative peace, because, more vulnerable than the East to domestic opposition, Western elites feared that the nuclear threat would lead to appeasement *à la* 'better red than dead'. Therefore, the West tried to fight the idea that negative peace should be an absolute aim.

Security became the watchword of the establishment in the West. In the world of academe and not least policy research, this split reproduced itself as one between strategic studies (security) and peace research.

This pattern changed in the 1980s. During what was then called the 'second Cold War', with the rise of peace movements especially in Western Europe aimed at preventing the deployment of new intermediate nuclear missiles, the intellectuals of and around the peace movements – including much of North European and especially German peace research – tried to adopt the term 'security', which had previously been a monopoly of the mainstream. This was controversial within peace research, because, being associated with the autistic syndrome of deterrence and arms racing (cf. Chapter 4), security has been seen as part of the problem, not the solution, by 'orthodox, critical peace research' since the 1970s. But both social–democratic intellectuals and many peace researchers linked to the peace movements tried to avoid the radicalism of 'peace' and 'disarmament'. This probably stemmed in part from the fact that these reformists actually believed in their own securitisation of the nuclear danger, and therefore it seemed irresponsible to abstain from all change with the argument that only by leaving the track of Western, exploitative, growth-oriented, materialistic capitalism all together could peace be achieved in a decentralised, autarchic, green, Buddhist alternative society based on holistic, spiritual values.

The reformists, in contrast, tried to move closer to the mainstream by picking up the term security, but redefining it. Much of the 'redefining security' business stems from this move. New concepts like 'common security' and 'security partnership' (and non-offensive defence) were introduced, and security itself was to be widened beyond its military constraints. Some of the radicals occasionally took to the task of redefining security too (partly as a reaction to the reformists?) and this led to some of the most extreme widenings in the history of security thinking (Galtung, Øberg).

Still, the peace movement was a *peace* movement – even in the 1980s. This conceptual non-accommodation (i.e. not becoming a security movement) befitted radical opposition. The word from the street was 'peace' exactly because it was shocking in its meaninglessness within Western mainstream thinking on international affairs, just as the form of the movement – masses in the street – was threatening in the political culture of Western liberal democracy. Both constituted metaphorical violence, with the advantage of shaking the edifice of the security state, but with the disadvantage of not being able to talk with it, and thus a tension-ridden dualism emerged with a movement talking peace and its intellectuals talking (reformed) security (Wæver 1989).

This mood of the early 1980s was well captured by Barry Buzan in a 1984 *Journal of Peace Research* article arguing that security was the inclusive middle-ground avoiding the extremism of peace (peace research) and power (IR realism and parts of strategic studies).

COPRI was created in the mid-1980s against this background. While COPRI was never very 'peace research'-like as prejudices go, it was not only because it got a tolerant and non-sectarian first director in Håkan Wiberg, but it was also because it was formed at the height of this neo-security wave within peace research.

'Peace' and 'security' after the Cold War

After the end of the Cold War, peace reappeared as a Western concept. The 'absolute' concept was revalued when it seemed closer to realisation. With the 'end of history' in sight, liberalism mutated back from scepticist, Popperian Cold War liberalism to the more evolutionary and optimist belief in its own truth. When the task of the West changed from fighting a Cold War to building a 'new world order', it suddenly remembered that it actually had a long-term vision of peace as democracy (and/or liberalism) (Rasmussen 2001; Williams 2001).

President Bush senior declared in 1989, 'Once again, it is a time for peace' (quoted by Rasmussen 2001: 341). The famous 'New World Order' speech at the end of the Gulf War (March 6, 1991) was phrased mostly in terms of peace – 'enduring peace must be our mission'. NATO enlargement is so hard for Russia and others to oppose because it is presented apolitically as the mere expansion of the democratic peace community (Williams 2001). The war on terror after 11 September 2001 has surprisingly few references to either peace or security – operation 'Enduring Freedom' – but President George W. Bush's address on 7 October 2001 ended with 'Peace and freedom will prevail', and the (in)famous 'axis of evil' was presented (29 January, 2002) in terms of a 'threat to peace'. Peace has become the overarching concept of the two examined in this chapter.

Security in turn, is gradually swallowed up into a generalised concern about 'risk'. Society's reflections on itself are increasingly in terms of risk ('risk society'). More and more dangers are the product of our own actions, and fewer and fewer attributable to forces completely external to ourselves – thus threats become risks (Luhmann 1990). This goes for forms of production and their effects on the environment, and it goes for international affairs, where it is hard to see the war on terrorism as a pure reaction to something coming to the West from elsewhere. Western actions in relation to Middle East peace processes, religion, migration and global economic policy are part of what might produce future terrorism. The short-term reaction to the 11 September attacks on the USA in 2001 might be a re-assertion of single-minded aspirations for absolute security with little concern for liberty and for boomerang effects on future security (Bigo 2002), but in general debates, the 'risk' way of thinking about international affairs is making itself increasingly felt. We have seen during the last twenty years a spread of the originally specifically international concept of security in its securitisation function to more and more spheres of 'domestic' life, and now society takes its revenge by transforming the concept of security along lines of risk thinking (Wæver 2002).

Politically, the concepts of peace and security are changing places in these years. 'Security studies' and 'peace research' were shaped in important ways by the particular Cold War context, though not the way it is often implied in fast politicians' statements about the post-Cold War irrelevance of peace research. 'Peace research' and 'security studies' (or rather 'strategic studies') meant, respectively, to oppose or to accept the official Western policy problematique. Today, it is the other way round. 'Peace research' might be dated because peace is so apologetic as to be intellectually uninteresting, while 'security' is potentially the name of a radical, subversive agenda.

Note

1 Nor – as we saw above (cf. Wæver 2002) – was 'security' in its Cold War meaning actually a well-established theoretical term in the West (although it was believed to be), but this was less of a problem in a less text-based political culture.

References

Arblaster, Anthony (1984) *The Rise and Decline of Western Liberalism*, Oxford: Blackwell.

Bigo, Didier (2002) *To reassure and protect, after September 11*. Online, available at: http://www.ssrc.org/sept11/essays/bigo.htm.

Buzan, Barry (1984) 'Peace, power, and security: contending concepts in the study of International Relations', *Journal of Peace Research* 21 (2): 109–25.

Carr, E.H. (1981 [1946]) *The Twenty Years' Crisis 1919–1939: An Introduction to the Study of International Relations*, second rev. edn, London/Basingstoke: Macmillan.

Cicero, Marcus Tullius (1971 [45 BC]) *Tusculan disputations (Tusculanae disputationes)*, with an English translation by J.E. King, The Loeb classical library, London: William Heinemann Ltd.

Conze, Werner (1984) 'Sicherheit, Schutz', in Otto Brunner, Werner Conze and Reinhart Koselleck (eds), *Geschichtliche Grundbegriffe. Historisches Lexikon zur politisch-sozialen Sprache in Deutschland*, vol. 5, Stuttgart: Ernst Klett Verlag: 831–62.

Delumeau, Jean (1986) *Rassurer et protéger: Le sentiment de sécurité dans l'Occident d'autrefois*, Paris: Fayard.

DUPI (2000) *Humanitarian Intervention: Legal and Political Aspects*, Copenhagen: Danish Institute of International Affairs.

Fassbender, Bardo (2000) '*Quis judicabit?* The Security Council, its powers and its legal control', *European Journal of International Law* 11 (1): 219–32.

Galtung, Johan (1981) 'Social cosmology and the concept of peace', *Journal of Peace Research* 18 (2): 183–200.

—— (1988 [1987]) 'What is meant by peace and security? Some options for the 1990s', reprinted in John Galtung, *Transarmament and the Cold War: Peace Research and the Peace Movement*, Essays in Peace Research vol. 6, Copenhagen: Christian Ejlers: 61–71.

Hassner, Pierre (1997 [1995]) *Violence and Peace: From the Atomic Bomb to Ethnic Cleansing*, Budapest: Central European University Press.

Herz, John H. (1950) 'Idealist internationalism and the security dilemma', *World Politics* 2 (2): 157–80.

Howard, Michael (2000) *The Invention of Peace: Reflections on War and International Order*, London: Profile Books.

Instinsky, Hans Ulrich (1952) *Sicherheit als politisches Problem des römischen Kaisertums*, Deutsche Beiträge zur Altertumswissenschaft, Heft 3, Baden-Baden: Verlag für Kunst und Wissenschaft.

Jahn, Egbert, Pierre Lemaitre and Ole Wæver (1987) *European Security: Problems of Research on Non-Military Aspects*, Copenhagen: Centre for Peace and Conflict Research, Copenhagen Papers 1.

Janssen, Wilhelm (1975) 'Friede', in Otto Brunner, Werner Conze and Reinhart Koselleck (eds), *Geschichtliche Grundbegriffe: Historisches Lexikon zur politisch-sozialen Sprache in Deutschland*, vol. 2, Stuttgart: Klett-Cotta: 543–91.

Kaufman, Franz-Xaver (1970) *Sicherheit als soziologisches und sozialpolitisches Problem: Untersuchungen zu einer Wertidee hochdifferenzierter Gesellschaften*, Stuttgart: Ferdinand Enke Verlag.

Koskenniemi, Martti (1995) 'The police in the temple. Order, justice and the UN: a dialectical view', *European Journal of International Law* 6: 325–48.

Luhmann, Niklas (1990) 'Risiko und Gefahr', in Niklas Luhmann, *Soziologische Aufklärung 5: Konstruktivistische Perspektiven*, Opladen: Westdeutscher Verlag: 131–69.

Meinecke, Friedrich (1976 [1923]) *Die Idee der Staatsräson in der neuren Geschichte*, Vienna, Munich: R. Oldenbourg.

Morgenthau, Hans J. (1948) *Politics Among Nations: The Struggle for Power and Peace*, New York, NY: Knopf.

Osiander, Andreas (1998) 'Begriffsgeschichte: Sicherheit, Frieden und Krieg', *AMI: Antimilitarismus-information*, 5: 13–27.

Rasmussen, Mikkel Vedby (2001) *A Time for Peace: The West, Civil Society and the Con-*

struction of Peace Following the First World War, the Second World War and the Cold War, PhD dissertation, University of Copenhagen.

Rotschild, Emma (1995) 'What is security?', *Dædalus* 124 (3): 53–98.

Schnur, Roman (ed.) (1975) *Staatsräson: Studien zur Geschichte eines politischen Begriffs*, Berlin: Duncker und Humblot.

Schrimm-Heins, Andrea (1991–2) 'Gewißheit und Sicherheit: Geschichte und Bedeutungswandel der Begriffe "certitudo" und "securitas"', *Archiv für Begriffsgeschichte* 34: 123–213; 35: 115–213.

Stephanson, Anders (1996) 'Fourteen notes on the very concept of the Cold War', published on the Web by 'H-Diplo', the H-NET discussion list dedicated to the study of diplomatic and international history: http://www.h-net.msu.edu/~diplo/stephanson.html.

Wæver, Ole (1989) 'Politics of movement: a contribution to political theory in and on peace movements', in K. Kodama and U. Vesa (eds), *Towards a Comparative Analysis of Peace Movements*, Aldershot: Dartmouth.

—— (1995) 'Securitization and desecuritization', in Ronnie Lipschutz (ed.), *On Security*, New York, NY: Columbia University Press: 46–86.

—— (2002) 'Security: a conceptual history for International Relations', paper presented at the annual meeting of the International Studies Association in New Orleans, 24–27 March.

Wiberg, Håkan (1987) 'The security of small nations: challenges and defences', *Journal of Peace Research* 24 (4): 339–63.

Williams, Michael C. (2001) 'The discipline of the Democratic Peace: Kant, liberalism and the social construction of security communities', *European Journal of International Relations* 7 (4): 525–53.

Winkler, Emil (1939) 'Sécurité', in *Abhandlungen der Preußische Akademie der Wissenschaften, Philosophisch-historische Klasse Nr. 10*, Berlin: Verlag der Akademie der Wissenschaften in Kommission bei Walter de Gruyter u. Co.

Wolfrum, Rüdiger (1995) 'Article 1', in Bruno Simma (ed.), *The Charter of the United Nations: A Commentary*, Oxford: Oxford University Press: 49–56.

Yergin, Daniel (1977) *Shattered Peace: The Origins of the Cold War and the National Security State*, Boston, MA: Houghton Mifflin Company.

Part II

Globalisation and contemporary security studies

6   Wars and the un-making of states

Taking Tilly seriously in the contemporary world[1]

Anna Leander

That war makes states has become part of International Relations (and political science) folklore. There are good reasons for this. The idea can be evoked with reference to venerable classical masters of our trade, including Weber, Hintze and Elias, or more recent ones such as Finer or Tilly. Moreover, the argument dovetails beautifully with the anti-liberalism underlying much realist thinking in International Relations. It stresses the violent foundations of power and states, as opposed to liberal stress on the role of power growing out of legitimacy and common action. Finally, the argument is useful from two perspectives. Analytically, it enables observers to make positive sense of the messy reality of war in large parts of the world: it is just an inevitable step on the way to state formation (Cohen *et al.* 1981). And politically it provides a welcome excuse for not getting too closely involved with that messy reality. If wars make states, well then the best thing is to allow them to be fought out (Herbst 1996–7).

The only trouble with all of this is that, in spite of its respectable origins, its realism and its usefulness, the 'war makes states' argument no longer holds. The main reason for this is that contemporary state building takes place in a globalised context which alters the effects of the central processes which Tilly (and others) argued placed war-making and state-making in a positive relationship. The thrust of the argument is that these mechanisms and processes continue to be useful and essential for understanding the relationship between wars and states. However, if we look at how they work, it soon becomes clear that they fail to create a positive link between wars and states. The point is therefore not to contest Tilly's analysis of European situation. Rather, the chapter shows that if we take Tilly seriously – i.e. follow the arguments he actually develops and grant his argument more than folklore status – it helps us to understand why wars at present do not make states, but rather unravel them.

In order to make this argument, I will begin by identifying the three key processes by which 'war made states' in Europe, according to Tilly. I will then proceed to look at how each of these processes work in the contemporary developing world in order to clarify the reason for which they not only fail to make states, but often lead to the unmaking of fragile state structures.

Three Tillian processes linking war-making and state-making in Europe

The general thrust of Tilly's argument is that states were produced as unintended consequences (rather than by grand design) by the competition among 'wielders of coercion' for control over capital and territory. I want to extrapolate the three central processes by which Tilly argues that wars made modern states so that I can then proceed to look at these processes in the contemporary context.

The first process involved is one whereby war-making pushed political leaders to establish a growing degree of centralised control over the means of coercion and of finance. To consolidate their power and defeat or pacify armed rivals, rulers had to disarm rival groups, as well as society at large, and establish the 'bifurcation of violence' typical of the modern state with violence increasingly contained to the state sphere (Tilly 1990: 68). And this in itself entailed a concentration of the means of violence at the central level. Moreover, protection against external threats required growing concentrations of means of coercion, as competition and technology increased the scales and costs of warfare. This process of concentrating the control over the means of coercion entailed a concentration of financial resources. This is so because controlling, producing or seizing the means of coercion, as well as waging war, is an expensive business which has to be financed. This is all the more the case as the scale and size of wars grows.

This drive to concentration led to a second process: it pushed power holders to develop state apparatuses to administer the increasingly centralised means of coercion and capital. Taxes had to be levied and debts contracted and repaid (Tilly 1990: 85). Arms, soldiers and police forces had to be managed and paid. All of this took a body of administrators. Moreover, the war-making effort in itself played an important part in the expansion and development of administrative state apparatuses. It justified the increasing intrusiveness of the state both into the economy (to extract resources) and into social life (to provide security). The expansion of the state administration during war times was rarely given up when peace came. On the contrary, the administrative apparatus either clung to its newly won prerogatives and functions or converted them to other (state) uses.

Administrative development and concentration led to a third process. It created (civilian) groups with claims on the state and hence produced 'the central paradox of European state formation' whereby 'the pursuit of war and military capacity [. . .] as a sort of by-product, led to a civilianisation of government and domestic politics' (Tilly 1990: 206). Extracting financial resources required bargaining with those controlling these resources. And, at the same time, the expansion of the administrative state apparatus created a body of civil servants who also made claims on the state. How important the resulting civilian grip on the state became varies greatly depending on the relative importance of coercion and capital in the state-building process. Tilly distinguishes three ideal–typical paths of state formation: coercion intensive; capital intensive; and capitalised coercion (1990: 30). However, *pace* variations, the grip of civilians on the state has grown in all contexts.

The importance and weight of these three processes (the competition to centralise control, the construction of administrative structures and the bargaining with civilians) varies in time. Thus, Tilly summarises his argument in terms of a 'cartoon history of Europe' (1990: 206), where the key figure, the ruler, takes on four different shapes which reflect this variation: (1) a *patrimonial* wielder of means of coercion (fighting with his own forces and extracting resources from a population and lands under his immediate control) eventually establishes himself as (2) a *broker* hiring mercenaries and using loans from independent capitalists (around 1400) between different groups. However, he eventually manages to (3) *nationalise* the use of armies and integrate a fiscal apparatus directly into the state (around 1800) and slowly gets to a point where controlling violence is only one of many (4) *specialised* functions (around 1900).

It is clear from Tilly's account of war-making/state-making in Europe that he sees the importance and outcome of the central processes as depending on time and context. It should therefore come as no surprise that, nowhere does Tilly claim that his argument is universally applicable. Instead his book concludes with a chapter on 'soldiers and states in 1992', where the thrust is that 'contrary to the apparent teaching of European history, the growth of big government, arbitrary rule, and militarization now seem to be going hand in hand' (1990: 204). Tilly's explanation for this absence of (the third) 'civilianising process' is that the 'drift from 'internal' to 'external' state formation which prevailed in Europe has continued into our own time' (1990: 195). The implications of this drift have been that states and military organisations receive their resources and legitimacy largely from without and that they do not therefore need to forge the kind of mutual ties that constrained the relationships between European rulers and ruled. Instead it gives the managers of military organisations an 'extraordinary power' and strong incentives to seize power (Tilly 1985: 186).

Next, I want to pursue this path initiated by Tilly, and argue that 'the drift from internal to external state building' has now gone even further than it had when Tilly wrote in the late 1980s. The consequence is that not only is war not leading to civilianisation, but it also fails to prompt the centralisation of the means of coercion and capital, and the construction of centralised administrative structures.

Decentralisation and privatisation of coercion and capital

If we start with the first building block in Tilly's argumentation, i.e. the competition which pushes rulers to concentrate means of coercion and capital, we quickly realise (and even if we don't, reading Tilly elucidates us) that the nature of this competition has been profoundly altered with the 'drift' towards external state building. The formal boundaries of states are sanctioned internationally, so the competition for controlling coercion is essentially internal. Inversely, the competition to control capital is largely about controlling international (or better put, transnational) capital flows and much less focused on the development of national taxation. The combination of these shifts has meant that the stakes and strategies involved in controlling coercion and capital have more to do with bargaining with local strong men, privatisation and decentralisation than with a monopolisation of control at the level of the central state.

First, for most developing countries, controlling capital has for a long time meant controlling access to international financial sources. Recent developments have compounded this with a trend to decentralise the control over capital. As a consequence of the increased importance of financial relations (debt and portfolio investments) and of the debt crisis, most governments have become far more sensitive to the preferred policies of international financial actors. Even if this sensitivity is epitomised by IMF and World Bank conditionality, it is important to recall that it runs far deeper and is a reflection of the direct and structural power of international financial actors (Patomäki 2001). Arguably IMF and World Bank conditionality is vaguely transparent and subject to negotiation, which is more than one can say about private conditionality (Williams 2000).

Privatisation, de-regulation and reduced budget deficits are central to these policy preferences. In theory (and in the minds of blueprint stand-by-agreements), it is possible to imagine that these policies were pursued without effects on the capacity of the state to centralise the control over financial resources. But practically, that tends to be an illusion. Rather, the policy translates as a reduced capacity of the central state to buy support, for example by offering positions in the state bureaucracy, by offering under-priced goods from state industries and by channelling money to local administrators. The reverse side of the coin is growth in the capacity of local power holders to control privatised assets, impoverished bureaucracies and subject populations.

In a context where access to international capital is fundamental, it comes as no surprise that local power holders use the relative weakness of state structures (and possibly their own growing strength) to establish relations of their own with wielders of international capital. Depending on the situation, they might cajole foreign investors, trading companies and aid organisations into paying them some form of tax and/or protection money. This is made easier by the fact that these foreign organisations will often find it more important to deal with the local (real) authorities than the central (state) ones. Local power holders use 'innovative strategies' to link up with transnational business networks to buttress their power (Reno 1998: 8–10). For the central state, this means, at a minimum, a need to bargain with the local authorities. And concretely, it often means accepting high degrees of decentralisation of the control over financial means. Some writers see this as a *sui generis* state-building process (Duffield 1998: 76). And this might be. However, it certainly is not one where centralised control over financial resources figures prominently.

Second, the drift towards external state building is also visible in the evolving strategies for controlling the means of coercion, which have also followed a trend towards decentralisation and privatisation. One reason is the pressure on budgets and on centralised control over finance, which is making itself felt also for the armed forces. This pressure has been particularly intense in the wake of the Cold War. The diminished interest of external powers in propping up armed forces for larger geo-political reasons has meant diminished external support in many places. Since this has coincided with pressure on budgets more generally, governments have had to look for alternative ways of not only financing their armies, but also reducing the costs of maintaining armed forces generally.

Three criss-crossing paths have been walked to deal with these difficulties.

i Local strongmen who have gained political and financial clout over the past twenty years have taken over a share of the cost of – and hence control over – the means of coercion. They run their own militias or armies and provide 'security' in a territory they control (Rufin 1993).
ii Armed forces are allowed to finance themselves by taxing economic activities, demanding protection money, looting civilians, or by engaging in various forms of independent, legal or illegal, income-generating activities (Howe 2001: Chapter 2).
iii The costs are reduced by outsourcing to private security and military companies (Leander 2002).

This outsourcing makes it possible to have non-state agents (e.g. private firms, international organisations and humanitarian NGOs) pay for their own security. Moreover, it makes security cheaper for governments. They only have to pay for the intervention they ask for, whereas a standing army and/or police force has to be paid independently of what it does. Additionally, firms accept payment in concession rights. This saves scarce foreign currency and has the advantage of making sure that the extractive activities can continue, hence securing continued revenues.[2]

These strategies are less disadvantageous to governments than conventional views on state authority might assume. Giving up a share of central control and monopolisation of the means of coercion in favour of a decentralised and bargained strategy has the political advantage of limiting the impact of one of the main threats to central political authority in many countries of the world. As pointed out by Tilly (1985: 286), the military is one of the strongest political institutions in many countries, and the temptation of military leaders to take over political power directly has been strong, as the prevalence of military coups testifies. From the perspective of rulers it is therefore not necessarily an evil that the military as a centralised institution is weakened. It takes away one of the main treats to the central authority of rulers. It paves the way for a divide and rule strategy that might prove more viable than attempts at centralising and monopolising the means of violence typical of the European state-building strategies.

In short, the importance of controlling the means of coercion and capital remains unaltered. But the best way of doing this has been profoundly altered. Rulers increasingly seem to broker between and bargain with armed forces and local strong men with various degrees of independence. Under these conditions, wars do not lead to leaps forward in centralisation. They deepen the dilemma of finding financial sources and the difficulties of controlling the means of violence.

Dismantling and criminalising administrations

The second process on which Tilly's state-building logic relies is the expansion of administrations to manage the centralised means of coercion and finance. However, this process has also been profoundly affected by the 'drift' towards external state building over the past decades. The decentralised and privatised control over the means of violence and finance wreaks havoc with the basic logic by which wars call for an expanded administration. Moreover, there is considerable pressure on rulers to reduce the weight and influence of a civil administration and on administrators to react to the changing situation. The result is that war in the contemporary developing world tends to trigger further dismantling and even a criminalisation of administrative structures rather than creating the centralised and hierarchical structures familiar from European history.

The strategies of controlling capital through privatisation and decentralisation have profound effects on the development of administrations. For one thing, it renders unnecessary the administrative expansion to manage the concentration and/or monopolisation of financial resources and means of coercion. For another, the prevailing decentralised and largely private form of control over financial resources and means of coercion entail that any such expansion would depend on the support of a variety of local power-wielders. Yet these groups have no reason to support increased administrative intrusiveness by central authorities, even if it is justified in terms of an external threat. Finally, extending the administration under these conditions might well mean lessening control, since it will come at the price of making concessions to local power holders.

In addition to this, the 'neo-utilitarian' view on the role of the state in the economy which has underpinned IMF and World Bank conditionality, as well as the world-view of many policy-makers, has been ominous for the fate of civil administrations. In this account, state involvement in the economy is the source of more harm than good, and bureaucrats do more rent seeking than provide services for society. Departing from these premises, it is not surprising that blue-print writers and policy-makers do their best to reduce the resources granted to the development of the public administration and certainly do not wish to see any expansion. The result is a self-fulfilling prophecy: an under- or un-paid administration produces incompetence and rent-seeking as those who have a choice leave, while those who don't have to develop survival strategies.

One consequence has been the privatisation of (or shared authority over) large chunks of policy-making. Even conventional strongholds of state power such as foreign policy-making is increasingly taken over by a variety of actors with a more or less independent status (Wright 1999). And the situation is even more marked in other areas, where private actors are effectively 'privatising' the state to various degrees. The consequence is that private and public blur and overlap within central and local authorities and an 'occult structure' of power surrounds or controls the official structures of power (Bayart *et al.* 1997: 42).

A second consequence is that administrations have themselves become increasingly imbricated in the criminalisation of economic activities. As the resources available to pay administrators are reduced, and their work de-legitimised, there is a strong incentive for them to draw income from sources available to them. Any document, permit or certificate (or its falsification) will cost a bribe. Moreover, the push to privatise state assets has opened new opportunities. 'Spontaneous privatisations' and other forms of administrative take-overs of state property much studied and decried in former socialist countries have their equivalents in other parts of the world (Hibou 1997; Stark 1996). Finally, there are signs that, at least in some parts of the world, administrations are increasingly being dragged into the networks and activities of organised crime. They are no longer merely paid to close their eyes on various illegal activities and trades (in e.g. dirty money, arms, diamonds, oil, drugs, organs or people), but take active part in them.

The trends towards shrinking, privatising and criminalising state administrations have taken place just as much (if not more) in countries at war. Wars have not made it easier for states to finance and control their largely decentralised administrations. They are often fought, at least in part, to consolidate the control of local power holders over economic activity, including through their grip on administrations. Moreover, war economies fuel informal and criminal economies and the imbrication of state administrations in them. In some cases war has become part of a 'complex emergency', where the war itself (e.g. via the aid generated by the humanitarian disaster) becomes a fundamental source of revenue for some power holders (administrators or war lords), who therefore have an interest in its continuation (Duffield 1994).

War and the unravelling of administrative structures seem to have gone hand-in-hand in many places. 'Internal wars' or 'wars of the third kind' are often explained by the weakness of central state structures. Holsti points out that war since 1945 is more often explained by anarchy within than anarchy between states. And he insists that this is likely to continue to be the case because of what he calls the 'state-strength dilemma': weak states are caught in a catch-22 situation. They have to consolidate their power and are pushed to resort to violent means, causing resistance and often war, which further weakens them (Holsti 1996: 115–18). The bottom line is that it is hard to claim administrations of notoriously war-torn societies (namely, Georgia, Angola, Columbia or Afghanistan) have been strengthened. Rather, 'wars in and of themselves do not make anything [. . .] Without institutional cohesion, wars will make for chaos and defeat. Wars provide an opportunity for those political organizations that are able to capitalize on it; they cannot create them' (Centeno 1997: 1570).

The changing civilian constituency of politics

So where does this leave us with regard to the last key process on which Tilly's war-makes-state argument relies, namely the paradoxical need created by wars to bargain with civilians? In Tilly's argument, the civilianisation of politics is a *consequence* of the expansion of the extractive and coercive activities of the state and the expansion of its administration. In view of what has been argued already, there is no reason to expect that war should still have this paradoxical effect. On the contrary, the changes in the way that war is financed, fought and administrated entail that the civilian constituency which gains claims over the state as a consequence of war is increasingly composed of external and/or local power-wielders and that profoundly alters the nature of the stakes in bargaining between states and societies resulting from war.

First, the actors who finance wars and can make claims on states are increasingly external, and this affects the kind of claims they make. The reliance on external sources of finance (foreign aid, debt, the sale of (legal and illegal) services and commodities, and customs) is mirrored by an 'externalisation of economic management and political accountability' (Clapham 1996). The state is accountable for its economic activity to actors who are actually outside the boundaries of the state. These actors are not under the legislation of the states accountable to them for most of their activities. Consequently, their prime concern is not likely to be general shifts in state authority, such as the 'civilianisation' of administration (although they might not oppose it). It is far more likely that the prime concern is the smooth operation of the part of the economy which is of direct concern to them.

The unravelling of central state authority might inhibit this. It is a minimal requirement for the functioning markets that property rights are established and protected. This presupposes a functional judicial system, which states have conventionally been responsible for providing. However, this does not entail that private business would be willing to invest in improving the functioning of states. Businesses will have an individual and immediate interest in deregulation, but a long-term collective interest in a well functioning state. *Pace* talk of corporate citizenship, the latter is unlikely to prevail at the expense of the former (Evans 1997). In fact, most studies of the political economy of regions plagued by violence and shrinking state authority indicate that foreign businesses tend to compensate for the lack of central authority by dealing with local strong men and/or buying their own private protection. They rely on para-statal systems of property-rights protection in the absence of state structures. That is, rather than contribute to the 'civilianisation', the grip of external actors on the state tends to work towards further fragmentation of state structures.

The second important shift is that the strategies of decentralising the control of capital and coercion has left states 'brokering' between different groups, rather than ruling them from a nationalised or specialised centre. And in this, the side favouring an expansion of the central state is weakening. On the one hand, there is no cohesive group (like Tilly's growing body of civil servants and members of national armies) that have an obvious interest in the expansion of the state or can advance claims for the civilianisation of the state. On the other hand, the groups with which the state is bargaining are concerned above all with defending special privileges against the expansion of central authority.

Limiting central state expansion is not necessarily bad. Where the state is the key source of violence, oppression and injustice, it might seem very attractive. Weakening central authority is hence welcomed as opening new spaces for political and social action, in particular through the development of issue-oriented movements and groups with ties to international NGOs. The underlying contention is that it might strengthen 'civil societies' and increase pressures for democratisation and civilianisation.[3] Unfortunately, this is a sadly inadequate description of actual developments, particularly in places where both coercion and administration have escaped state control. The flourishing of civil society and social movements requires a relatively strong state capable of protecting civil society and enforcing rights. The groups that do get into a position to bargain with the state often bargain for things less noble than democratisation and civilianisation.

The real drama is that there are groups which are not linked to any power-wielder (local strong man or central state) and who have no one to defend their interests. Increasing chunks of population are not useful to anyone. They can offer nothing in exchange and hence are not worth extending protection to or organising administration for. There is a roll-back of the state from certain areas or groups. The issue is not people 'exiting' from state structure. It is that 'rulers abandon people who could contribute little to a political alliance and would make demands on scarce political resources' (Reno 1998: 10). State building is increasingly Swiss-cheese-like.

War in this kind of context is not likely to work in a unifying way. At best, it might reflect and reproduce societal divisions, as the following joke aptly illustrates:

> During the Israeli-Arab war of 1948 a Greek Catholic platoon of the Lebanese army is found in a state of complete inactivity despite the unabating and still vigorous exchange of fire on the Lebanese–Israeli front. When a Maronite lieutenant appears and rebukes the men, they reply that they lost one of their men and are therefore waiting for each of the other ethnic groups to pay their proportional toll before they engage in any additional fighting. War in Lebanon is merely a continuation of confessional politics, not by different means but by the same means.
>
> (Barak 2001)

At worst, war might be used to make societal divisions unbridgeable. The point of war is often to produce the enemy to cement the networks of (ethnic, religious, tribal) extremism. Wars of this kind are not caused by extremism, 'rather, the spread and strengthening of these ideologies are the consequences of war' (Kaldor 2001: 5). In some cases new 'quasi states' emerge (King 2001). But these tend to come at the cost of deeper and more violent social divisions and a reinforced role for local strong-men. These wars carry the threat of spirals of violence which can only be stopped by outside intervention.

In short, the prospect that wars could civilianise states is bleak. The main constituencies who gain control over states through wars are foreign and/or local power-wielders who are not particularly interested in such a process. Worse, bargaining with these constituencies might work against civilianisation or even prompt further violence.

Conclusion

This chapter has argued that the processes described by Tilly's war-makes-states argument continue to be absolutely central for the analysis of the relationship between violence and state building. This said, globalisation has accentuated the 'drift towards external state building' and this has fundamentally altered the way that these processes link war and state building: war no longer makes states. Controlling finance and capital is an increasingly decentralised business, which does not go hand-in-hand with an expansion of central administrations and the two things produce a state which is brokering between competing groups rather than ruling them from a centre. The consequence is that war – in the context of most developing countries – at best leaves states where they are and at worst speeds up their unravelling. It therefore seems particularly unwise to follow the recommendations of those who advocate giving war a chance in building states. More generally, the argument underscores the importance of a basic insight we all share but ignore when we turn arguments into folklore. There is no predetermined path of development (of states, democracies, economies or anything else). Many roads can be taken and they do not necessarily end up in the same place. Some might even lead backwards. Hence, classical arguments are useful. They tell us what processes to look at. But they cannot tell us what outcome the processes have. On the contrary, processes which made war central to European state building are making war a major obstacle for state building in the developing world today.

Notes

1 This chapter has its roots in a conversation with Håkan Wiberg. Mette Lykke Knudsen provided valuable research assistance for its completion, and it draws on helpful comments by Barry Buzan, Stefano Guzzini, Dietrich Jung, Pertti Joeniemi, Morten Kelstrup, Viatcheslav Morozov, Noel Parker and Ole Wæver.
2 It is difficult to know exactly how important this 'EO model' (after the now closed Executive Outcome, which was the most well-known firm practising this) is, since most of the military/security firms deny having received this form of payment and the links between the companies and other firms in the business groups they belong to are far from transparent.
3 Migdal (1988, 2001) is often used as a foil by those arguing along these lines.

References

Barak, Oren (2001) 'Commemorating Malakiyya', *History and Memory* 13 (1): 60–84.
Bayart, Jean François, Stephen Ellis and Béatrice Hibou (1997) 'De l'Etat kleptocrate à l'Etat malfaiteur?', in Jean François Bayart, Stephen Ellis and Béatrice Hibou (eds), *La criminalisation de l'Etat en Afrique*, Paris: Editions Complexe: 17–54.
Centeno, Miguel Angel (1997) 'Blood and debt: war and taxation in nineteenth-century Latin America', *American Journal of Sociology* 102 (6): 1565–605.
Clapham, Christopher (1996) *Africa and the International System: the Politics of State Survival*, Cambridge: Cambridge University Press.
Cohen, Youssef, Brian R. Brown and A.F.K. Organski (1981) 'The paradoxical nature of state making: the violent creation of order', *The American Political Science Review* 75 (4): 901–10.

Duffield, Mark (1994) 'The political economy of internal war: asset transfer, complex emergencies and international aid', in Joanna Macrae, Anthony Zwi with Mark Duffield and Hugo Slim (eds), *War and Hunger. Rethinking International Responses to Complex Emergencies*, London and New Jersey: Zed Books: 50–69.

—— (1998) 'Post-modern conflict: warlords, post-adjustment states and private protection', *Civil Wars* 1 (1): 65–102.

Evans, Peter (1997) 'The eclipse of the state? Reflections on stateness in an era of globalization', *World Politics* 50 (1): 62–87.

Herbst, Jeffry (1996–7) 'Responding to state failure in Africa', *International Security* 21 (1): 120–44.

Hibou, Béatrice (1997) 'Le "capital social" de l'Etat falsificateur, ou les ruses de l'intelligence économique', in Jean François Bayart, Stephen Ellis and Béatrice Hibou (eds), *La criminalisation de l'Etat en Afrique*, Paris: Editions Complexe: 105–58.

Holsti, Kalevi J. (1996) *The State, War, and the State of War*, Cambridge: Cambridge University Press.

Howe, Herbert M. (2001) *Ambiguous Order: Military Forces in African States*, Boulder, CO: Lynne Rienner.

Kaldor, Mary (2001) 'Beyond militarism, arms races and arms control', Paper prepared for the Nobel Peace Prize Centennial Symposium (6–8 December), 16 pp.

King, Charles (2001) 'The benefits of ethnic war: understanding Eurasia's unrecognized states', *World Politics* 53 (4): 524–52.

Leander, Anna (2002) 'Global ungovernance: mercenaries and the control over violence', Copenhagen: COPRI Working Paper, 4/2002.

Migdal, Joel S. (1988) *Strong Societies and Weak States: State – Society Relations and State Capabilities in the Third World*, Princeton, NJ: Princeton University Press.

—— (2001) *State in Society. Studying How States and Societies Transform and Constitute One Another*, Cambridge: Cambridge University Press.

Patomäki, Heikki (2001) *Democratising Globalisation: The Leverage of the Tobin Tax*, London: Zed Books.

Reno, William (1998) *Warlord Politics and African States*, Boulder, CO, London: Lynne Rienner.

Rufin, Jean-Christophe (1993) 'Les économies de guerre dans les conflits internes', in François Jean and Jean-Christophe Rufin (eds), *Économie des guerres civiles*, Paris: Hachette: 19–59.

Stark, David (1996) 'Networks of assets, chains of debt: recombinant property in Hungary', in Roman Frydamn, Cheryl W. Gray and Andrzej Rapaczynski (eds), *Corporate Governance in Central Europe and Russia*: 109–51.

Tilly, Charles (1985) 'War making and state making as organized crime', in Peter Evans, Dietrich Rueschemeyer and Theda Skocpol (eds), *Bringing the State Back In*, Cambridge: Cambridge University Press: 169–91.

—— (1990) *Coercion, Capital and European States, AD 990–1992*, Cambridge, MA, Oxford: Blackwell.

Williams, David (2000) 'Aid and sovereignty: quasi-states and the international financial institutions', *Review of International Studies* 26 (4): 557–73.

Wright, Stephen (ed.) (1999) *African Foreign Policies*, Boulder, CO: Westview.

7 Post-trinitarian war and the regulation of violence

Bjørn Møller

The paradigm of 'trinitarian war'

The term 'trinitarian war' was coined by the Israeli military historian Martin Van Creveld in his path-breaking work, *The Transformation of War* (1991). It described more or less war as waged by European states since Napoleon and as analysed by Clausewitz, Jomini and the other classical European strategic writers (Bonaparte 1985; Clausewitz 1980; Jomini 1811). War was conceived of as a means to an end, more precisely, a military means to the political ends of the state in its relations with other states. While politics could be conducted by the states directly, war was predominantly waged by state-controlled armies against their respective counterparts, but on behalf of the opposing states in pursuit of their political ends. Moreover, states were presumed to somehow 'represent' their citizens, i.e. the people or nation, on the basis of a 'Hobbesian', 'Lockean' or 'Rousseauist' form of 'social contract' (Hobbes 1968; Locke 1978; Rousseau 1966).

This paradigm rested on a number of assumptions about the three corners of the triangle, the state, the people and the army, as shorthand for the armed forces (see Figure 7.1).

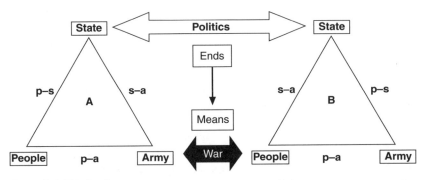

Figure 7.1 Trinitarian war.

- The people was supposed to be a meaningful unity, either in the sense of comprising the citizens of the State (as in France) or as forming a '*Blut und Boden*' community (as in Germany of the eighteenth century), in either case referred to as 'the nation'.
- The state was supposedly a 'Weberian' rational state, enjoying a monopoly on the legitimate use of violence within its border (Weber 1947, 1958: 78). It should thus not only possess the requisite administrative capacity to exercise actual control, but also enjoy legitimacy, and it would be recognised by others as a sovereign entity (Fowler and Bunck 1995).
- The army was mainly envisaged as a unitary, hierarchically organised service, operating according to 'rational' principles as set out in 'scientific' works on strategy and tactics (e.g. Clausewitz 1980; Jomini 1811) and the principles of war (Fuller 1926).

The paradigm also entailed assumptions about the relations between the three corners:

- people/state relations should conform to the social contract which obliged the state to protect its citizens against each other and external foes (Hobbes 1968), to which were subsequently added demands for representativity and democracy (Locke 1978; Rousseau 1966). In the course of the nineteenth century, the new norm emerged that the borders of the state should preferably conform to the spatial extent of the nation, i.e. that the ideal state was the nation-state (Hutchinson and Smith 1994).
- state/army relations (i.e. what is today referred to as civil–military relations) were envisaged as a clear subordination of the latter to the former, the state setting out the ends and the army providing the means to these ends. It should thus be 'professional' in the sense of Samuel Huntington (1957) and Morton Janowitz (1960), i.e. as a malleable tool of politics.
- people/army relations were to be harmonious in so far as the people manned the army as 'citoyens-soldats' or 'Staatsbürger in uniform', either via conscription or in the form of professional armed forces. Arguably such people–army relations also had implications for people–state relations, as the people were entitled to a say in affairs of the state in return for their military service. Democracy could thus be viewed as the siamese twin of universal conscription (Foerster 1994; Opitz and Rödiger 1994; Posen 1993).

War was supposedly waged between such 'trinities', i.e. between states somehow representing peoples and employing their armies for war as a 'continuation of politics by other means' (Clausewitz 1980: 34).

Hence arose the possibility of regulating which political ends could justify resorting to war, as entailed by the *jus ad bellum* criteria, representing one subset of the 'just war' regulations (Hallett 1999). Only legitimate rulers of (recognised) states were entitled to wage wars (to which were later added international organisations such as the League of Nations and its successor, the United Nations), and they were only allowed to do so for certain ends, regarded as legitimate. Gradually, the resort to war was almost outlawed and limited to self-defence and the restoration of the *status quo ante bellum* (Baretta 1993).

The trinitarian war paradigm also permitted a distinction between civilians and combatants, which in turn allowed for a certain regulation of how war could legitimately be fought, as set out in the *jus in bello* criteria (Elshtain 1992; Johnson 1981). Wars could only legitimately be waged against combatants, i.e. in an army-versus-army mode, whereas war against civilians was unjust, as already argued by Rousseau:

> La guerre n'est donc point une relation d'homme à homme, mais une relation d'État à État, dans laquelle les particuliers ne sont ennemies qu'accidentellement, ne point comme hommes ni même comme citoyens, mais comme soldats; non point comme membres de la patrie, mais comme ses défenseurs.
>
> (Rousseau 1963: 47)

This was indeed a neat and convenient paradigm. However, it was arguably never in conformity with reality, at least not universally, and it may provide an increasingly inadequate conceptualisation of modern wars.

Inherent limitations of the paradigm

One of the main deficiencies of the paradigm of trinitarian war has been its ahistorical nature. Far from being perennial or 'natural', its main pillars are revealed by closer analysis as products of evolution and social construction.

- 'Peoples' in the sense of nations (or even ethnic groups) are 'imagined communities' of rather recent vintage (Anderson 1991), and this imagination may change, either simply because of the passage of time or as a result of traumatic events or political manipulation. As a result, ethnic conflicts may flare up within what was previously a seemingly harmonious 'nation' – or a nation may be forged from disparate and even mutually hostile elements.
- States are very much a product of fairly recent, and quite violent, struggles, which might well have produced different results (Spruyt 1994; Tilly 1990).
- Armies played an important role in this process (Krippendorff 1984;

Giddens 1995; Porter 1994), but most of these armies were far from the trinitarian ideal of 'the nation in arms'. In fact most of them consisted of mercenaries, boosted with levies from the peasantry (Anderson 1998; Hale 1998; Tallet 1992; Thomson 1994).

Moreover, the Westphalian order had specific, but often overlooked, limitations. For instance, the associated conception of sovereignty has entailed a division into 'inside' and outside (Walker 1993) which has, to a large extent, been an illusion, even in Europe, where states have habitually intervened in each other's 'internal affairs' (Krasner 1999). Outside Europe, borders (separating inside from outside) were often artificial and externally imposed, and the state (to the extent that there was one) was merely one among several competing authorities. European authors may thus have drawn quite unwarranted conclusions from a rather short and geographically limited experience, elevating it to being the 'quintessential war'.

Arguably, trinitarian war contained the seeds of its own demise or obsolescence in an almost Hegelian (i.e. dialectical) way. While it began as a means to protect the state, in its turn protecting the people, the increasing destructiveness of war from the late nineteenth century (the Crimean War and the American Civil War followed by the two World Wars) undermined the utility of war and produced increasingly strong pressure for outlawing it as a means of politics (Baratta 1993). At the dawn of the nuclear age, Bernard Brodie thus expressed what was soon to become commonplace: 'Thus far the chief purpose of a military establishment has been to win wars. From now on its chief purpose must be to avert them. It can have no other useful purpose' (Brodie 1946: 76). Others have argued that major war has been rendered obsolete as a result of a (painful) learning process, as a result of which states have come to realise that war does not pay off (Mueller 1989).

To the extent that this holds true, the relationship between armies and states must logically change, as armies no longer perform vital functions for the states, much less their peoples. By implication, the relationship between peoples and armies is also deprived of its foundations, which may explain why a growing number of countries have abandoned conscription in favour of professional armed forces, and why it is no longer viewed as a national duty to risk one's life in mortal combat. Hence the growing demand for what Edward Luttwak (1995) has called 'post-heroic warfare'.

This proclivity for casualty-free warfare is hard to reconcile with the kinds of military interventions which even the Western countries have been facing in recent years, and even more so with the likely ones of the future: military interventions in situations of intense ethnic strife of sometimes genocidal proportions; and peacekeeping operations when there is no real peace to keep (as in the former Yugoslavia); the struggle against international terrorism, etc. One of several problems with such engagement has been that the armed struggles have not conformed to the paradigm of warfare outlined above, but have been instances of non- or 'post-trinitarian war'.

Post-trinitarian war

There are many terms for these 'new wars', as they have been labelled by Mary Kaldor (1999), including 'uncivil wars' (Snow 1996), 'wars of the third kind' (Holsti 1996); 'post-modern war' (Gray 1997; Møller 1999a) or 'neo-archaic war' (Møller 1999b). For all their diversity, they exhibit certain common features, which are set out in Table 7.1. As they do not at all conform to the paradigm of trinitarian war, such wars might also be labelled 'non-trinitarian' or 'post-trinitarian wars'.

While such post-trinitarian or neo-archaic wars may be most common in Africa and elsewhere in the Third World, developments in the former Yugoslavia seem to imply that the developed world may not be immune. In any case, quantitative studies of war seem to indicate that such wars (or 'major armed conflicts') have almost outcrowded traditional war (Wallensteen and Sollenberg 2001), hence that they may be the predominant form of war in the future.

First of all, such wars rarely observe any delimitations of 'inside' from the 'outside'. Rather they tend to be intra-state, but very often they transcend borders (Brown 1996; Lake and Rothchild 1998), either because they involve ethnic groups straddling borders, or because neighbouring states feel the need to establish an extended defence perimeter well

Table 7.1 Pre-modern, modern/trinitarian and neo-archaic/non-trinitarian war

War	Pre-modern	Modern/trinitarian	Neo-archaic/non-trinitarian
Who?	Mercenaries, 'amateurs'	Conscripts, professionals	Militias, terrorists, mercenaries, child soldiers
On whose behalf?	Clan or tribe, feudal rulers, warlords	The state	Nation, ethnic or religious group, warlords
Against whom?	Soldiers	Soldiers, civilians	Civilians
Why?	Economic ends: booty	Political ends: territory, sovereignty	Individual and group ends
Where?	Inside/outside	Outside as the norm/ inside as the aberration	Inside/outside
How?	Disorderly	Principles of war, scientific strategy	Asymmetrical strategy (guerrilla warfare, terrorism)

beyond their borders – or simply because they exploit the opportunity to loot, as in the present war in the Democratic Republic of Congo (*Report* 2001). Second, such wars involve other actors and different relationships between the actors than the peoples, states and armies of trinitarian wars.

Peoples are usually at the core of such conflicts, yet not as unitary and cohesive entities. Rather, the struggles are often about the delimitation of would-be nations or ethnic groups from others – and the struggle is all too often waged by one segment of a 'people' against another, sometimes tantamount to genocide, as in Rwanda (Adelman and Suhrke 2000; Prunier 1999) and arguably in Bosnia (Kaldor 1999). According to the most pessimistic analyses, such violence may even be a precondition of forging national identity (Neumann 1998).

States tend to exhibit variable degrees of weakness, both with regard to (lack of) legitimacy and cohesion and in terms of deficient administrative capacities – ranging from 'cleptocracies' or 'vampire states' (Bayart, Ellis and Hibou 1999), over quasi-states (Jackson 1990), where merely an empty shell of statehood remains as a cover for warlordism (Reno 1998), to failed or collapsed states, where the situation has regressed to an antediluvian chaos and a Hobbesian *bellum omnium contra omnes* has ensued (Zartmann 1995). This may not be all that surprising, considering that most African states have merely had as many decades to complete their state-building as their European counterparts had centuries – and they have had to accomplish this within the constraints of much more rigid rules (Ayoob 1995; Tilly 1990).

As a consequence, many states in the Third World, and not least in Africa, are far from enjoying any monopoly on the legitimate use of force. On the contrary, beyond a certain point, even internal security tends to become privatised, as citizens and companies resort to armed self-help, but thereby simply adding to the total number of arms and armed personnel in society, thus setting in motion a vicious circle (Cilliers and Mason 1999; Mills and Stremlau 1999).

As set out in Table 7.2, armed forces are much more amorphous in the global South than in the North. Hence the term 'security sector' seems preferable to that of 'army', with the caveat that it may sometimes produce *in*security rather than actual security for the two other corners of the triangle, the state and the people.

• The distinctions between external and internal security functions are blurred, to say the least, and the internal functions usually predominate (Ayoob 1995). They range from crime prevention and similar law-and-order tasks to counter-insurgency – and it cannot be taken for granted that the state is always in the right and the insurgents wrong. All too often, the state blatantly violates human rights, *inter alia* by means of its security forces, and in a few cases they have even perpe-

Table 7.2 The amorphous security sector

	External security		Internal security
	North		
Mission	National Defence		Domestic order
State agencies	Army, navy, air force		Police
	Military and foreign intelligence service(s)		Internal intelligence service(s)
Non-state agencies	None		Relatively few and insignificant
	South		
Mission	National defence	Counter-insurgency	Domestic order
State agencies	Army, navy, air force	Army	Police, army
	Military and foreign intelligence service(s)	Internal intelligence service(s)	
Non-state agencies	Private military companies	Private Military Companies	Private security firms Neighbourhood watch and vigilante groups

trated genocide, as did the FAR (*Forces Armées Rouandaises*) in Rwanda in the spring of 1994 (Prunier 1999).

- Security functions are often shared between state institutions and private entrepreneurs, the latter ranging from private security companies to warlords (Reno 1998), clan leaders (as in Afghanistan, see Cooley 1999) and various groups of armed civilians. The latter group, in turn, ranges from neighbourhood watch groups to genocidal maniacs armed with machetes such as the Rwandan *Interahamwe* militias (in collaboration with FAR, see Prunier 1999). Both counter-insurgency tasks and certain external security functions such as national defence have occasionally been outsourced by states to private military companies (PMCs), employing old-fashioned mercenaries within a modern corporate framework (Cilliers and Mason 1999; Mills and Stremlau 1999; Musah and Fayemi 2000).

Not only are the corners of the trinity thus much less unitary than in the trinitarian paradigm, but the relationships between them are also much less harmonious.

- State/people relations are often in stark contrast to the Weberian ideal, as states oppress, abuse and exploit the people just as often as they protect them – or the leaders of the state simply neglect the people in favour of an unscrupulous pursuit of personal wealth, as in Mobuto's Zaire (Wrong 2001).
- State/army relations often exhibit the exact opposite of that implied by the ideal of modern civil–military relations, as armies run the states, rather than the other way around – either directly as a result of a military *coup d'état* or other praetorian activities (Pearlmutter 1977) or, more discreetly, by 'pulling strings' and defining the borders of what is 'legitimate' for the civilian politicians, as in Turkey or Pakistan (Hale 1994; Shafquat 1997). Sometimes armies, or parts thereof, even effectively sever their links with state and society to operate independently under the leadership of a warlord, usually for private gain (Reno 1998), as seems to have happened with the various foreign forces in the DR Congo (*Report* 2001).
- People/army relations come in a variety of shapes. Sometimes armies do serve as 'melting pots', helping to forge diverse social strata and ethnic groups into cohesive nations, but just as often they do not (Peled 1998). Either the army is composed of (or at least commanded by) one ethnic group and used as a means of ethnic domination or even cleansing (or even genocide); or a multi-ethnic army disintegrates under the strains of ethnic conflict, as happened in Yugoslavia (Gow 1992). In many cases, armies do not even consist of nationals, but are manned with foreigners – as is not only the case of the aforementioned PMCs, but also, for instance, of the French Foreign Legion (Porch 1992).

In addition to all of the above 'security forces' which are somehow working *for* the state, there are all those who are working *against* it. They are, likewise, much more amorphous and diffuse that the regular troops of opposing armies which formed the basis of the paradigm of trinitarian war.

- Guerrillas are, of course, an ancient phenomenon (Laqueur 1978), but they are just as hard for today's armed forces to defeat as they were for the armies of Napoleon (Gates 1986) because of their elusive nature, their blending in with the civilian population and their deliberate avoidance of battle. Moreover, as has always been the case, guerrillas often combine the armed struggle with various criminal activities such as drug or diamond trafficking (Clapham 1998; Cooley 1999; Malaquis 2001), thereby requiring a combination, on the part of state forces, of policing with counter-insurgency.
- Child soldiers are, of course, to be found in both insurgent and government forces, but the most destitute are surely found among the former (Goodwin-Gill and Cohn 1994).

- Traditionally, mercenaries and PMCs have just as often sold their services to insurgents as to governments – even though the major PMCs, in line with their recent quest for legitimacy and legality, appear increasingly reluctant to work for non-state clients.
- Terrorists have, like guerrillas, been around for centuries or even millennia. However, their activities have been expanded from the 'traditional' assassinations of kings and presidents, or the hostage takings and plane hijackings of the 1970s, to something more ominous. The attacks against the World Trade Center and the Pentagon on 11 September 2001 may thus be harbingers of even worse events to come, say if terrorist groups should somehow gain possession of weapons of mass destruction (Gurr and Cole 2000; Tucker 2000). Moreover, while individual terrorists or terrorist organisations (such as the *al-Qaida*) may be defeated and/or evicted from their host countries (such as Afghanistan), a method to defeat the terrorist threat as such has yet to be devised. In any case, it would require efforts well beyond those of the armed forces.

Moreover, just as these forces bear little resemblance to regular armies, they are also not mainly directed against opposing armies (or even security forces), but rather against the people itself, i.e. civilians.

Regulation of post-trinitarian war

Post-trinitarian war is thus much more multidimensional and multifaceted than trinitarian war, but no less violent or destructive for that (for a preliminary estimate of costs, see Cranna 1994). Unfortunately, the 'toolbox' of legal and other instruments to regulate trinitarian war (in a 'Westphalian setting') is entirely inadequate for containing or regulating whatever violence or war falls beyond its confines.

With a few exceptions (pertaining mainly to 'semi-regular guerrillas'), the Geneva conventions and other pieces of international law have nothing to say about post-trinitarian war. Neither are there regulations for how the irregular warring parties may or may not conduct their struggle, nor for how they may be fought by states – and it remains unclear how they should be treated if defeated or captured (e.g. the USA's creative play with various neologisms for captured al-Qaida fighters).

There are certainly various regulations (in the form of regional conventions and UN resolutions) of the kinds of armed forces that states may employ, e.g. banning the use of mercenaries (in Musah and Fayemi 2001: 275–88) or prohibiting the recruitment of children (Goodwin-Gill and Cohn 1994: 148–64, 183–208), but there is scant evidence of any actual impact on the behaviour of warring parties. The reason is probably that the very legal framework is much too narrow for the challenges of non-trinitarian war.

The time has thus come for innovative thinking which rejects former prejudices as obsolete and goes beyond legal instruments intended to control activities of states. Some of the requisite instruments might well be of a juridical nature, such as the following:

- the establishment of an International Criminal Court (decided in 1998, see *Rome Statute* 1998), which might bring to justice non-state actors guilty of war crimes and crimes against humanity (including terrorism).
- a combined legalisation and regulation of PMCs and mercenaries (for an elaboration, see Møller 2001).

Other instruments, however, might be of an entirely different nature such as, for instance, 'security sector reform' (Wulf 2000) or programmes for the disarmament, demobilisation, resettlement and reintegration of former (state and other) combatants (Kingma 2000). Such initiatives may be a *conditio sine qua non* of preventing wars from flaring up again, along with other forms of 'post-conflict peace-building' of an entirely non-military nature, such as a strengthening of human rights, empowering of women, poverty reduction, etc. All of these are indirect approaches to the control of violence and war, but as long-term measures they may be much more effective in removing the roots of violence.

References

Adelman, Howard and Astri Suhrke (eds) (2000) *The Path of a Genocide: The Rwanda Crisis from Uganda to Zaire*, New Brunswick: Transaction Publishers.

Anderson, Benedict (1991) *Imagined Communities*, rev. edn, London: Verso.

Anderson, M.S. (1998) *War and Society in Europe of the Old Regime 1618–1789*, Phoenix Mill: Sutton Publishing.

Ayoob, Mohammed (1995) *The Third World Security Predicament: State Making, Regional Conflict, and the International System*, Boulder, CO: Lynne Rienner.

Baretta, Joseph Preston (1993) 'The Kellogg–Briand pact and the outlawry of war', in Richard Dean Burns (ed.), *Encyclopedia of Arms Control and Disarmament, Vol. II*, New York, NY: Charles Scribner's Sons: 695–705.

Bayart, Jean-François, Stephen Ellis and Béatrice Hibou (1999) *The Criminalization of the State in Africa*, Oxford: James Currey.

Bonaparte, Napoleon (1985) 'Maxims of war', in T.R. Phillips (ed.), *Roots of Strategy: The 5 Greatest Military Classics of All Time*, Harrisburg, PA: Stackpole Press: 401–41.

Brodie, Bernard (ed.) (1946) *The Absolute Weapon*, New York, NY: Harcourt Brace.

Brown, Michael E. (ed.) (1996) *The International Dimensions of Internal Conflict*, Cambridge, MA: MIT Press.

Cilliers, Jakkie and Peggy Mason (eds) (1999) *Peace, Profit or Plunder? The Privatisation of Security in War-Torn African Societies*, Pretoria: Institute for Security Studies.

Clapham, Christopher (ed.) (1998) *African Guerillas*, Oxford: James Currey.

Clausewitz, Carl von (1980) *Vom Kriege*, Frankfurt am Main: Ullstein Verlag.
Cooley, John K. (1999) *Unholy Wars. Afghanistan, America and International Terrorism*, London: Pluto Press.
Cranna, Michael (ed.) (1994) *The True Costs of Conflict*, London: Earthscan.
Creveld, Martin Van (1991) *The Transformation of War*, New York, NY: Free Press.
Elshtain, Jean Bethke (ed.) (1992) *Just War Theory*, Oxford: Blackwell.
Foerster, Roland G. (ed.) (1994) *Die Wehrpflicht. Entstehung, Erscheinungsformen und politisch-militärische Wirkung*, München: R. Oldenbourg Verlag.
Fowler, Michael Ross and Julie Marie Bunck (1995) *Law, Power, and the Sovereign State: The Evolution and Application of the Concept of Sovereignty*, University Park, PA: Pennsylvania State University Press.
Fuller, J.F.C. (1926) *The Foundations of the Science of War*, London: Hutchinson.
Gates, David (1986) *The Spanish Ulcer: A History of the Peninsular War*, New York, NY: W.W. Norton.
Giddens, Anthony (1995) *The Nation-State and Violence*, Oxford: Polity Press.
Goodwin-Gill, Guy and Ilene Cohn (1994) *Child Soldiers: The Role of Children in Armed Conflicts*, Oxford: Clarendon Press.
Gow, James (1992) *Legitimacy and the Military: The Yugoslav Crisis*, London: Pinter Publishers.
Gray, Chris Hables (1997) *Postmodern War: The New Politics of Conflict*, London: Routledge.
Gurr, Nadine and Benjamin Cole (2000) *The New Face of Terrorism: Threats from Weapons of Mass Destruction*, London: I.B. Tauris.
Hale, William (1994) *Turkish Policies and the Military*, London: Routledge.
Hallett, Brien (1999) 'Just war criteria', in Lester Kurtz (ed.), *Encyclopedia of Violence, Peace and Conflict*, vol. 2, San Diego, CA: Academic Press: 283–93.
Hobbes, Thomas (1968) *Leviathan*, Harmondsworth: Penguin Books.
Holsti, Kalevi J. (1996) *The State, War, and the State of War*, Cambridge: Cambridge University Press.
Huntington, Samuel P. (1957) *The Soldier and the State: The Theory and Politics of Civil–Military Relations*, Cambridge, MA: Belknap Press.
Hutchinson, John and Anthony D. Smith (eds) (1994) *Nationalism*, Oxford: Oxford University Press.
Jackson, Robert (1990) *Quasi-States: Sovereignty, International Relations and the Third World*, Cambridge: Cambridge University Press.
Janowitz, Morris (1960) *The Professional Soldier: A Social and Political Portrait*, New York, NY: Free Press.
Johnson, James Turner (1981) *Just War Tradition and the Restraint of War: A Moral and Political Inquiry*, Princeton, NJ: Princeton University Press.
Jomini, Antoine-Henri de (1811) *Traité des grandes operations militaires*, second edn, Paris: Magimel.
Kaldor, Mary (1999) *New and Old Wars: Organized Violence in a Global Era*, Oxford: Polity Press.
Kingma, Kees (ed.) (2000) *Demobilization in Sub-Saharan Africa: The Development and Security Impacts*, Basingstoke: Macmillan.
Krasner, Stephen D. (1999): *Sovereignty: Organized Hypocrisy*, Princeton, NJ: Princeton University Press.
Krippendorff, Ekkehardt (1984) *Staat und Krieg. Die historische Logik politischer Unvernunft*, Frankfurt am Main: Suhrkamp Verlag.

Lake, David A. and Donald Rothchild (eds) (1998) *The International Spread of Ethnic Conflict: Fear, Diffusion and Escalation*, Princeton, NJ: Princeton University Press.

Laqueur, Walter (ed.) (1978) *The Guerrilla Reader: A Historical Anthology*, London: Wildwood House.

Locke, John (1978) *Two Treatises on Government*, London: Everyman's Library.

Luttwak, Edward N. (1995) 'Post-heroic warfare', *Foreign Affairs* 74 (3): 109–22.

Malaquis, Assis (2001) 'Diamonds are a guerilla's best friend: the impact of illicit wealth on insurgency strategy', *Third World Quarterly* 22 (3): 311–25.

Mills, Greg and John Stremlau (eds) (1999) *The Privatisation of Security in Africa*, Braamfontein: South African Institute of International Affairs.

Møller, Bjørn (1999a) 'The faces of war', in Håkan Wiberg and Christian P. Scherrer (eds), *Ethnicity and Intra-State Conflict: Types, Causes and Peace Strategies*, Aldershot: Ashgate: 15–34.

—— (1999b) 'The role of military power in the third millennium', in Young Seek Choue (ed.), *Will World Peace Be Achievable in the 21st Century?*, Seoul: Institute of International Peace Studies, Kyung Hee University: 91–126.

—— (2001) 'Private militære virksomheder og fredsoperationer i Afrika', *Militært Tidsskrift* 130 (3): 175–99.

Mueller, John (1989) *Retreat from Doomsday: The Obsolescence of Major War*, New York, NY: Basic Books.

Musah, A.-F. and J.-K. Fayemi (eds) (2000) *Mercenaries. An African Security Dilemma*, London: Pluto Press.

Neumann, Iver B. (1998) 'Identity and the outbreak of war: or why the Copenhagen School should include the idea of "violisation" in its framework of analysis', *International Journal of Peace Studies* 3 (1): 7–22.

Opitz, Eckhardt and Frank S. Rödiger (eds) (1994) *Allgemeine Wehrpflicht. Geschichte, Probleme, Perspektiven*, Bremen: Edition Trennen.

Pearlmutter, Amos (1977) *The Military and Politics and Modern Times: On Professionals, Praetorians, and Revolutionary Soldiers*, New Haven, CT: Yale University Press.

Peled, Alon (1998) *A Question of Loyalty. Military Manpower Policy in Multiethnic States*, Ithaca, NY: Cornell University Press.

Porch, Douglas (1992) *The French Foreign Legion: A Complete History of the Legendary Fighting Force*, London: Harper.

Porter, Bruce (1994) *War and the Rise of the State*, New York, NY: Free Press.

Posen, Barry R. (1993) 'Nationalism, the mass army, and military power', *International Security* 18 (2): 80–124.

Prunier, Gérard (1999) *The Rwanda Crisis. History of a Genocide*, second edn, Kampala: Fountain Publishers.

Reno, William (1998) *Warlord Politics and African States*, Boulder, CO: Lynne Rienner.

Report of the Panel of Experts on Illegal Exploitation of Natural Resources and Other Forms of Wealth of the Democratic Republic of the Congo (2001) United Nations document S/2001/357. Online, available at: www.un.org/Docs/sc/letters/2001/357e.pdf.

Rome Statute of the International Criminal Court (1998) Online, available at: www.un.org/law/icc/statute/romefra.htm.

Rousseau, Jean Jacques (1966) *Du Contrat Social*, Paris: Garnier-Flammarion.

Shafquat, Saeed (1997) *Civil–Military Relations in Pakistan*, Boulder, CO: Westview Press.

Snow, Donald M. (1996) *UnCivil Wars: International Security and the New Pattern of Internal War*, Boulder, CO: Lynne Rienner.

Spruyt, Hendrik (1994) *The Sovereign State and Its Competitors*, Princeton, NJ: Princeton University Press.

Tallett, F. (1992) *War and Society in Early-Modern Europe, 1494–1715*, London: Routledge.

Thomson, Janice E. (1994) *Mercenaries, Pirates and Sovereigns: State-Building and Extraterritorial Violence in Early Modern Europe*, Princeton, NJ: Princeton University Press.

Tilly, Charles (1990) *Coercion, Capital and European States, AD 990–1990*, Cambridge: Basil Blackwell.

Tucker, Johnathan (ed.) (2000) *Toxic Terror: Assessing Terrorist Use of Chemical and Biological Weapons*, Cambridge, MA: MIT Press.

Walker, R.B.J. (1993) *Inside/Outside: International Relations as Political Theory*, Cambridge: Cambridge University Press.

Wallensteen, Peter and Margareta Sollenberg (2001) 'Armed conflict, 1989–2000', *Journal of Peace Research* 38 (5): 629–44.

Weber, Max (1947) *The Theory of Social and Economic Organization*, New York, NY: Oxford University Press.

—— (1958) 'Politics as vocation', in H.H. Gerth and C. Wright Mills (eds), *From Max Weber: Essays in Sociology*, New York, NY: Galaxy Books: 77–128.

Wrong, Michaela (2001) *In the Footsteps of Mr Kurtz*, London: Fourth Estate.

Wulf, Herbert (ed.) (2000) 'Security sector reform', *BICC Brief*, no. 15 Bonn: Bonn International Centre for Conversion.

Zartmann, I. William (ed.) (1995) *Collapsed States: The Disintegration and Restoration of Legitimate Authority*, Boulder, CO: Lynne Rienner.

8   'Civil' and 'uncivil' in world society

Barry Buzan

Introduction

This chapter uses an English-school lens to look at the current enthusiasm for the idea of global civil society (GCS). Its particular focus is to bring together the idea of GCS and the English-school concept of 'world society'. Both concepts highlight the political dimension of the non-state universe, and both also carry a liberal programme aimed at constraining and/or reforming state power. Both therefore share two problems: how to define the content of the non-state universe; and how to handle the tensions between the needs of activists pursuing a normative agenda on the one hand, and those of analysts needing a concept with which to capture the non-state, deterritorialised elements in world politics on the other. These problems are linked, and examining the better-developed GCS debate throws useful light on how to develop the world society concept. Activists are constrained not only by their campaigning needs, but also by a dual meaning inherent in 'civil', to define GCS in ways that construct it as 'nice'. Doing so raises two questions: how to handle the dark side of the non-state world represented by various kinds of organised extremists and criminals; and how to handle the global economy and its non-state actors (whether as part of GCS or as one of its targets). Analysts need a concept that captures the non-state political universe whether 'nice' or 'nasty'. The argument is that the needs of activists and analysts may well be irreconcilable. The debates around these concepts have roots in classical ideological divisions. Until recently, they opened a divide between economic and social liberals, but with the rise of concern about terrorism, they may return to a much older and deeper clash between liberal and conservative views of the relationship between state and society.

English-school theory (Buzan 2001) divides world politics into three domains: international system (also known as 'Hobbesian': representing a power-politics view of inter-state relations), international society (also known as 'Grotian': representing the social order that states construct among themselves), and world society (also known as 'Kantian': representing non-state actors – individuals and transnationals – and their relationship with the states system). World society has always been the least-well developed of these three pillars, and this makes it useful to bring together English-school theory and the parallel political-theory discourse about GCS. The two share a common foundation in the tradition of liberal thinking about civil society, which stretches back to the eighteenth century. The English school's concept of world society can be understood as the first systematic attempt to lift the liberal conceptualisation of civil society based on individualism and the right of association out of the state and place it alongside international society as part of a toolkit for understanding the international system. It was, in this sense, more ambitious than the Kantian idea of an eventual convergence amongst republican states, from which it mistakenly took its label. It was also distinct from both early liberal versions of civil society, and Marxian reactions to them, that linked civil society closely to the social structures of capitalism, the liberals positively, the Marxians negatively (Alexander 1998). If world society shared anything with the Marxists, it was the attempt to question, and possibly transcend, the dominant framework of states and nations as the defining entities at the international level. The early liberal version of civil society was an assault on the aristocratic social structures, just as the Marxian was an assault on capitalist social structures. Both sought to capture the state as an ally for their projects.

The state and (un)civil society

The liberal idea of civil society always carried some cosmopolitan assumptions about civilised communities separate from, and transcending, the framework of states, and having distinct social and/or legal codes (Lipschutz 1996: 106–9). But the main thrust of civil society was at the domestic level, counterpointing the state, though at the same time being deeply entangled with it. Depending on one's view of human nature, the state might be seen, in Hobbesian terms, as a necessary condition for civil society (because civil society is dependent for its own functioning on the defended civil space created by the state), or as irrelevant, or even obstructive, to civil society (because human beings are perfectly capable of forming societies without an oppressive Leviathan).

Hobbes was quite radical for his day and is claimed as a founder by both conservatives (for the necessity of the state) and liberals (for his emphasis on individualism and a disarmed civil society). For him, the Leviathan state was necessary to contain the anarchic and violent qualities of an ungoverned (and uncivil) society (the war of each against all). The assumption was that, unless constrained by a superior power, human society lacks the ability to regulate itself and falls into thuggery and warlordism. Later (eighteenth-century and onward) liberal thinking starts both from a more positive view of human nature, giving better prospects for uncoerced cooperation, and from a sharp historical consciousness that

Leviathan has often been a profoundly flawed saviour, itself generating unacceptable amounts of violence and repression. In this view, if humans were properly educated and left more to themselves, both a more efficient political economy and a more 'civil' society would be the probable outcome. The civil society tradition thus reflects not only an analytical distinction between state and non-state modes of social organisation, but also a deep and longstanding ideological battle between conservative and liberal understandings of the human condition, and views about how best to achieve the good life.

Civil society thus has descriptive functions (that which is not the state, where 'civil' takes its meaning from 'civilian') and normative ones (still non-state, but where 'civil' takes its meaning more from 'civilised', representing a particular preferred form of social order). In descriptive mode, civil society is neutral about whether what composes it is good or bad, or a mixture of the two. Those with a conservative view of human nature will tend to see civil society as the problem (because the power-seeking, ruthless and self-interested nature of human beings generates conflict, criminality, injustice, inequality) and the state as the solution (by imposing disarmament and enforced laws). Those with a more liberal view of human nature see the state as the problem (because nothing constrains its monopoly of force, which is therefore too frequently abused), and civil society as the solution because of the natural sociability of humans and their rational tendency to seek joint gains (in the less radical version, as an organised democratic counterweight that can constrain the state and keep it minimal; in the more radical version, as an alternative to the state).

This normative side of civil society is both a great strength and a main weakness. It is a strength because it opens up powerful opportunities for political mobilisations both within the state (aimed at redefining the relationship between citizens and government) and outside it (possibly with the same aim of reforming the state, possibly aimed at bypassing and superseding the state). In this mode, civil society had its most recent airing in the last decades of the Cold War, when both state and non-state actors in the West cultivated the emergence of civil society within the Soviet bloc as a way of undermining the totalitarian control and social atomisation that was the key to the power of communist parties (Lipschutz 1996: 103). Both state and non-state actors in the West, and non-state actors in the East, aimed at reforming the communist states by changing the balance within them between civil society and government. Some of the non-state actors in the West also aimed at reforming the Western states, which they saw as equally responsible for generating the Cold War and the threat of nuclear obliteration (Burke, forthcoming).

The problem with defining civil society in this normative, politically activist way is that it almost inevitably opens up a gap between what is incorporated in the wider descriptive meaning and what is incorporated in the narrower normative one. In descriptive mode, civil society equates with 'non-state', and therefore includes mafias, pornography merchants and a host of other dark-side entities as well as the nicer side of civil society. There is of course plenty of room for disagreement about what counts as 'nice', and what 'nasty': religious organisations, or terrorists, might be placed in either camp according to individual taste. There is a substantial grey zone occupied, for example, by those prepared to use 'nasty' means (violence against the property and staff of abortion clinics and research facilities that use live animals) for 'good' ends. But regardless of either disagreements or grey zones, it remains the case that a normative understanding of civil society will almost inevitably represent only a partial selection of what exists in the non-state world. Therefore if the term 'civil society' is used in this narrower way, it cannot avoid both casting civil society as 'nice' and leaving a vacuum about what term is to be used analytically to label the whole of the non-state social world.

The rise of global civil society

The shift to global civil society as a primary focus occurred during the 1990s, and in one sense can be seen as a result of the stunning intellectual and political victory of liberalism represented by the end of the Cold War and the ideological collapse of communism (Fukuyama 1992). With the communist Leviathan routed and democracy spreading, two changes became apparent. First, and demonstrated in part by the role played by transnational civil-society forces in the victory against communism, it was clear that both the power of GCS and its scope for operation had increased. A more liberal-democratic system of states wound down the significance of national borders as barriers to many (not all) types of interaction, and in doing so opened up substantial transnational economic, societal, legal and political space in which non-state actors could operate. This development was already underway during the Cold War, with many firms and some international non-governmental organisations (INGOs) moving into transnational space. But the ending of the Cold War gave neoliberal ideology more scope to blow away geopolitical barriers, both opening up new areas for non-state actors and giving them more leeway in areas already open.

The second change resulting from the ending of the Cold War was that, with the spread of democratic states, the domestic agenda of civil society versus Leviathan became less relevant, at least within core areas of Western civilisation. It remained relevant in parts of the Third World, but there the problem was as much the failure of states as it was the impositions of overbearing Leviathans. Failed states provided a new arena for the transnational vanguard of GCS in the form of aid and development INGOs. Where there were still repressive Leviathans posing political and/or cultural barriers to civil society, the issue was no longer largely one between particular states and their citizens, but between such states and coalitions of transnational and domestic civil-society forces.

The ending of the Cold War thus strengthened both the descriptive and the normative aspects of what was now referred to as 'global civil society'. In the descriptive sense, GCS was a kind of synonym for globalisation. It captured the general understanding that non-state actors, entities and structures of all sorts were a more influential part of International Relations than they had been during the Cold War. Transnational actors of all stripes were now out there, some of them enabled by the liberal character of the leading states, some of them enabled by the political vacuums opening up where failed states were tearing holes in the fabric of international society. Not everyone agreed that this added up to global civil society: Peterson (1992: 388), for example, saw instead 'strongly connected national civil societies living in a system of many states'. But most analysts, whether or not they advocated the continued primacy of the state, were happy to concede that the transnational domain was uncommonly lively, and there was little doubt that GCS in this sense was making a difference to international norms and rules through successful campaigns on issues ranging from land mines and famine relief, through debt and terms of trade, to human rights and the environment.

But in the normative sense, and in an ironic twist, a substantial part of the newly confident political forces of GCS constructed 'globalisation', which is mainly seen as the operation of neo-liberal global capitalism, as their principal target. The most prominent public manifestation of GCS in the decade after the implosion of the Soviet Union was an anti-globalisation movement that bundled together a diverse transnational coalition ranging from environmentalists and humanitarians, through various kinds of cultural nationalists and socialists, to outright anarchists. Rather than pitching liberals against conservatives, this move opened up the split always present in liberalism between economic liberals (who put the market first and see it as the key to delivering the other goods on the liberal agenda) and social ones (who start from individualism and human rights and are much less tolerant of the inequalities generated by unconstrained operation of markets) (McKinlay and Little 1986).

The development of an anti-globalisation global civil society is rich with contradictions, and highly instructive for any attempt to understand the English school's concept of world society. Among other things, many of the transnational actors that compose GCS are in alliance with, employed by, funded by, and sometimes even created by, states and/or state-dominated intergovernmental organisations (Risse 2002). If globalisation is understood superficially to be a neoliberal alliance of state and corporate elites, then the opposition to it of GCS makes sense. Globalisation is posed either as a conspiracy or as a set of impersonal structural forces. In the hope of maintaining the engine of growth, state elites rejig legal and political frameworks to facilitate the operation of capital. Corporate elites promise economic efficiency and growth and fatten themselves at the expense of workers, the environment and civil society at large. In this reading, GCS is an activist manifesto picking up the Marxian tradition. As Anheier, Glasius and Kaldor (2001: 15) frankly admit, GCS 'has increasingly occupied the emancipatory space left by the demise of socialism and national liberation'. This means that it often comes in the clothes of an aspirational left oppositional project aimed at creating a third force to resist both the state system and global capitalism.

Defining global civil society: activists versus analysts

Partly because it is a carrier of this ideological energy, the definition of GCS remains hotly contested, and not just in the details, but also in the basic conceptualisation. The narrower, more political understanding is rooted in the Gramscian conception of civil society as a social force standing between state and market and attempting to call their power to account. Anheier, Glasius and Kaldor (2001: 17) define it as: 'the sphere of ideas, values, institutions, organizations, networks and individuals located between the family, the state and the market and operating beyond the confines of national societies, polities and economies.' Tacked on to this is the idea that GCS is 'nice', because it rests on ideas of trust and nonviolence, and carries a commitment to 'common human values that go beyond ethnic, religious or national boundaries' (Anheier, Glasius and Kaldor 2001: 15). This definition feels close to what must have been in the minds of Bull (1977), and up to a point Vincent (1986) and his followers, when they talked of world society. It rests on the same idea of individuals and non-state organisations as carriers of values in opposition to the impositions of a state-created Westphalian international society. This view of GCS, however, is more clearly formulated than the English school's concept of world society, particularly so in relation to the economic sector. English-school thinkers have been largely silent about the economic sector, and it could be inferred from that silence that they agree with the political proponents of GCS in differentiating the two in order to exclude the economic from the civil.

But on a deeper reading of globalisation, GCS is itself part of the process. Capitalism is a principal mover in the process of globalisation, but not the only one, and not necessarily the principal definition of what globalisation is about. In this reading, interestingly prefigured by Rosenau (1990), the key is the development of 'powerful people' and a consequent across-the-board shift in the nature of authority structures and political relationships. Starting from the industrial revolution, it has served the interests of both state and capital to have better educated, healthier and wealthier citizens and workers. Only by improving the capacities of their citizens/workers could the state increase its power and capital increase its returns. But as more and more individuals have become more capable, they have become less subservient to authority, more willing to define their own agendas and more able to create their own nodes and networks in pursuit of those agendas. This development underpinned the flowering of Western democracy during the twentieth century and has a certain teleological force. The question is not only the happy liberal one of what happens if democratising and decentralising forces begin seriously to transcend the state, but also the darker Hobbesian one of what happens if 'powerful people' express themselves by organising crime and pursuing extremist agendas.

Rosenau's scheme (1990: 40) generates an international system divided between 'sovereignty-bound' and 'sovereignty-free' actors whose fate depends on both the balance of power between the two worlds and, with echoes of the Stanford school's approach (Meyer *et al.* 1997), on whether or not they agree or differ on what the prevailing norms of the system should be. This comes very close to the English school's division between international and world society and reflects the same dilemma about whether the two are in tension or in harmony. It reflects a complex interplay among political, economic and social structures in which a strong historical line of development is changing the capabilities and requirements of all kinds of actors simultaneously. Since capitalism is immensely effective at stimulating and spreading technological innovation, this whole package is pushed and pulled by opportunities and dangers arising from new technological capabilities. Powers of destruction become so great that total war becomes absurd and the planetary environment moves from being a background constant to a foreground variable. Powers of communication become so widespread, and so cheap, that geography no longer determines the shape of community and the world becomes a single information space. Powers of transportation become so efficient and so dense that the world becomes a single market and interdependence effects ripple easily from one end of the planet to the other. In this wider view of globalisation, GCS cannot be separated from capitalism and can only be understood as part of it. GCS exists through, between and around states rather than just within them. Rather than being counterpointed against a global state – as civil society sometimes was against the territorial state – it is itself part of and entangled with a loose and rather hazy structure of global governance. This structure has mostly been generated by the leading capitalist states, but now has a quasi-autonomous standing.

A recent reflection on this wider, more analytical understanding of global civil society is offered by John Keane (2001). He rejects the Gramscian separation of civil society from the economic sector on the grounds that this generates a major misunderstanding of what GCS is and how it works. Like Rosenau, he sees the global economy as part of GCS, with 'turbo-capitalism' as one of the driving forces underpinning it:

> the contemporary thickening and stretching of networks of socio-economic institutions across borders to all four corners of the earth, such that peaceful or 'civil' effects of these non-governmental net-

works are felt everywhere. . . . It comprises . . . organisations, civic and business initiatives, coalitions, social movements, linguistic communities and cultural identities. All of them . . . deliberately organise themselves and conduct their cross-border social activities, business, and politics outside the boundaries of governmental structures, with a minimum of violence and a maximum of respect for the principle of civilised power-sharing among different ways of life.

(Keane 2001: 23–4)

Keane's more comprehensive definition fleshes out an understanding of GCS that goes much further towards filling the non-state side of a state/non-state distinction. He correctly points out that there is no sharp line between state and non-state (Keane 2001: 35). Within democratic states there are numerous quasi-autonomous non-governmental organisations (QUANGOs) that blur the boundary, and during the Cold War communist states were notorious for constructing short-leash versions of QUANGOs such as the various official peace councils. Similarly at the global level many INGOs receive support and funding from governments, whether they be humanitarian aid organisations or various forms of ideological fifth-column. The Red Cross, for example, is closely integrated into the state system as a key supporter for some aspects of international law. Keane seems absolutely right in insisting that the non-state dimension cannot be understood without incorporating the economic sector, even though doing so necessarily wrecks some of the emancipatory political agenda that the activists want to pin onto the concept.

But although Keane's definition is more analytical, he does not wholly abandon the political project. Keane is also committed to the idea that GCS is 'nice', in the sense of committed to non-violence, civility and tolerance. His incorporation of the economic sector, however, makes it difficult for him to maintain coherence on this issue. Although he rightly points out that the corporate world by and large supports the value of nonviolence in the interests of business efficiency, he also concedes that: 'Inequalities of power, bullying, and fanatical, violent attempts to de-globalise are chronic features of global civil society' (Keane 2001: 33, 39). This hints strongly, though it does not explore, that there is a dark side to GCS. He is also rightly aware (2001: 40) that GCS does not stand above the grimy issues of force and coercion. Because it is vulnerable to ruthless uncivil elements, whether state-based or not, GCS needs protection and can most easily acquire it from states. On the grounds that 'civil' carries two meanings (non-state and civilised), both Keane (although he comes closer to acknowledging it) and Anheier, Glasius and Kaldor marginalise the dark side of the non-state world from their definitions of GCS. If the narrower and/or 'nicer' view of GCS is accepted, then for analytical purposes one would need a parallel concept of global uncivil society to cover what has been left out of the non-state picture. This would be true whether or not one's purpose was primarily analytical or primarily political. The existence of such uncivil society, and the need to contain it, is of course the prime (Hobbesian) justification for the existence of the state and, by extension, also of the existence of an international society created and maintained by states. Nothing could illustrate this more clearly than the terrorist attacks on the USA on September 11, 2001.

Global uncivil society

The dark side of the non-state world is a problem for the advocates of both global civil society and world society. The GCS school, especially its activist wing, is stuck with the 'nice' meaning of 'civil', which pushes it towards regarding the non-state as inherently a good thing. It does not take a vast amount of empirical research to demonstrate that both the benign and the malign views of civil society are incorrect as characterisations of the whole non-state world. In reality, there is always a mixture of the two. The 'nice', non-violent side of civil society both domestic and global is to be found everywhere in voluntary associations, NGOs, INGOs and firms. But the 'nasty' side is everywhere too, in the form of crime, hoodlum anarchism and self-righteous extremists of all stripes. The anti-globalisation movement has run up against this in the form of its anarchist wing, which is useful at generating media attention, but destructive to its political image. The neoliberal-driven globalisation of the last decade also has to come to terms with the consequence that opening borders for commerce is a boon to organised crime and extremists. Indeed, after the events of September 11, there are firm grounds for expecting that the politics of global civil society/world society will shift away from economic versus social liberal, and back more into the frame of liberal versus conservative. Al-Qaida has highlighted the dark side of global (un)civil society, and in doing so has strengthened the Hobbesian case for the state as a necessary defence against the disorders of an under-regulated human condition.

Because GCS rests on the same distinction between state and non-state as does world society, there are many useful lessons here for English-school thinking. The GCS literature has a better-developed view of the economic sector than can be found in English-school thinking. Its normative commitments run in parallel to the solidarist wing of the English school (Dunne and Wheeler 1996; Vincent 1986; Wheeler 2000) but, in principle, the English school is better placed to take into account the dark side of the non-state world. First, its concept of world society is not restricted to 'civil' and therefore has an easier time in incorporating the whole of the non-state world. Second, it is less focused on transnational actors and therefore better placed to deal with the non-state identity components of world politics such as Islam. Islam is an excellent example of a world society element that is not in itself a transnational actor. It is a non-state identity that does not have actor quality itself, but which carries a mobilising power that enables a range of non-state (and state) actors. When it mobilises terrorism, it is a much stronger challenge to international society than human rights, because it privatises the use of force, thus undermining the foundations of the Westphalian political order. Third, world society is better adapted to thinking about the global level, having originally been designed for that purpose. GCS is still hung about with many of the political trappings carried over from its roots in the debates about civil society. These make it an effective idea for activists, but a problematic one for analysts.

Conclusion: where to from here?

Whatever their flaws, concepts such as GCS and world society are an essential part of the toolkit that we need to develop if we are to equip ourselves to think meaningfully about globalisation. If the discussion in this chapter highlights anything, it is the necessity to encompass the whole of the non-state political universe when trying to conceptualise the politics of globalisation. Particularly in the political sector, it is useful to distinguish between civil and uncivil society, both domestically and globally. Among other things, this distinction offers a helpful way into classifying the types of violence that occur in a globalised international system, and therefore of tracking the changes that differentiate such a system from its Westphalian predecessor. Using the basic frame of the debates about world society and GCS, one can identify four distinct structures of violence:

- *state versus state.* This structure of violence is the traditional concern of Westphalian International Relations about the disorders of a second-order form of anarchy in which sovereign states play balance of power and regularly end up at war with each other. This concern has declined overall with the end of the Cold War and the rise of a zone of democratic peace at the core of the international system. It still remains active in the periphery, especially in the Middle East and Asia, where increasing numbers of states are equipped with weapons of mass destruction. Whether it will become active in the form of military threats from the periphery to the core remains to be seen, but the potential is indicated by the willingness of the sole superpower, the USA, to securitise North Korea, Iraq and Iran.
- *state versus uncivil society.* This is the traditional Hobbesian agenda where the state is the solution to civil disorder typical of primary anarchy. The state protects its citizens against each other by creating a legal framework and enforcing a monopoly of legitimate violence against warlords, terrorists, organised crime and whatever uncivil elements seek to disrupt the peace or deploy force against the citizenry. But under globalisation, a wider dimension is added. The openness of

a liberalised economy provides opportunities for transnational criminals, terrorists and extremists of all sorts to operate on a global scale.
As a consequence, the traditional Hobbesian domestic security
agenda gets pushed up to the international level, becoming a
problem for international society against global uncivil society.

- *state versus civil society*. This is the core concern of those who see the
  state more as an agent of repression and a vehicle for elite interests
  than as a Hobbesian ringholder. In the present international system it
  exposes a large agenda of state elites abusing their political primacy
  and their control of police, law and military to suppress civil society in
  pursuit of their own interests, whether self-enrichment or hanging on
  to power. Of the many current examples, one might note the military
  junta in Burma; Robert Mugabe's reign of terror in Zimbabwe; the
  North's war against the South in Sudan; the regime of dynastic
  communism in North Korea; the massacre of Tutsis in Rwanda; and
  the Indonesian attempt to prevent the secession of East Timor. Such
  repression becomes a concern both for international society and for
  global civil society elements such as the human rights movement.

- *civil versus uncivil society*. This is perhaps the most worrying and distinctive structure of violence under globalisation. It is where the state
  more or less ceases to exist, thereby removing the previous three
  options and leaving the civil and uncivil aspects of society in an
  unmediated 'state of nature' relationship with each other and the rest
  of the world. This is most easily illustrated by the uncivil wars common
  in Africa, where, as in Congo, Liberia, Sierra Leone, Somalia and
  Angola, the state structures fail, leaving various warlords, 'big men'
  and suchlike to battle out their territorial and political claims. Some
  of these will claim to *be* the state, but in practice control only part of
  its territory and exercise few if any of its functions. State failure poses
  problems for international society in how to react politically to the
  holes torn in its fabric. It poses problems for GCS in terms of how to
  deal with humanitarian and human rights consequences of chaos. It
  poses opportunities for global uncivil society in terms of providing
  safe-havens for all sorts of illegal and/or anti-social activities.

References

Alexander, Jeffrey C. (1998) 'Introduction – civil society I, II, III', in J.C. Alexan-
der (ed.), *Real Civil Societies*, London: Sage: 1–19.
Anheier, Helmut, Marlies Glasius and Mary Kaldor (2001) 'Introducing global civil
society', in Helmut Anheier, Marlies Glasius and Mary Kaldor (eds), *Global Civil
Society 2001*, Oxford: Oxford University Press: 3–22.
Bull, Hedley (1977) *The Anarchical Society. A Study of Order in World Politics*, London:
Macmillan.
Burke, Patrick (forthcoming) *'European Nuclear Disarmament' (END): A Study of Its*

Successes and Failures with Particular Emphasis on Its Work in the UK, PhD thesis, University of Westminster.

Buzan, Barry (2001) 'The English School: an underexploited resource in IR', *Review of International Studies* 27 (3): 471–88.

Dunne, Tim and Nicholas Wheeler (1996) 'Hedley Bull's pluralism of the intellect and solidarism of the will', *International Affairs (London)* 72 (1): 91–107.

Fukuyama, Francis (1992) *The End of History and the Last Man*, London: Penguin.

Keane, John (2001) 'Global civil society?', in Helmut Anheier, Marlies Glasius and Mary Kaldor (eds), *Global Civil Society 2001*, Oxford: Oxford University Press: 23–47.

Lipschutz, Ronnie D. (1996) 'Reconstructing world politics: the emergence of global civil society', in Rick Fawn and Jeremy Larkin (eds), *International Society After the Cold War*, Basingstoke: Macmillan: 101–31.

McKinlay, R.D. and Richard Little (1986) *Global Problems and World Order*, London: Pinter.

Meyer, John W., John Boli, George M. Thomas and Francisco O. Ramirez (1997) 'World society and the nation-state', *American Journal of Sociology* 103 (1): 144–81.

Peterson, M.J. (1992) Transnational activity, international society and world politics', *Millennium* 21 (3): 371–88.

Risse, Thomas (2002) 'Transnational actors and world politics', in Walter Carlsnaes, Thomas Risse and Beth A. Simmons (eds), *Handbook of International Relations*, London: Sage: 255–74.

Rosenau, James N. (1990) *Turbulence in World Politics: A Theory of Change and Continuity*, London: Harvester Wheatsheaf.

Vincent, R.J. (1986) *Human Rights and International Relations: Issues and Responses*, Cambridge: Cambridge University Press.

Wheeler, Nicholas J. (2000) *Saving Strangers: Humanitarian Intervention in International Society*, Oxford: Oxford University Press.

9 Globalisation and societal insecurity

The securitisation of terrorism and competing strategies for global governance

Morten Kelstrup

The purpose of this chapter is to discuss the relationship between globalisation and societal insecurity, and to relate this to the events of 11 September 2001. The main perspective is that globalisation increases the importance of societal insecurity, and that the events of 11 September marked an important step in the globalisation of a specific form of societal insecurity: terrorism. Further, these events and the reactions in their aftermath created a new, 'formative' situation in global politics in which the threat from terrorism was 'securitised' and attempts are made to legitimise new security policies and strategies. The result is that we experience a new competition between different strategies not only for security, but also for governance in the global system.

Globalisation and the dislocation of politics

The concept of globalisation shall here in all brevity be taken to refer to the development of social systems which transcend the borders of the nation-states. This definition lies close to the definition which regards globalisation as social processes creating transnational social space (Leander 2001a). Yet, it is added that the different kinds of transnationalisation are seen as being so strong that they get their own dynamics, dynamics which cannot be contained within the traditional nation-states (Beck 1998). In this perspective, globalisation is in its main features equal to 'denationalisation' (Zürn 1998: 63ff.).

The processes of globalisation have many dimensions, and they are complex and contradictory, because globalisation provokes national and other forms of reaction. Economic globalisation implies the emergence and strengthening of transnational economic systems, encompassing intensification of trade, financial flows, investments and labour movements across state borders. It has long been seen as the most important dimension of globalisation. But other dimensions are of growing importance, for instance transnationalisation of cultures, media, ecological systems and so on. Such processes of transnationalisation get their own dynamics and develop in different ways beyond the control of the individual states.

Politics is, of course, influenced and changed by globalisation in rather fundamental ways, but it is far too simplified just to claim that we experience a 'political globalisation'. The complex and often contradictory political processes also include the 'dislocation of politics', indicating that the place and structure of 'the political' is changing (Beck 1998: 13f.; Leander 2001a). Often reference is made to the view that globalisation affects the ability of states to govern within their territory, and that the 'locus' of politics, which until now has been mainly in the political systems of nation-states, is pushed 'upwards' to the supranational level *and* 'downwards' to the local level. But this interpretation should also be differentiated. Although we have seen an impressive growth of international organisations and regimes, we also see trends which undermine the strength of governance through international regimes. And the tendencies towards 'localisation' are contradictory. Sometimes they might involve more political 'empowerment' to local entities, but maybe the opposite is the dominant trend.

Even if states are weakened, we have open questions with regard to how weakened they are. Part of the picture is that states remain actors, but get new functions, and that the character of statehood is transformed in differentiated ways in the processes of globalisation. We now have one super-power (the United States), 'transnational states' (as in the EU), relatively normal, modern states, and weak states and 'quasi-states' with huge internal problems. The very different states all operate in the same international system and all interact with non-states actors.

The effect is that, in the transnationalising world, we see a move from government to governance. Governance might, in all brevity, be understood as the ability of social systems with many different actors to govern through the constitution of norms and rules even without any fixed formal structure (as we find in states). We see growing regulation through networks of different kinds of actors, for instance involving states' representatives, actors below the state level (such as firms or NGOs), above the state level (international organisations with special competences) and transnational actors (MNCs and INGOs) in the same processes (for instance, in the system of 'multi-level governance' in the European Union). These developments should direct our attention to strategies for shaping transnational and global governance, a task which, of course, is difficult because systems of governance are very fluid in their structures.

From military insecurity to societal insecurity

Of course, the processes of globalisation also affect security and the ways in which social systems of different kinds experience security problems.

Our answer to the question of how we shall understand globalisation in relation to security clearly depends on our understanding of 'security' and related concepts. Here I take the view that insecurity of a certain entity (reference object) exists when the entity is threatened in a basic way (with regard to survival of identity, basic structures or vital functions). Security exists either when there are no threats or when there is an ability to neutralise the threats so that basic survival is not affected. Security is relational and relative. It has the character of a 'social fact', which can be and will be interpreted by observers as well as by the agents themselves.

I use the concept of 'societal insecurity' as encompassing situations in which societal entities, collectives *or* individuals, are (and/or feels) threatened. My terminology here is a little different from that used in Wæver *et al.* (1993) and Buzan *et al.* (1998). Basically, societal security has, in the terminology of Buzan *et al.*, to do with threats against 'large, self-sustaining identity groups' (1998: 119–20) or what we might call communities or macro-identities. The most commonly used example of threatened societal identity is nations, although this, as the authors mention, is not the only relevant collective identity in understanding societal security. I prefer a broader use of the concept of societal insecurity which not only includes that collective identities might be threatened, but also includes situations in which many and maybe all individuals in a society are threatened or experience threats, as well as situations in which these threats are not articulated against a greater collective identity. Thus, there might be threats towards individuals or threats towards the 'social order' (or both). Such insecurity is in my view 'societal insecurity'.

Returning to the question of how globalisation affects security, it should first be clear that the political–military sector has been globalised for a very long time. The sector has been globalised in the sense that states were exposed to threats of military aggression and – as members of an anarchic international political system – part of a system which had a dynamic of its own beyond the control of the individual states. The world wars and, in particular, the creation of the atom bomb and the subsequent emergence of the terror balance can be seen as a globalisation of the political–military sector and of military-based insecurity.

In addition, globalisation in other sectors than the military tends to increase societal insecurity. Globalisation in non-military sectors might cause societal insecurity and even new patterns of conflict and war. In particular, we have a debate on the effects of the neoliberal, economic globalisation (for instance Brand *et al.* 2000; Geertsen 2001). Basically, it is claimed that the expansion of transnational markets leads to a weakening of the states' legitimacy and power (Leander 2001b). One problem is the transnationalisation of organised crime. Another is the increasing pressure for migration and the securitisation of this issue. Others will go even further and argue that the increased importance of markets and privatisation combined with difficulties in public control of transnational flows lead to new risks, for instance, with regard to food insecurity, spread of ill-nesses, etc. Further, it is claimed that the neoliberal form of economic globalisation leads to new ecological problems and through this – and in particular through its effects on weak states – to new societal insecurity and increasing potentials for clashes of interests, for instance in raw materials, including water and oil. Of course, these rather negative views on the neoliberal form of economic globalisation should be balanced by pointing to the positive effects which the globalisation of markets might have with regard to, for instance, economic growth and spread of techno-logy and skills on a global scale. But even if these effects are taken into account, it can hardly be denied that a major effect of an uncontrolled neoliberal economic globalisation is increased societal insecurity.

Some find that globalisation even leads to new kinds of conflicts and wars. Mary Kaldor, in her book *New and Old Wars*, has claimed that globali-sation affects our traditional views on war (Kaldor 1999). Her interpreta-tion is that we experience a new type of organised violence identified as 'new wars'. These are characterised as a mixture of military conflict, organised crime and massive violations of human rights. The actors are global and local, public and private. The wars are fought on the basis of political interests of special groups, and actors use terror and destabilising intervention, which is prohibited by international law.

An obvious counterargument is that the so-called 'new' kind of mixed war is rather old. It seems, though, that we are experiencing new develop-ments and changed patterns with regard to conflict and war. For instance, out of fifty-six major armed conflicts after the Cold War, only three have been interstate wars, and while the UN had fourteen peace missions in the period 1948–88, all in peacekeeping, it had fifty-seven peace missions, including twelve political and peace-building missions in the period 1989–2000 (SIPRI 2001). The new picture includes both a growing number of peace missions and 'humanitarian interventions', and, in this connection, there is also the use of military force and privatisation of mili-tary forces. The debate on this might be continued, for instance with ref-erence to Mark Duffield, who claims that with new wars we also see a merging of security and development. In addition he says: 'In response to the new wars and the merging of development and security, innovative, strategic complexes – linking state and non-state actors, public and private organisations, military and civilian organisations, and so on – have emerged' (Duffield 2001: 45). These 'innovative, strategic complexes' might be seen as examples of the new form of governance systems which was mentioned earlier in this chapter. They have developed, at least partly, in response to the effects of the globalisation of societal insecurity.

Many will argue that globalisation creates societal insecurity much more directly than through effects of neoliberal globalisation. If globalisa-tion is seen as social processes which irreversibly change societies to a world society (Beck 1999), then change would be a direct result of these

social processes, not mediated by markets. Changes in institutions, traditions, lifestyles and identities create a higher degree of 'ontological insecurity' (Giddens 1994). In this way societal globalisation also implies
societal insecurity.

Here we might leave it open as to how much emphasis one should put
on indirect or direct effects of globalisation. The general picture is that
the different forms of globalisation create a move from a world in which
military concerns dominate questions of security to a world in which societal insecurity plays a much greater role, not in the sense that military
means are unimportant, but rather in the sense that new complexities of
societal insecurity become the primary security concern.

11 September and the globalisation of terrorism

Now, we might ask whether the general picture described already in this
chapter has changed in an important way after the attacks on the World
Trade Center and the Pentagon on 11 September 2001? My view is that
the events of 11 September can be seen as a radical step in the globalisation of a specific form of societal insecurity: terrorism. The effects of the
actions were, of course, in the first place a cynical and massive destruction
and killing. But the secondary effect was a recognition of an increased
societal insecurity caused by new dimensions of terrorism.

The new dimensions in the attacks were, in particular, compared to
earlier terrorist acts, that:

1   these actions caused more death to innocent people in one event
    than we had experienced earlier in non-war situations. We saw a
    'mega-terrorism', which might be characterised as a terrorism in
    which violence hits many innocent people very suddenly.
2   This action represented, because of its suicidal character, a kind of
    threat against which it is very difficult to defend oneself.
3   This action was, through its means (planes hijacked using razor blades
    and then being used as missiles entailing the sacrifice of the lives of
    those on board), of an extraordinarily cynical nature.
4   At the same time, it was extraordinarily 'civilian' in its character.
5   No one, no 'adversary' or 'enemy', took explicit and immediate
    responsibility for the action.

The immediate effect of the attacks was quite naturally an escalation in
the 'distrust' or feeling of insecurity, in particular of the people in the
United States, but also more generally. Basic questions were: if some
people are able to act like this, what will then prevent others from doing
the same – or even from committing crimes that are worse? And if this
cannot be prevented in the heart of the United States, the world's only
superpower, can it then be prevented at all? A new, collective vulnerability

was recognised. And since the roots of network behind the persons that caused the attacks go to other parts of the world and to a – more or less – non-state, transnational, terrorist organisation, al-Qaida, the terrorist threat was recognised as an effect of transnationalisation and globalisation.

Of course, the effects of the events of 11 September depends not only on what happened, but also on the way in which the events are interpreted. Somehow, the events are also constituted by their interpretations. In one interpretation, the new terrorism was seen as directed against the identity of the American people and American power, hitting some of its main symbols. Another interpretation was to see it as a symbolic 'clash of civilisations'. A third perspective was to interpret the attacks as an endangerment of the life of 'common people' and to relate it more to civic culture and the survival of individual people and the kind of civilisation they represent. And a fourth interpretation was to see the events as signifying the kind of ontological insecurity which characterises an age of globalisation.

It lies beyond the scope of this chapter to analyse the 'discursive battle' between different interpretations of 11 September. It seems, though, that the dominant interpretation – in particular in the Western world – became that transnational and global networks of terrorists are threatening civil society, not only the civil society in the United States, but civilisation in general and civil society as such. Even though we might argue that it was not entirely new to see such a transnationalisation of terrorism, the events became – through the way they were interpreted – nearly a symbolic indication of a sudden rise in societal insecurity.

Thus, the events of 11 September have basically strengthened the general picture presented in this chapter that globalisation indirectly as well as directly leads to increased societal insecurity. But the events had another great importance. In the following I suggest that we might use the concept of securitisation in understanding how the events of 11 September are used in legitimising a new strategy for global governance.

Securitisation in the global system?

The concept of securitisation seems very useful in grasping some phenomena related to security which otherwise are difficult to identify. Basically, securitisation can be understood as 'the intersubjective establishment of an existential threat with a saliency sufficient to have substantial political effects' (Buzan *et al.* 1998: 25). Securitisation might be initiated through a

> speech act where a securitizing actor designates a threat to a specified referent object and declares an existential threat implying a right to use extraordinary means to fence it off. The issue is securitized –

becomes a security issue, a part of what is 'security' – if the relevant audience accepts this claim and thus grants the actor a right to violate rules that otherwise would bind.

(Wæver 2000: 251)

It was, in some ways, a part of the events of 11 September (as they were interpreted) that they included a securitisation of the new 'mass terrorism': the attacks – and the threat which such attacks represent – were articulated through 'speech acts' by important actors, not least the president of the United States, as a threat which made extraordinary action legitimate. This 'securitization move' by the American government was followed by most other state leaders and other important representatives in most societies. There were exceptions, but the reactions to 11 September were remarkable in articulating a 'new' security situation. The 'extraordinary actions' for which the 'securitizing actor(s)' sought acceptance and thus some kind of legitimacy were, in particular, the declared 'war against terror', and this was – at least to a large extent – accepted by 'the relevant audience'. Said differently: with the new terrorism we have experienced not only a new dimension in the globalisation of societal insecurity. We have also experienced what might be seen as rather remarkable 'successful' securitisation in the global system.

The reactions to the events of 11 September were not only the declaration of the 'war against terror' but also the many subsequent actions which in this period are changing global security perspectives. One element in these was the coalition which the USA formed behind the intervention in Afghanistan in the pursuance of the al-Qaida network. But the 'war against terror' has expanded into many fields and areas. The war with Iraq in the spring 2003 is, so far, the most serious and remarkable event following 11 September. This war has, like other actions after 11 September, been legitimised as part of the 'war against terror'. We have seen many actions legitimised as 'extraordinary' in the sense that they, arguably, do not follow established international law but rest on special interpretations. In this 'exceptionalist' perspective they fit with the concept of securitisation. It should be added, though, that we have some difficulties in deciding *how* extraordinary are the actions we are dealing with, because we do not have a clear concept of what would be ordinary action in such exceptional cases.

Another element in the reactions after 11 September is what we might call the strengthening of the international regime on the prevention of terrorism. This implies that the domestic laws in many states – including the EU – are reviewed, that control mechanisms are strengthened and that the national practices are put under stronger international surveillance. These actions can also be understood as 'extraordinary'. Yet here we have uncertain interpretations of the question of whether the new international rules and norms affect what we might characterise as 'normal'. They might affect the exclusive sovereignty of states, but can we any longer regard such a view of sovereignty as normal?

The new securitisation is remarkable because it is taking place not only in relation to the American public, but in the global system. It is not entirely new that securitisation is undertaken with reference to a 'referent object' at the systemic level; see how threats to the global environment or mankind have also been objects for securitisation moves (Buzan *et al.* 1998: 36). But this time it was the president of the USA who, together with other, mainly Western, state leaders, was the leading 'securitizing actor', and even though there was no unanimous agreement on the securitisation, it can be seen as 'successful' – as such, and so far! Of course we might question how basic an acceptance we are dealing with. For some actors, for instance Ariel Sharon, Robert Mugabe and Vladimir Putin, the declaration of war against terror seemed to be a very instrumental way to attempt to legitimise themselves in their already established, suppressive policies. The American-led coalition is probably rather fragile and depends on delicate political conditions and uncertain future developments. But maybe we should recognise that in some social systems even fragile securitisation might be 'successful'.

The use of the concept of securitisation to characterise the reactions to the events of 11 September illustrates some important problems in understanding global security as compared to national security. A major difficulty in talking about securitisation in the global system is, as indicated, that it is rather unclear what this perspective implies with regard to normality and 'extraordinary means'. What do we in the global or international system understand by 'rules that would otherwise bind' or 'normal politics'(cf. Wæver 2000: 251)? How are we in the global system, to understand the relationship between securitisation and politicisation? In the normal use of the concept, 'securitization can . . . be seen as a more extreme version of politicization' (Buzan *et al.* 1998: 23). But politicisation is normally defined in relation to established political systems, and it is unclear what we mean by politicisation in relation to global politics.

Perhaps it is more fruitful in social systems with no clear or generally accepted institutionalisation of normality to see securitisation as attempts to create 'formative moments', situations in which new norms and maybe new kinds of agency can be constituted and legitimised. Securitisation can be regarded as appeals for legitimacy in extraordinary situations for new kinds of action and maybe also for new actors. Thus, talking about threats towards civilisation and of responses from 'the world community' implies that the 'world community' is somehow articulated as a rather strong identity, and that actions are legitimised with reference to the defence of this entity. The securitisation can in this view be seen as a quest for a new basis for legitimacy or for 'extraordinary' legitimacy. This leads us to the last point in this chapter: the securitisation of terrorism after 11 September can be seen as a turning point in which a new strategy is launched, not only a strategy for security, but a new strategy for governance in the global system. The securitisation in the global system can be seen as an attempt to legitimise such a new, global strategy.

Competing strategies for governance in the global system

The general interpretation that has been proposed in this chapter is that we have seen an example of successful securitisation in the global system which has been – and still is – used to legitimise 'extraordinary actions' lead by the USA. The events of 11 September 2001 and their interpretations have, through an American-led securitisation, created a 'formative moment' in the global system, a situation which allows for the formation of new norms and maybe new agencies. The result is that, in the complex picture after the events of 11 September, new questions about what is – and what is not – legitimate in the global system are emerging.

We might interpret this new uncertainty as the emergence of competing strategies for governance in the global system. In a somewhat sketchy presentation, we might distinguish between (1) a traditional vision of international law – in an extended version, and (2) a new, power-based strategy of dominance based on the new securitisation.

The first strategy for global governance is rather well known. It is embedded in a traditional understanding of the international system as, basically, a system of sovereign territorial states. The states are sovereign on their own territory and have – through international law, i.e. the Charter of the United Nations – agreed not to interfere in the internal affairs of other states. They have a recognised right to self-defence, and the only possibility of military intervention is the right accorded to the Security Council to act in order to maintain or restore international peace and security. This basic understanding is extended through what we might call a traditional approach to global governance (see, for instance, Brand *et al.* 2000). This approach emphasises the importance of established international regimes and organisations and works for a strengthening of these, not least the United Nations. The strategy is pursued through a growing number of conventions, agreements and organisations which regulate different sectors internationally. Such a thinking is found in the different UN commissions about global problems and their work for better governance and conflict solution. Important contributions are the report of the so-called 'Brandt-Commission' from 1979, followed by the 'Palme-Commission' (1982), the 'Brundtland-Commission' (1987) and the report came from the Commission on Global Governance (1995). The same approach dominates the big thematic UN conferences. Many important steps have been taken in the UN system in accordance with this strategy. The UN has, for instance, in the period since the end of the Cold War, gained a much more important – if not totally successful – role in peacekeeping and peace-building operations. The establishment of the UN Tribunal on Crime in The Hague is one of the latest, important steps in the attempts to give the UN a stronger role in relation to global governance.

This strategy is, it seems, challenged by a new, power-based strategy of dominance based on a global securitisation. Of course, a strategy of power and power projection is not entirely new, but it – and in particular its legitimation – is being reinforced through the securitisation of the globalisation of the threat from terrorism. The new strategy might be viewed as the action which a superpower might undertake relatively unrestricted by existing international law, but – because, through securitisation, it involves legitimation – it is also a project for the reformulation of legitimising norms and rules in the global system. It is clear that the USA, as the only superpower, has the possibility of disregarding the rather weak elements of existing international law and acting unilaterally. Much in the USA's attitude towards the UN system indicates that the USA does not support the traditional strategy for global governance, but aims at establishing an alternative. The USA's attitude towards international agreements and its withdrawal of its signature on the agreement on the UN Tribunal on Crime in The Hague is a rather clear manifestation of this. The problem for such a new power-based strategy, which at least partly rests on USA unilateralism, is not only whether the USA has the capacity to act, but also how it might be possible for the USA to get its policy accepted from others, i.e. to give it legitimation. In this, securitisation plays an important role. Securitisation might change a basically unilateral strategy into a much broader and more legitimate power project. Through securitisation it might be possible to generate support for a strategy for global governance led by the only superpower in defence of 'humanity' or 'civilisation'. The interpretation suggested here is that securitisation and the 'war on terror' is part of such a strategy.

Conclusions

The conclusions of this chapter are that we are experiencing processes of globalisation, which – albeit in complex and contradictory ways – implies a globalisation of societal insecurity, and that the events of the 11 September 2001 mark an even stronger globalisation of societal insecurity in the form of terrorism. In addition, the events have triggered a massive US-dominated securitisation with reference to 'humanity' and 'civilisation'. This securitisation has – with all its lack of clarity – led to a new, 'formative' moment in the global system. In this situation, we see a competition between different strategies for global governance. The traditional UN-based strategy for global governance seems challenged by a new, US-based strategy which rests on a combination of unilateralism and securitisation. The perspectives of this change are manifold. One perspective is that it might strengthen the formation of one global polity and that, in the future, we might get a global political system in which we have a 'real politicisation' of strategies for global governance.

References

Beck, Ulrich (ed.) (1998) *Politik der Globalisierung,* Frankfurt am Main: Suhrkamp.
—— (1999) *Was ist Globalisierung? Irrtümer des Globalismus – Antworten auf Global-isierung,* Frankfurt am Main: Suhrkamp.
Brand, Ulrich *et al.* (2000) *Global Governance. Alternative zur neoliberalen Global-isierung,* Münster: Westfälisches Dampfboot.
Buzan, Barry, Ole Wæver and Jaap de Wilde (1998) *Security: A New Framework for Analysis,* Boulder, CO: Lynne Rienner.
Duffield, Mark (2001) *Global Governance and the New Wars: The Merging of Develop-ment and Security,* London, New York, NY: Zed Books.
Geertsen, Uffe (ed.) (2001) *Globale Udfordringer. Miljø, udvikling og sikkerhed.* 2000, København: Mellemfolkeligt Samvirke.
Giddens, Anthony (1994) 'Living in a post-traditional society', in Ulrich Beck, Anthony Giddens and Scott Lash (eds), *Reflexive Modernization: Politics, Tradition and Aesthetics in the Modern Social Order,* Cambridge: Polity Press: 56–109.
Kaldor, Mary (1999) *New and Old Wars,* Cambridge: Polity Press.
Kelstrup, Morten (1995) 'Societal aspects of European security', in Birthe Hansen (ed.) *European Security 2000,* Copenhagen: Copenhagen Political Studies Press: 172–97.
Leander, Anna (2001a) 'Globalisation, transnational politics and the dislocation of politics', Copenhagen: COPRI Working Paper 12/2001.
—— (2001b) 'Globalisation and the eroding state monopoly of legitimate viol-ence', Copenhagen: COPRI Working Paper 24/2001.
SIPRI (2001) *SIPRI Yearbook 2000. Armaments, Disarmamant and International Security,* Oxford: Oxford University Press
Wæver, Ole (2000) 'The EU as a security actor. Reflections from a pessimistic con-structivist on post-sovereign security orders', in Morten Kelstrup and Michel Williams (eds), *International Relations Theory and the Politics of European Integration. Power, Security and Community,* London, New York, NY: Routledge: 250–94.
——, Barry Buzan, Morten Kelstrup and Pierre Lemaitre (1993) *Identity, Migration and the New Security Agenda in Europe,* London: Pinter Publishers.
Zürn, Michael (1998) *Regieren jenseits des Nationalstaates. Globalisierung und Denation-alisierung als Chance,* Frankfurt am Main: Suhrkamp.

10 From Bentham to Bush

Surveillance, security and the quest for visibility[1]

Lene Hansen

> The terrorist threat to America takes many forms, has many places to hide, and is often invisible.
>
> (Bush 2001: 2)

In the aftermath of September 11 2001, criticism was raised of American intelligence. How was it possible, it was asked, that future terrorists with ties to Bin Laden and Islamic Chechen units could attend American flight academies showing no interest in the skills of landing or take-off without causing any concern? How could men who had trained in Afghanistan enter the United States on regular tourist visa? When the existence of the Phoenix memo – filed by a local agent in July 2001, but ignored by the FBI – which had pointed to Al Qaeda supporters attending flight academies in Arizona appeared in the American news in May 2002, criticism turned to the procedures and bureaucracy of the FBI. Institutional inertia, atrophied hierarchies and top officers' lack of attention were identified as hindering the acquisition of pertinent information.

Others argued that the success of the 9–11 hijackers was due not only to intelligence blunders or institutional inefficiencies, but that the attacks were made possible by a more fundamental misunderstanding of the post-Cold War security agenda. Ashton B. Carter claimed, for example, in an article in *International Security*, that the USA and its allies had become mistakenly convinced that ethnic and internal conflicts in the Balkans, Africa, Haiti and Asia were indeed the proper security problems of the West. As a consequence, the 'A-list' security problems – including 'catastrophic terrorism' – and vital interests of the USA had not been properly attended to (Carter 2001/2: 5–6).

On 20 September 2001, nine days after the attacks, Bush responded by announcing the creation of a new Cabinet-level position, the Office of Homeland Security. As underscored by his lengthy report, *Securing the Homeland, Strengthening the Nation*, combating terrorism was neither going to be swift nor easy (Bush 2001: 2). Faced with the daunting task of casting light on the 'often invisible' terrorist threat, Bush proposed a dual strategy: intelligence gathering should be increased, and more integrated systems built to facilitate information sharing in an Information Integration Office. Knowing that expanding the government's right to tap cell phones, monitor emails and Web browsing, track financial transactions and freeze assets might provoke criticism, Bush declared that civil liberties and the need for privacy would not be compromised (Lormel 2002; Penenberg 2001).[2] A little over a year later, in November 2002, the Office of Homeland Security was transformed into a new Department by a 90–9 Senate majority, creating the third largest department, with 170,000 employees, and uniting twenty-two agencies, amongst them the Immigration and Naturalization Service, Secret Service, Customs Service, Border Patrol, and the U.S. Coast Guard.[3]

The increased use of surveillance and its heightened institutionalisation might at first seem like a vindication of a narrow realist conception of security: of military security as ultimately privileged over non-military issues; of the state as the reference object for security; of 'vital security issues' as more important than peacekeeping and humanitarian intervention; and of 'security' as a concept which can be objectively defined (see, for example, Walt 1991). In this reading, integrated surveillance becomes a means to counter the terrorist threat and reinstall security in the face of 'The War Against Terror'. But this chapter will argue that the analytical and political pressures to conceptualise security in these terms notwithstanding, this conceptualisation of security has an inherent instability in particular when surveillance is seen as the objective mechanism through which security can be achieved, and furthermore that reliance upon this understanding produces severe political dangers. The argument, to be developed further below, is that practices of surveillance while claiming to produce visibility and security by identifying 'threats' rely upon particular constructions of identity, that they imply a particular construction of the subject of surveillance prior to the process of surveillance itself. This subject is, however, not infrequently trying to avoid surveillance by adapting to the new technologies and the definitions of the surveying agencies.

Seeking to address these questions, this chapter begins with an account of Foucault's classical work on surveillance, specifically of his exploration of Bentham's Panopticon, an invention which completely reconstructed the relationship between the individual prison inmate and the government represented by the prison guards. The second section of the chapter holds that while Foucault's analysis offers crucial insights into the self-disciplining effects of surveillance, it might not fully capture the nature of surveillance in a (post)modern world of monitors and visual data storage. It is suggested that two important transformations have occurred: that the acceleration of time works against easy surveillance and that the 'information-surveillance' nexus, as well as the omni-presence of cameras and the digital storage of data accentuate the importance of coding and decoding surveillance. The third section discusses the ambiguous role of surveillance for September 11, where the terrorists were simultaneously evading and captured by technologies of surveillance. Returning to Bush's Home-land Security initiative, the fourth section points to the political dangers of conceptualising intelligence in terms of seamless, objective and instan-taneous computer networks.

Panoptic surveillance

Alan Sheridan, the translator of Foucault's *Surveiller et punir: Naissance de la prison* into English had difficulties with the translation of '*surveiller*': the English word 'surveillance' 'has an altogether too restricted and technical use' (Sheridan 1977: ix). In response, Sheridan's chosen title – *Discipline and Punish: The Birth of the Prison* – points to the emphasis on discipline as crucial to Foucault's analysis.

The specific focus of Foucault's analysis is Jeremy Bentham's Peniten-tiary Panopticon, an architectural structure designed to individualise by dividing the old prison-house crowds into single-person cells and making all inmates' actions visible. Visibility is ensured by locating the inmates in a circular structure with a tower, patrolled by guards, at the centre. Each cell had one window on the inside of the building corresponding to the windows of the tower and another on the outside of the building, which made light flow through the cell. This backlighting would guarantee that the guards could see the contours of the inmate. But blinds and a particu-lar structure of corridors inside the prison tower protected the guards from the gaze of the inmates. As a result, a hierarchy between the guard and the observed inmate was constructed with the latter as 'the object of information, never a subject in communication' (Foucault 1977: 200). Since the inmate never saw any guards, he could never be sure he was not being watched, thus the panoptic power was, in Foucault's words, 'visible and unverifiable' (Foucault 1977: 201). In terms of prison regimes, this introduced an entirely new disciplinary programme: 'there were no more bars, no more chains, no more heavy locks; all that was needed was that the separations should be clear and the openings well arranged' (Foucault 1977: 202). One moved from 'houses of security' to 'houses of certainty' (Foucault 1977: 202). But more important than the architectural design itself, this constituted a shift within the disciplined subject:

> He who is subjected to a field of visibility, and who knows it, assumes responsibility for the constraints of power; he makes them play spon-taneously upon himself; he inscribes in himself the power relation in which he simultaneously plays both roles; he becomes the principle of his own subjection.
>
> (Foucault 1977: 202–3)

The prisoner would, in other words, internalise the possibility of the gaze of the prison guard and thereby abstain from any rebellious actions.

While Bentham developed the Panoptic design for the prison system, its application was by no means thought to be restricted to this. Schools and factories were two other major institutions to undergo a Panoptic transformation within 'the disciplinary society' (Foucault 1977: 209). But as a utilitarian liberalist, Bentham did not advocate an omnipresent state, the Panoptic principle was not, in other words, an argument in favour of pervasive state intervention, but articulated within a political philosophy which centred on ensuring the security of individual goods and property (Held 1996: 94–8). Bentham argued that the pursuit of individual interests would cause conflict, but these conflicts could be managed through the dual employment of state arbitration, which would eliminate arbitrary outcomes, and a structure of punishment and surveillance, which would prevent transgressive behaviour through deterrence and (self)-discipline.

Surveillance flowed, as the disciplinary society developed further, from the prison, the school and the factory into the social fabric. More and more parts of life became observable and observed, not least because the clear division between guard and inmate dissolved. It was not only the state who sought to guard its citizens/inmates, but also citizens who observed one another. This was perhaps taken to its fullest extent in Eastern Germany, where the excavation of the STASI files after German unification made clear that an extraordinary number of people had informed the state about the minute details of the behaviour of their neighbours, colleges and sometimes even family (Darnton 2002). But McCarthy's hunt for American communists in the 1950s can also be seen as installing a similar, in Campbell's words, 'society of security' (Campbell 1992: 171–5). With surveillance moving out of the prison and the factory and into the fabric of the entire society, there followed an expansion of 'suspicious behaviour' and a deeper transformation of the subject of surveillance: every individual might now be under surveillance and thus subjecting oneself to self-disciplining practices.

As Foucault brought out in his reading of Bentham, the Panoptic society relied upon a complex articulation of the relationship between architecture and technology on the one hand, and political practices and subject formation on the other. The architectural design of the Panoptic prison brought forward a particular subjectivity in the prisoner (and the guard), and it might therefore be tempting to see technology as determining the constitution of the subject. But technology is itself influenced by, sometimes even constituted through, political desires to install a particular subjectivity. To put it differently, the Panoptic prison did not simply materialise independently of Bentham's ideas of the individual and the proper governance of society. Nor have the disciplined subject fully conformed to the Panoptic vision; rather, a historical analysis of surveillance points to the strategies of avoidance which appears in response to (imperfect) surveillance.

Post-Panoptic surveillance

Since Bentham's late-eighteenth-century Panopticon, the societal spread of surveillance has been greatly facilitated by technological advances, in particular in the area of photography and video. Numerous encounters with surveillance occur throughout everyday Western life; the roadside camera connected to sensors detecting speed violations, the monitors of stores and apartment buildings and ATM cameras are all parts of the constitution of an increasingly monitored society. There are, however, important differences to Bentham's era, differences which might be significant enough that a post-Panoptic programme has crystallised. These differences hinge on how technological innovations have reconstructed the (metaphorical) Panoptic prison and thereby the subject under surveillance.

It is possible to track every individual, physically via cameras and electronically through bank flows, credit card use, plane tickets, etc. The guard is, however, no longer in/out of sight. There is no agent at the centre, no site of authority distinct from the inmates, or, necessarily any mailman watching your newspaper subscriptions. These technological changes transform the dynamic of surveillance and the subjectivity of the surveyed individual in (at least) four different ways.

First, there is a transition from the visibility of the contour of the backlit inmate's body to the specificity of the face. This move is related to the more general developments of digitalised surveillance: images are stored by surveillance cameras, and the corporate photo ID card has become an omnipresent means of entrance into public and private workspaces. With the possibility of swiping or scanning these cards upon entry and departure, a building's inhabitants can be determined at any given point. This emphasis on the face and visual surveillance means that appropriation of fake picture ID becomes a way of circumventing security, and, moreover, that the face is ranked above the name as a means of identification. In response, the use of disguises or clothes which blurs the visibility, and thereby identity, of the subject has been appropriated by a large variety of groups and individuals.

Second, the technology of video recording has made affordable 'complete surveillance' a possibility. The inmates of the Panoptic prison did not know whether the guard was watching, but the possibility itself had a self-disciplining effect; those passing by the surveillance cameras of today's airports and bank machines know that cameras are recording and storing data at all times.[4] Surveillance changes from being a possibility to being set within a framework of documentation, and as a consequence the question of deterrence changes from one of self-disciplining due to the possibility of being watched/caught, to highlighting identification in time. The disturbance of video documentation combines disguises, from the Palestinian scarf to the veils of the Chechen female terrorists in Moscow, with speedy operations, where getting away and timing is of critical importance.

Third, surveillance has changed from being instantaneous to being, possibly, delayed. The Panoptic guard offered on-site surveillance; and while his function was to prevent riots and unruliness, he was also to have the capacity to meet those resisting inmates who might not be subdued by surveillance itself. Many of the current cameras have the same effect, especially if they are located inside larger structures such as department stores and office buildings. Fewer guards and split-screen constructions keep costs down while still trading on the surveillance effect. But most of these cameras and numerous others offer an additional delayed surveillance, which further underscores the need for disguising one's identity.

This also shows, fourthly, that with the omnipresence of surveillance cameras and the continuous production of millions of data, surveillance confronts the problem of selection. A guard watching twelve monitors in a department store employs codes; either he or she has been greeted by management's profile of the usual shoplifter or has developed his/her own profile of who is a likely candidate. On a much larger scale, systems used to monitor global communication, like the Eschelon of the United States National Security Agency, produce millions of inputs, which necessitates the use of 'filters' – or codes – to search out the important messages from the irrelevant 'noise' in order to get at 'information' (Campbell 2002). With computerised data, codes can be digitalised and used as a filter. A person 'fitting' the terrorist code can thus, at least in principle, be selected by electronic surveillance and, for example, stopped by the airport gate.

Taken as a whole, these four changes imply an important reconfiguration of the relationship between the constitution of the subject and the agents of surveillance. The new technologies offer, on the one hand, the possibilities of surveillance at a level and with a pervasiveness previously unknown. The subject might thus be even more subjected to self-discipline and internalisation, yet the increase in the possibilities of surveillance also brings the danger of the system's collapse: if everything is on the screen or processed, the possibility of selecting 'the suspicious' collapses. The transgressing subject can escape surveillance precisely because everybody is equally under surveillance; as a consequence the system needs to respond by the elaboration of codes, for example by using key words as filters for emails or phone calls, or racial features at border crossings, or bodily characteristics at airports (Campbell 1992: 164, 168). But if codes are employed to make surveillance meaningful, it follows that the construction of codes is of the outmost importance. Where do codes come from? Not surprisingly, it is difficult to get security agencies – be that governmental or commercial – to publicise their checklists, but at a more general level, the identification of code will usually be highly path-dependent, that is based upon knowledge of past terrorists or shoplifters.

Yet, as a consequence, the system becomes vulnerable to those who do not fall within the parameters identified by the coding, and it also subjects those who do meet the code – by being, for example, of Middle Eastern or Muslim descent – to heightened levels of scrutiny and surveillance. There is not, in other words, an unmediated subject prior to the construction of codes; rather, it is the practice of code construction itself which constitutes the subject onto whom surveillance is employed. The construction of the subject and the practice of surveillance are thus deeply embedded within each other.

Avoiding surveillance – September 11 and beyond

The September 11 hijackers were both captured by and avoiding the surveillance of the post-Panoptic regime. The first photo to circulate the global media was indeed from airport surveillance cameras, which had captured Mohamed Atta and Abdulaziz Alomari as they were boarding their flight from Portland, Maine, to Logan Airport, Boston. Later, footage of Atta and Alomari from an ATM Portland cash machine was released, showing a stern Atta, whereas Alomari appeared to be in a much lighter mood, lending support to the theory that only the leading terrorists on each plane knew their operation was suicidal.

But while cameras had captured and stored images of Atta and Alomari in Portland, they had not been of any use in preventing the September 11 attacks. The hijackers knew that speed was crucial, making the simultaneity of the hijackings and downing of the planes essential. Even so, they had perhaps underestimated the electronic saturation of American society as passengers on board the fourth plane, which crashed in Pennsylvania, were alerted by cell phone calls notifying them of the fate of the first three planes.

If surveillance cameras are to be of use for fighting terrorism, data needs to be transformed into information. Some of the hijackers had already crossed the searchlight of the FBI and the INS, most too late. Two of them, Khalid Almihdhar and Salem Alhazmi, were already on a watch list; the former was known to have met in Kuala Lumpur, Malaysia, with a senior aide who masterminded the attack on the *USS Cole*. 'According to a law enforcement source, the CIA transmitted this information about Almidhar to the FBI and the INS and his name was placed on the INS watch list. However, he had already entered the United States by the time his name was placed on the list August 24' (ABCNews.com 2001). Interestingly, in terms of 'de-coding' terrorist activity, Habbi Zacarias Moussaoui, the so-called twentieth hijacker, had already been detained in August when flight instructors in Minnesota brought his disinterest in learning how to take off and land to the attention of the FBI. However, several of the September 11 hijackers had attended American flight academies and behaved similarly without this leading to their arrest. Post-September 11, this kind of behaviour will, of course, be de-coded much more quickly and with more seriousness. And the coding of suspicious behaviour itself might be expanded, one example being the so-called 'Hazmat-suspects', individuals who attempted to obtain 'Hazmat licenses' which 'allowed them to drive large tanker trucks carrying hazardous materials' (ABCNews.com 2001).

Trying to code behaviour is, however, complicated by the difficulty of grounding identity in a name. In response to the identification of one of the hijackers as Abdulaziz Alomari, a Saudi man reported that he was 'the real Abdulaziz Alomari', but that his passport had been stolen in 1995 when he was a student of electrical engineering at the University of Denver. Several other hijackers were apparently using different names and taking the names of others.

This brief account of some of the key movements of the September 11 terrorists point to the difficulties connected with encoding terrorist activity and of tracing specific individuals. It also, at a more general level, points to the collapse of the nation-state as a reliable generator of identity and thus as a key to coding. The Hamburg cell had spent years studying in Germany; other hijackers had lived for months in the United States, and all seemed to have blended sufficiently in with their surroundings not to create any concern. Beyond September 11 the cases of Richard Reid, the shoe-bomber, a British citizen who converted to Islam while living in London, subdued on a flight from Paris to Miami when he tried to ignite explosives in his shoes; of a Puerto Rican American, Jose Padilla, born in Brooklyn, NY, arrested in Chicago's O'Hare airport on charges of being part of an Al Qaeda plot to explode a dirty bomb; and of Astrid Eyza-guirre, a German–American, and Osman Petmezci, a German-born Turkish national, arrested in Germany charged with plans to attack American military interests, all point out that there are no simple alignments between national identity and citizenship and terrorism (Hansen 2002). Nor is gender, one might add, a reliable code either, as the cases of Palestinian female suicide bombers and the female Chechens who were part of the siege of a Moscow theatre in October 2002 brought an end to easy binary divisions between peaceful women and aggressive men. The subject of surveillance is thus jamming any simple national or regional coding, but equally importantly, the global spread of suicidal terrorism challenges the value of deterrence as the modus operandi of surveillance. For a subject who no longer fears for his or her loss of life, death does not function as a principle of deterrence; this, in turn, accentuates the question of speed, which puts further pressure on the agencies of surveillance.

The politics of institutionalising surveillance

Increased surveillance and 'interagency information architecture' might seem a credible solution to the perceived intelligence failure of September 11. Yet it is important to bear in mind, as argued above (p. 122), that information without selection is not 'information' but endless flows of data. The Bush administration has trodden the path of selection carefully with Bush consoling the general public that civil liberties and privacy have not been endangered. Much discursive effort has also been applied to assure Muslim–Americans, Arab–Americans and Muslims internationally that they are not the targets of the 'War on Terror'. But how is the data noise ratio to be reduced without selecting certain groups, countries, drinking habits, or sexual preferences as more worthy of tracking than others? Which directives are to be sent out to the President's enhanced Neighborhood Watch Program?

Bush's Homeland Security policy hinges on the creation of an information system, but this system cannot by itself identify 'terrorist threats'. This means that increasing the information load, for example through the implementation of a new INS entry–exit system, makes the identification of 'terrorism' all the more dependent on designating behaviour and features as 'terrorist'. As a consequence, Bush's declaration that the Information Integration Office 'will support United States effort to find, track, and respond to terrorist threats within the United States and around the world, in a way that improves both the time of response and the quality of decision' (Bush 2001: 17) simplifies slightly more complicated questions. 'Finding and tracking' terrorists is not a straightforward two-step procedure. In practice, it is through the 'tracking' of behaviour that is already considered suspicious that the terrorist is 'found'.

But it was not only intelligence which failed on September 11, but also the intellectual capacity for fathoming the possibility that someone would hijack a plane and force it into the World Trade Center and the Pentagon. Reptile monsters (*Godzilla*), meteoric waves (*Deep Impact*) and future human self-destruction (*A.I.*) had laid New York City to waste in recent Hollywood years, but a migration of suicide bombs from buses to planes had not registered as a possible threat. Indeed, when the first plane hit the World Trade Center, it was reported as an 'accident' (Der Derian 2001b: 687).

This suggests that the surveillance–information nexus will always be both path dependent and dependent on creative imagination. But Bush's desire to construct an integrated system which improves both 'the time of response and the quality of decision' runs the risk of eliminating rather than expanding the imaginative realm. Unless, of course, the cooperation between the intelligence community and Hollywood (described in detail by Der Derian 2001a) becomes further integrated with blockbuster scenarios feeding into the behavioural sensors of the Integrated Information System. Computerising intelligence might be useful to secure a better response time – granted, of course, that the infrastructure is equipped accordingly – but the suggestion that this simultaneously improves 'decision quality' is troubling. One only need bear in mind *War Games* to

have one's faith in the superiority of technological procedures desta-
bilised. As pointed out by James Der Derian, after all, the National Security Council had had thirteen days to resolve the Cuban Missile Crisis; a
possible response time reduced to thirteen minutes or thirteen seconds
might have allowed for a radically different outcome with reflexes standing in for reflection (Der Derian 2001b).

Some might argue with Adam Penenberg that recent American legislation is going to make little difference to an American society that was
already used to omnipresent cameras and the tracking of bank records
prior to September 11, a society which perhaps even celebrated surveillance through reality TV shows such as 'Big Brother' (Penenberg 2001).
And, following the governmental logic of classical surveillance, 'if you do
no wrong you have nothing to be concerned about'. Yet, if surveillance is
never politically neutral, the current increase in surveillance intensity
might well be unequally felt. Not only America but the Western world
more generally might be entering a dual society, where people – Bush's
claims to the contrary – who belong to (more) suspicious ethnicities, faiths
or sexualities are more in the searchlight than others – and not just the
searchlight of the authorities but of the friendly neighbourhood watch.

Over the past fifteen months, the attacks of September 11 have been
followed by the bombs in the Bali disco, the siege of the Moscow theatre,
and the attacks on an Israeli hotel and planes in Kenya, and it is understandable that the pressure for a politically potent and an unambiguously
defined concept of security is large. It is equally understandable that surveillance is appointed as an important means through which security is
sought. Yet, as this chapter has argued, surveillance is not simply a means
through which objective threats can be identified by employing a neutral
scheme of codes. Rather, surveillance should be seen as a political practice, which mediates technologies with particular constructions of subjectivity, and it is never neutral in its application or political effect, nor will it
be immune to strategies of avoidance and manipulation.

Notes

1 I wish to thank Barry Buzan, Ulla Holm, Stefano Guzzini, Dietrich Jung, Anna
  Leander, Thomas Levin, John Phillip Santos and Ole Wæver for valuable criticism and suggestions.
2 Not that much concern was expressed at this point. As Senate Republican Trent
  Lott put it, 'When you're in this type of conflict – when you're at war – civil liberties are treated differently' (quoted in Penenberg 2001).
3 See under: http://www.cnn.com/2002/US/11/20/facts.homeland/index.html.
  As one of the few opposing the bill, Russ Feingold (Democrat, Wisconsin)
  argued that the bill was 'weakening protections against unwarranted government intrusion into the lives of ordinary Americans' (http:// www.cnn.com/
  2002/ALLPOLITICS/11/20/homeland.security/index.html).
4 The question of how long electronic data is stored and by whom is another –
  important – question.

References

ABCNews.com (2001) *Who did it? FBI links names to terror attacks*. Online, available at: http://www.abcnews.go.com/sections/us/DailyNews/WTC_suspects.html (accessed 30 September).

Bush, George W. (2001) *Securing the Homeland, Strengthening the Nation*. Online, available at: http://www.whitehouse.gov/homeland/homeland_security_book. html.

Campbell, David (1992) *Writing Security: United States Foreign Policy and the Politics of Identity*, Manchester: Manchester University Press.

Carter, Ashton B. (2001/02) 'The architecture of government and the face of terrorism', *International Security* 26 (3): 2–23.

Darnton, Robert (2002 [1991]) 'The Stasi files', in Thomas Y. Levin, Ursula Frohne and Peter Weibel (eds), *CTRL[SPACE]: Rhetorics of Surveillance from Bentham to Big Brother*, Cambridge, MA: The MIT Press: 170–4.

Der Derian, James (2001a) *Virtuous War: Mapping the Military–Industrial–Media–Entertainment Network*, Boulder, CO: Westview.

—— (2001b) 'Global events, national security, and virtual theory', *Millennium* 30 (3): 669–90.

Foucault, Michel (1977) *Discipline and Punish: The Birth of the Prison*, London: Penguin.

Hansen, Lene (2002) 'Territoriality and deterrence in the wake of 9/11', *Security Dialogue* 33 (1): 109–11.

Held, David (1996) *Models of Democracy*, second edn, Cambridge: Polity.

Lormel, Dennis M. (2002) 'Statement for the Record. Dennis M. Lormel, Chief, Financial Crimes Section, FBI, Before the House Committee on Financial Services, Subcommittee on Oversight and Investigations, Washington, D.C', 12 February.

Penenberg, Adam (2001) 'The surveillance society', *Wired Magazine* 12 (9). Online, available at: http://www.wired.com/wired/archive/9.12/surveillance.html.

Sheridan, Alan (1977) 'Translator's note', in Michel Foucault, *Discipline and Punish: The Birth of the Prison*, London: Penguin.

Walt, Stephen M. (1991) 'The renaissance of security studies', *International Studies Quarterly* 35 (2): 211–39.

—— (2002) 'Inside Echelon: the history, structure, and function of the global surveillance system known as Echelon', in Thomas Y. Levin, Ursula Frohne and Petu Wiebel (eds), *ETRL [SPACE]: Rhetoric of Surveillance from Bentham to Big Brother*, Cambridge, MA: The MIT Press: 158–69.

11 The subversion of borders[1]

Thomas Diez

Scandinavian prologue

Scandinavia is in many ways different from other parts of the world. At least that is how we tend to think of 'Norden', as Scandinavians like to call the place themselves, thereby including Finland and Iceland (see Wiberg 1993: 209). Among other things, it was what we usually refer to as a security community long before the rest of Western Europe, or for that matter, before the term became part of political science dictionaries (see Wæver 1998: 72–4). This security community manifests itself, as Håkan Wiberg (1993, 2000) has aptly illustrated, in the peaceful resolution of conflicts that could have led to war elsewhere (in Wiberg's terms, 'non-wars', see Wiberg 1993: 210). Examples include the Norwegian secession from Sweden in 1905, and the political and cultural autonomy enjoyed by the (mostly Swedish-speaking) Åland Islands after they became part of Finland following the First World War (Joenniemi 1997). The islands have set an example for a peaceful settlement that is nowadays often quoted when discussing the Cyprus conflict (see Diez 2002: 207; Emerson and Tocci 2002: 38–9).

Following the Deutschian understanding of security communities (Deutsch *et al.* 1957), it is important to note the density of transactions among Nordic countries. While the question of whether this density is particularly strong in Scandinavia is contested (see Wæver 1998: 73 for the opposite claim), there can be no doubt that in terms of cultural exchange, for instance, the closeness of the languages, at least in Denmark, Sweden and Norway, means that television from the other Nordic countries is not only readily available, but can also be relatively easily understood (see Wiberg 2000: 296). Similarly, books can be read, movies watched and so on.

However, 'Norden' is not a typical security community throughout. It lacks, for instance, strong common political institutions, and while there are shared sources of identity, these have not developed into a single common identity. Instead, I argue that at the heart of this security community is the role of borders. Whereas in many places of the world, state borders are still heavily contested and fiercely guarded, they have become porous in Scandinavia without being dissolved. A case in point is that the free movement of people between Nordic countries had for long been a stumbling block for the implementation of the Schengen agreement in the Scandinavian EU member states, which has only recently been solved. Whereas the significance of borders for the daily life of people in Norden is therefore diminished, borders themselves have not disappeared. They remain as administrative boundaries, and to many they are still signifiers of identity, a sense that is perhaps strongest in Norway (on Norway, see Neumann 2002). Instead, borders have become part of 'normal' political life, rather than being at the centre of securitisations, i.e. representations of existential threats to the identity of Scandinavian communities that have to be met by extraordinary measures (for this definition, see Buzan *et al.* 1998: 23–4). In that sense, Scandinavia is a security community because of a relative lack of internal securitisations (see Wæver 1998), a lack that is manifest in what one could call a desecuritisation of borders.

This poses a normative as well as a political puzzle. Normatively, cosmopolitans and post-structuralists, although for various reasons, are critics of territorial borders, but the Scandinavian case seems to suggest that their arguments would at least have to be qualified in that borders are not always harmful to the freedom and identity of people. Politically, this implies that those concerned with the issues of freedom, especially in areas of border conflict such as in Cyprus, will have to re-think their strategy in that the abolition of borders may not be the appropriate and most effective means to achieve the subversion of borders. In this chapter, my aim is to address this puzzle by providing some initial thoughts on the normative status of borders, as well as on the dialectic of borders that leads to their subversion.

Borders and order in international society

Borders are a defining feature of modern international society. The states that this society is made up of are territorial (see, for example, Bull 1977). The existence of a definable state territory is one of the four criteria for the recognition of states in international law according to the 1933 Montevideo convention, alongside a government, a permanent population and the capacity 'to enter into relations with other states' (Ipsen 1990: 236–7). But such a state territory presupposes borders, for otherwise it would not be definable. Without borders, there would therefore be no international society, or an international society that would have little in common with the one we know today.

Because borders play such a crucial defining role, they are often contested. Borders regulate access to natural resources; they allocate identities to people. Many times in history, those governing have therefore sought to change them and to lay claim on territory and people beyond the recognised confines of their state. While borders therefore provide a particular order of international society by defining its constitutive units, this very function makes them a source of conflicts bringing about disorder.

The problem with the ordering function of borders, however, and the reason why borders are often contested, is that any such order of the international society is an imposed order. This imposition of order may be mutually agreed between those affected by the border or it may be achieved through violence – whatever the mode of its imposition, none such order comes naturally, and any border is ultimately a discursive rather than a 'natural' fact. This makes borders contestable, but it also, and perhaps more significantly, forces particular identities on people and restricts their freedom of movement and exchange. Many International Relations theorists are therefore critical towards territorial borders, and some engage in the search for alternative political spaces that would not rely on the clear demarcation of borders and would radically change the nature of international society. Furthermore, in concrete border conflicts, this line of thought has led to resisting the acknowledgement of the border and the order that it implies.

In what follows, I advance the argument that there is a dialectical nature to borders in that their acknowledgement implies, in the long run, and as the Scandinavian case suggests, their subversion. Put differently: those opposed to a border would be better advised to take steps towards the recognition of this border, for this will eventually bring them closer to their aim than continued contestation. Subversion does not necessarily mean disappearance, however. Rather, the argument is that as long as borders are 'important' to people in the sense that they are contested, they cannot fulfil their ordering function on a systemic level. It is when they become 'unimportant', when they are recognised and 'normalised', that they can bring about order, but ironically, in doing so, allow for more freedom and the articulation of a variety of identities cutting across borders.

The following section prepares the argument by discussing the normative implications of borders. In order to make the claim that the subversion of borders is a good thing, I need to revisit the debate about the value and perils of borders. After this, I will then elaborate on the dialectics of borders. My argument in this section will make particular use of the concept of securitisation, and the linkage between securitisation and identity, and will discuss the conditions required for the subversion of borders to be successful.

The problem with borders

Arguments in favour of territorial borders

The case for or against territorial borders is far from clear-cut. To start with, it should be noted that a borderless world is a world beyond imagination. One way or another, we need to talk about places and refer to particular groups of people. All of these need to be bounded if we are to identify them; they need to be differentiated from another place, another group. This implies the necessity of boundaries, some of which inevitably function as borders dividing one space from another.

Given the inevitability of borders in such a general sense, these are not my concern here. Rather, the main problem with borders as we know them is their linkage to the modern state and their overriding nature as state borders. But even in this specific context, normative judgement is contested.

Let me start by reviewing some of the arguments in favour of borders. In all of them, borders are seen as positive because of their defining and preserving function. There are four broad arguments of this kind, which, as I will discuss, can be seen as linked, although this is not normally the case when they are made.

The first argument in favour of borders is Herderian. Herder made the case in favour of a territorial division of nations in the name of diversity. In the context of the break-up of the Austro-Hungarian Empire, he saw nation-states as the political entity that would allow ethnic groups to survive and prosper on their own territory, with their own language and their own set of institutions (Breuilly 1985, 336–9). Borders in this argument serve to preserve the diversity of national identities. While the context of Herder's time might have changed, this argument of the preservation of identities is still very much alive today. Consider, for instance, the reasoning of those who want to strengthen the nation-state against the forces of globalisation. Often, their argument is based on the concern for the preservation of what is seen as a particular way of life or a particular language. In a different context, the demand of 'ethnic' groups to form their own state, such as in former Yugoslavia, is based on a similar logic. This is not to say that anti-globalisation forces and the nationalist politicians of former Yugoslavia are of the same political persuasion. However, their defence of borders ultimately rests on the same Herderian argument of a defence of identity.

The second argument in favour of borders is communitarian. While communitarians stress the role of identity, as does the Herderian argument, there is another significant rationale to their defence of borders, which is the definition of a sphere of rights and responsibilities. For communitarians, at least, not all rights and responsibilities can be universal. Redistribution in particular is meant to presuppose a shared sense of responsibility that cannot be endless. The nation-state's borders provided the boundaries of such responsibility and rights against the authorities and fellow citizens (for example, Miller 1995, Chapter 3). While there may be arguments about whether the size of the nation-state is adequate, the principal communitarian argument is one about the definition of political and moral spaces, in which 'communities of fate' are formed that underpin a sense of mutual responsibilities (Brown 2001: 129).

Related to the first two is a third, republican argument, which sees the protection of borders as a protection of the political values of a particular republican society. In the modern society of states, a variety of rights and freedoms are guaranteed through and limited by the state. Borders therefore need to be safeguarded against intrusions from outside which would threaten these rights and freedoms by imposing a non-republican rule. A version of this argument is made in defence of the borders of the welfare state as long as opening these borders would threaten its supposed social achievements but not contribute to a better life outside (for a critical view, see Brown 2001: 127).

Fourth, a defence of borders can be made on the systemic level of international society. This argument builds on the ordering function of borders. In the pluralist conception of international society, transferring the Herderian argument to the systemic level, borders guarantee diversity. Respecting these borders means maintaining order: good fences make good neighbours (Williams 2001). Cross-border traffic is regulated by the control of borders so as to minimise the disruption of international order. Most importantly, violations of borders are seen as violations of international order, ultimately providing an *jus ad bellum*, a justification for war.

While the four defences of borders make distinct arguments, they are nonetheless linked. As noted already in this chapter, the systemic defence is to some extent the macro-level flipside of the Herderian argument. Similarly, the sense of responsibility that communitarians seek to establish and preserve within bounded communities is based on the sense of a common identity. Taken together, the three defences provide an overarching rationale for the preservation of the modern state system. However, they do so on assumptions that are contestable.

Arguments against territorial borders

Some of the arguments against take their starting point in a reversal of the arguments in favour of territorial borders. It is to these that I want to turn first.

The Herderian defence of borders is in the name of preserving difference and preserving identities. But this is a double-edged sword. As much as they have preserved and often created identities, borders have also served to suppress identities, namely those that were not in line with the official identity of the nation-state. The fate of minorities in many countries all over the world is testimony to this, as well as, ironically although not surprisingly, the difficulties of communities living close to and across borders to articulate their own distinctiveness. Increasingly, migrants are coming under similar pressure to assume the identity of the state they live in. While identities are, by definition, exclusive, they become particularly suppressive if they are linked to a specific territory, since then there is no escape but to leave that territory. True, the Herderian argument sought the freedom to articulate one's identity through the linkage to a state territory, but this only followed the logic of the modern state system, which presupposes borders. The challenge is to conceptualise a political space that would not tie 'national' identity to a particular territory.

The communitarian argument claims a similarly progressive rationale. By establishing spaces of responsibility, borders allow for redistributive policies and can, following this logic, be seen as the basis of the welfare state. The problem is that these spaces are arbitrary once they become detached from the notion of a single underlying identity. Why should a Brit living in Dover be more concerned about her fellow citizens in Newcastle or Aberdeen than about someone living across the channel in Calais, with whom she might now share much more of a common economic space? The communitarian argument can then at best be a pragmatic one, but this in turn raises questions about the adequacy of any community as to which size it should have and where its borders should be drawn.[2] Eventually, as much as borders preserve and suppress identities in the Herderian argument, they establish and cut responsibilities in the communitarian argument, often standing against a cosmopolitan or in general transnational forms of responsibility.

The republican argument is couched in equally progressive terms. It rests, however, on the assumption that life inside state borders is indeed better than life outside. While this may be the case for some values in some circumstances, it is hardly ever true for all values and all citizens. Instead, the reference to the preserving of republican values is often part of the construction of a particular republican identity as such, marking this identity and the values attached as better than alternative identities and values, or denying the existence of similar values in other states. Often, citizens would therefore view other state systems, from democracy to healthcare, with scepticism, while criticising their own system domestically. Defending republican values against a threat also assumes that there *is* a threat and that this threat is located outside the state borders. The existence of a threat can, of course, be 'real', but importantly, the republican defence characterises something as a threat: it 'constructs' a threat, independent of whether this is a 'real' threat, which more often than not is subject to considerable argument (cf. Campbell 1992). As much as the republican argument can therefore be seen as preserving progressive ideals, it can come in parochial terms, constructing the identity of a clear inside that it claims to defend, and constructing a dangerous, anarchical outside against which it claims the inside has to be defended.

Finally, the systemic function of preserving order ultimately rests on the imposition of a particular order. The systemic concern is not so much about the effect of this order on identities and responsibilities, covered by the discussion above (pp. 132–3), but about the limits it imposes on the imagination of alternative orders. In other words, its problem lies with its discursive power, with its prescription that order is only possible within the confines of a bordered world of states. The rising interest in the study of borders over the past decade may be seen as part of an endeavour to refute this discursive power by analysing the constitution of borders and how their meaning has been changing throughout the centuries. Still, our imagination of an order beyond borders continues to be hampered by the vocabulary that the discourse of borders imposes on us.

The ambiguity of borders in international society

In many recent critical studies of international politics, the problematic side of borders has been given more weight than their positive aspects. For Critical Theorists, borders should ultimately give way to a cosmopolitan world society. For others, borders are part of a discursive power that, following the argument above, inhibits the free articulation of identities and destroys the multitude of relationships between people in border regions.

In his work on the Western intervention in Bosnia, for instance, David Campbell (1998) criticises the international community for buying into Milosevic's representation of the conflict as one between given ethnic identities that cannot live together – a representation that follows the logic of the Herderian argument. They therefore de facto segregated the 'ethnic' communities on a territorial basis and erected borders even though formally, Bosnia was to retain a single state personality. The linkage between territorial space and segregated identities, or what Campbell calls 'ontopology', resulted in tearing neighbours and even families apart in a complex social network that did not match the clear boundaries in the thinking of policy-makers, both in former Yugoslavia and of the international community. Campbell therefore wants us to resist the ontopological assumptions and to look instead for alternative articulations of identities that are non-exclusive and, consequently, do not operate on the basis of strict borders.

On the basis of the above arguments, I share with Campbell the principal scepticism towards borders, and especially the conviction that, in situations of ethnic conflict, borders are unjust. Yet I differ with Campbell's arguments on two accounts: First, as the discussion in this section has shown, borders are not only negative. Their ordering function in particular is a valuable contribution to peace in international society and should therefore not be underrated. I therefore suggest that, although the importance of borders should be greatly diminished in the daily life of people, we may not wish to do away with borders as such. In other words, we may wish to preserve the ordering function of borders without these borders or the order that they constitute becoming oppressive.

Second, I suggest that there may be situations in which the acceptance of borders, rather than their criticism or denial, has led to their losing importance. There are theoretical and empirical arguments in favour of such a solution. In fact, in most cases in which borders have been overcome, this has followed their recognition or quasi-recognition. I am not suggesting that this would have been the case in Bosnia; however, my argument is that under certain conditions, which I will discuss in the conclusion, those critical of borders should consider the acceptance of borders as a way of reducing their significance.

I call this process 'the subversion of borders'. Such subversion may or may not lead to the disappearance of borders. It is a subversion that comes as a result of the dialectic inherent to borders.

The dialectic of borders

Borders and securitisation

In most of the arguments in defence of borders, borders have a security function. In the Herderian argument, they are to secure the identity of a particular group of people, the nation. In the communitarian argument, they secure the definition of the community that establishes responsibility. In the republican argument, they are to defend the norms and values of a state. And in the systemic argument, they are to secure order in the international society. Borders are therefore closely intertwined with processes of securitisation. On one level, they are the means with which an existential threat is met. But they are also the sites of securitisation, because if they are seen as threatened themselves, the existence of the group that they circumscribe is seen as being threatened.

In cases where borders are openly contested, they are the objects of the rhetorical move to invoke security. But they are so not in their own right, but as a signifier for a particular identity that is supposed to be existentially threatened. This is why the Herderian argument cuts both ways, enabling and suppressing difference. Through the securitisation of a border, an identity is re-inscribed into the discourse, as any securitisation claims to defend an identity that it has to but cannot presuppose. Through this reinscription, other identities are marginalised, and often criminalised and constructed as not belonging to the real 'self', made 'foreign' (Campbell 1992). The securitisation of borders therefore has a crucial identity function, and thinking about the contestation of borders in these ways helps to clarify the Herderian ambiguity noted earlier (p. 133).

The Cyprus example is useful to illustrate this ambiguity. Here we have a case where, since Turkey's military intervention on the island in 1974, there has been a de facto border separating the northern part of the island from the south, with a UN-patrolled buffer zone and a so-called 'Green Line' between. In 1983, the 'Turkish Republic of Northern Cyprus' was declared by politicians in the north, but subsequently recognised by Turkey alone. The rest of international society recognises the (now purely Greek–Cypriot) government of the Republic of Cyprus, which, however, has effective administrative control only over the southern part of the island. This is a classic case of a contested border, decried in the dominant Greek–Cypriot discourse as unjust, declared in the dominant Turkish–Cypriot discourse as a necessary border between two states that (note the Herderian argument) separates two people who would not be able to live together in peace.[3]

The contestation of the de facto border of the Green Line and buffer zone delimits the possibilities of articulating identities on both sides of the island as Greek– and Turkish–Cypriot. However, the border is also contested by some who promote a single Cypriot identity, often constructed against both Greece and Turkey. In this case, the border threatens a single identity and therefore is likewise an 'other' that inscribes such an identity. But ironically, through this use, the border itself is re-inscribed, defying the object. At the same time, all of these securitising moves ultimately exclude alternative identities, and therefore set limits to difference. In contrast to some of the thinking in bi-communal grassroots groups, these moves are expressions of an impoverished, modernist conception of identity that does not allow for multiple identities to co-exist, and therefore operates with an understanding of borders in which borders are the sites of securitisation and practices of inclusion and exclusion.

Recognition, 'normalisation' and desecuritisation of borders

At first sight, it may be surprising that some bi-communal groups in Cyprus have been advocates of a normalisation, if not a full legal recognition, of the border. After all, it is these groups that should be most opposed to the de facto border and the division it imposes on the island. But it is amongst these groups where, perhaps intuitively, the link between borders, securitisation and identity has been understood. In very practical terms, the securitisation of the 'border' has, before the events of 2003, made it more difficult for these groups to meet and articulate visions of a Cyprus with multiple identities. Steps towards recognition, in contrast, would at least potentially provide the space to do so, and it should be noted that the idea of 'component' states and a 'common' state as floated in the UN proposal for a resolution put forward at the end of 2002 can be seen as such a step without implying full sovereignty for either Greek or Turkish Cypriots.

From a theoretical point of view, steps towards recognition are making the articulation of multiple identities easier to the extent that recognition is linked with desecuritisation. For Wæver, desecuritisation involves moving a subject from the realm of security to the realm of 'normal politics', in which claims can be discussed and met with counter-claims without invoking the rhetoric of 'existential threat' necessitating and justifying 'extraordinary means' (see Wæver 1995). Not only the Scandinavian case, but also post-Second World War developments in Western Europe, illustrate the possibility of such a 'normalisation' of borders. The literature often stresses the identity function of borders. However, the importance of this function is heightened in situations of securitisation. Ironically, in the context of desecuritised borders, for instance at the German–French border, borders may take on a completely new significance and allow for the construction of alternative, multiple and overlapping identities, with the border as a common reference point rather than the dividing line (see Albert and Brock 1996; Diez 1997).

Locating the dialectic of borders

The subversion of borders is therefore often made possible by the acceptance of those very borders, rather than by their contestation. The concepts of securitisation and desecuritisation help to understand the dialectic of borders that underlies this argument. The aggressive contestation of borders involves the securitisation of borders, and this securitisation reinforces the border through its discursive invocation, and limits the possibilities of articulating identities, even if the intention is otherwise. The acceptance of borders, through steps towards recognition, involves a normalisation of cross-border dealings in the sense of a desecuritisation, and through this desecuritisation allows different identities to be articulated and co-exist.

It should be stressed that I use dialectic in a loose sense. One of the caveats that need to be made is that there is no automatism between the recognition of a border and the dialectic that is described above to set in. It is ultimately up to those engaged in cross-border communication on all levels as to what to make of a border once it is accepted. There are, after all, recognised borders that are hermetically sealed. Having said that, most of these borders will, on a continuum between securitised and desecuritised borders, find themselves leaning towards the desecuritised end. As so often, the point is not to sign a piece of paper, although this may be of high symbolic importance; rather desecuritisation is to happen in and through daily discursive practices. The argument is that steps towards recognition enable actors to pursue alternative identity projects more freely, but of course, this does not mean that they will or that the process of recognition is irreversible.

Facilitating conditions

There are a number of conditions that may facilitate, and others that may prevent, the subversion of borders taking place. What follows is a list of three hypotheses that would have to be subjected to more thorough empirical studies that go beyond the scope of this chapter. We could expect that the subversion of borders is more likely to happen:

- if we are indeed dealing with a contested border, as in the Cyprus case, and not with a case of pure border aggression.
- if there is an international framework that can support the desecuriti-sation process. The supranational framework of the European Union may, for instance, speed up the subversion of borders by downgrading their importance in the larger context of the *acquis communautaire*, which is why the EU membership of Cyprus as a whole would be desirable (see Diez 2002).
- if there is relative economic equality between the two sides. This is not a sine qua non, but exchange is easier to institutionalise if one side does not have a clear economic advantage over the other, so that there is no attitude of 'buying the other side up'.

Conclusions

To many peace researchers, the argument about the dialectic of borders is perhaps not surprising. In many ways, it is reminiscent of the practices of détente advocated by peace researchers and carried out by governments in the 1970s. Similarly, many International Relations scholars may argue that borders today are anyway subverted through the processes of globali-sation. But both of these caveats neglect that there are still many conflicts in which the détente argument is not widely accepted and in which global-isation has not yet had an obvious effect on the securitisation of the border. In these cases, such as in Cyprus, the 'one state' option is pro-moted by some as the only just solution, whereas the border would inflict injustices on the people who live there. In this chapter, I have tried to develop the argument, prompted by the Scandinavian puzzle, that while it is true that borders are problematic because they inhibit the freedom of people, they also have some, perhaps more positive, functions, but that more importantly, their subversion is better achieved through their recog-nition than their contestation.

Much of what I have developed in this chapter from theoretical consid-erations deserves greater empirical attention. I will end with a final caveat, to which the same applies: there may be a case that the subversion of borders on the one hand has the consequence of erecting new or (further) securitising old borders on the other hand. In other words, the subversion of borders inside may go hand-in-hand with the erection of borders outside. This is why bringing Scandinavia into the Schengen agreement proved complicated, and the very development of Schengen and the securitisations of the EU's eastern border may further support this argument. If it were true, then normatively, nothing would be won. Empirically, however, the picture is not necessarily as clear-cut as it seems, as the application of the Interreg-program on the EU's borders suggests. But most importantly, this necessitates a call for political practice: the replacement of securitisations of some borders with the securitisation of other borders is to be resisted politically.

Notes

1 This chapter has benefited from discussions of an earlier paper focusing on Cyprus at the 2001 ISA and BISA conferences and at the London School of Economics. Thanks are due in particular to Barry Buzan, Jeff Checkel, Madeleine Demetriou and John Williams. Helpful comments during the process of writing this chapter came from my colleague Colin Farrelly at the University of Birmingham, Dietrich Jung and audiences at the Centre for Global Ethics at Birmingham, especially Donna Dickenson, the London Centre for International Relations of the University of Kent and the Department of Political Science at the Ludwig-Maximilians-Universitaet Munich.
2 Miller (1995: 68) maintains that nationality provides the required additional glue and a common set of understandings at the basis of mutual responsibilities, but this seems to make use of and therefore to run into the same problems as the Herderian argument.
3 For useful introductions to the Cyprus conflict, see Brewin (2001), Dodd (2002), Joseph (1999) and Richmond (1998).

References

Albert, Mathias and Lothar Brock (1996) 'De-bordering the world of states: new spaces in international relations', *New Political Science* 35 (1): 69–109.
Breuilly, John (1985) *Nationalism and the State*, second edn, Chicago, IL: University of Chicago Press.
Brewin, Chris (2001) *The European Union and Cyprus*, Huntingdon: Eothen Press.
Brown, Chris (2001) 'Borders and identity in international political theory', in Mathias Albert *et al.* (eds), *Identities Borders Orders: Rethinking International Relations Theory*, Minneapolis, MN: University of Minnesota Press: 117–36.
Bull, Hedley (1977) *The Anarchical Society: A Study of Order in World Politics*, London: Macmillan.
Buzan, Barry *et al.* (1998) *Security: A New Framework for Analysis*, Boulder, CO: Lynne Rienner.
Campbell, David (1992) *Writing Security: U.S. Foreign Policy and the Politics of Identity*, Minneapolis, MN: University of Minnesota Press.
—— (1998) *National Deconstruction: Violence, Identity and Justice in Bosnia*, Minneapolis, MN: University of Minnesota Press.
Deutsch, Karl *et al.* (1957) *Political Community and the North Atlantic Area: International Organization in the Light of Historical Experience*, Princeton, NJ: Princeton University Press.

Diez, Thomas (1997) 'International ethics and European integration: federal state or network horizon?', *Alternatives* 22 (3): 287–312.

—— (2002) 'Conclusion: Cyprus and the European Union – an opening', in Thomas Diez (ed.), *The European Union and the Cyprus Conflict: Modern Conflict, Postmodern Union*, Manchester: Manchester University Press: 202–12.

Dodd, Clement (2002) *Storm Clouds over Cyprus: A Briefing*, second edn, Huntingdon: Eothen Press.

Emerson, Michael and Nathalie Tocci (2002) *Cyprus as Lighthouse of the East Mediterranean*, Brussels: Centre for European Policy Studies.

Ipsen, Knut (1990) *Völkerrecht*, third edn, Munich: C.H. Beck.

Joenniemi, Pertti (1997) 'Åland in the new Europe: a case of post-sovereign political life', in L. Hannikainen and F. Horn (eds), *Autonomy and Demilitarisation in International Law: The Åland Islands in a Changing Europe*, The Hague: Kluwer Law International: 9–22.

Joseph, Joseph S. (1999) *Cyprus: Ethnic Conflict and International Politics*, Basingstoke: Macmillan.

Miller, David (1995) *On Nationality*, Oxford: Oxford University Press.

Neumann, Iver (2002) 'This little piggy stayed at home: why Norway is not a member of the EU', in Lene Hansen and Ole Wæver (eds), *European Integration and National Identity: The Challenge of the Nordic States*, London: Routledge: 88–129.

Richmond, Oliver (1998) *Mediating in Cyprus: The Cypriot Communities and the United Nations*, London: Frank Cass.

Wæver, Ole (1995) 'Securitization and desecuritization', in Ronnie D. Lipshutz (ed.), *On Security*, New York, NY: Columbia University Press: 46–86.

—— (1998) 'Insecurity, security and asecurity in the West European non-war community', in Emanuel Adler and Michael Barnett (eds), *Security Communities*, Cambridge: Cambridge University Press: 69–118.

Wiberg, Håkan (1993) 'Scandinavia', in Richard Dean Burns (ed.), *Encyclopedia of Arms Control and Disarmament*, vol. 1, New York, NY: Charles Scribner's Sons: 209–26.

—— (2000) 'Emanuel Adler, Michael Barnett and anomalous Northerners', *Cooperation and Conflict* 35 (3): 289–98.

Williams, John (2001) ' "Good fences make good neighbours": international ethics and territorial borders as dynamic norms', paper presented at the Annual Convention of the International Studies Association, Chicago, March.

Part III

Security analysis in the larger European context

12 A Deutschian security community?

Nordic peace reframed

Pertti Joenniemi

Admired from afar

The Nordic area, once rife with war, has become free of interstate violence. It challenges profoundly the ordinary, anarchy-oriented accounts of International Relations, and this is not just evidenced by statistics since 1815; it also applies to expectations and attitudes, in the sense that war among the Nordic countries (Denmark, Finland, Iceland, Norway and Sweden) has become inconceivable as a means of resolving conflicts. Actors in the region have, on numerous occasions, found their way out of situations that would have typically led to war (see Archer 1996; Archer and Joenniemi 2003; Wiberg 1993).

The scholarly community has, for its part, contributed to the image of Norden as an area of stable peace. The case is widely recognised, although less explored in any thorough terms despite Nordic peace challenging, by its very existence, mainstream International Relations theory. Peace is seen to be there in a rather durable fashion, but it has been more celebrated than investigated, or – as Emanuel Adler and Michael Barnett (1998a: 8–9) put it – 'admired from afar'.

One obstacle to any closer scrutiny appears to consist of the Nordic case having the firm reputation of being a 'security community'. It has been depicted as a Deutschian security community par excellence, a case to be extended and exported to cover northern Europe more extensively (Wallensteen *et al.* 1994). The concept appears to operate like a spell: efforts to explore the Nordic achievement more profoundly come immediately to a halt once those magic words are applied and extended to cover Nordic peace. The Nordic case is framed, by a policy of naming, to resonate with a set of integration-related theory, this largely satisfying the need to sort out the Nordic record on a more principal level.

The crucial question thus concerns whether the Nordic area really corresponds to the requirements of such a conceptualisation. Is it truly a security community along the lines indicated by the Deutschian approach? The departure here is that this is hardly the case. This critical stance implies, more generally, that the success of the Nordics in settling their grievances short of war calls for a revision of the conceptual departure applied in arresting the case. Approaches are required that better correspond to its very nature. It is claimed, in other words, that the comprehension of Nordic peace still rests on a shaky theoretical ground or, as asserted by Ole Wæver (1998: 68), it remains undertheoretised. The peacefulness of the area has stood the test of time, but it has not been, one may argue, properly accounted for in terms of International Relations theory.

This chapter, then, endeavours to reconsider the way Norden has been approached and treated in scholarly terms. It aims, by probing into some basic questions, at bolstering the standing of the Nordic case in conceptual as well as theoretical terms. The search for alternative avenues departs from a reviewing of some recent contributions that have, in their own way, articulated doubts about Norden's path towards a security community and have, in some instances, even raised the question of whether the concept is really applicable to the case.

A case in point

For most of its existence the Nordic instance has been there to be comprehended as an anomaly and a peculiar deviation. It emerged at an early juncture – a bit less than two hundred years ago – gaining a rather recognised position, and yet there was no flurry of theoretical inquiry or, for that matter, much empirical treatment. A breakthrough came first in the mid-1950s when Karl W. Deutsch – a Czech/German emigrant and American scholar – included the Nordic configuration in his seminal study on the prospects of peace through integration in the North Atlantic area.

Deutsch endeavoured to explain the peacefulness of relations between states in terms of interaction of their societies and the nature of their polities. He thought that states may, by their qualities and a developing of special ties, alter the configuration of violence and the dilemmas of security both within and between themselves. Integration could amount, in his view, to a security community. Integration means the attainment of a 'sense of community' and of institutions and practices sufficiently strong and widespread enough to assure for a lengthy, dependable expectation of peaceful change among the population. The sense of community refers to the belief on the part of individuals in the group that they have to come to agreement on at least one point: that common social problems must and can be resolved by processes of 'peaceful change' (Deutsch *et al.* 1957: 5–7, 30–2).

Particularly in the case of the emergence of the Nordic security community, an integrative process consisting of mutual responsiveness, a kind of we-feeling, perpetual attention, communication and perception of needs and of responsiveness was regarded as central (Deutsch *et al.* 1957: 7–8). In the context of the overall endeavour, Norden stood out as one of the few cases upon which Deutsch could premise his theory of communality settling issues of security.

The Deutschian treatment, although it remained at the fringes of IR theory in general, gave the Nordic case additional legitimacy and provided ground for a certain self-understanding. 'Security community' has since become something of a dogma; it provides a frame for the Nordic case, and there has been little need of any more detailed inquiry or alternative explanation.

Deviant voices

However, this state of affairs is under doubt. Håkan Wiberg, for one, has pointed out that some essential aspects of the Nordic case do not fully tie in with the Deutschian conceptualisation. There are 'dependable expectations of peaceful change', and many of the specific qualities – such as solidarity, common values and an ease of communication – are also present, although some discrepancy is present as well. Joint Nordic perceptions of external threat – assumed to be there by Deutsch – emerged only in the context of the Cold War. Prior to that, the Nordic countries were mostly divided in their views on danger and threat. The Nordics have occasionally failed, even at crucial junctures, to be responsive to the needs of each other. Wiberg also points out that the institutional and integrative aspects pertaining to Nordic communality have been rather weak and, in general, emerged well after the occurrence of a we-feeling rather than auguring it. Particularly in relation to the construction of communality around any forms of military cooperation, 'Norden is a continuous failure' (Wiberg 2000: 293).

Ole Wæver has advocated similar views (1998: 72–3). He points out, in singling out the path to Nordic peace, that neither is the configuration strongly institutionalised, nor does it reflect exceptionally dense societal transactions in terms of being based on economic foundations. More importantly, Wæver emphasises that the stable Nordic expectations of peace should not be equated with security institutions. There is a different ontology present: 'security and insecurity are not exhaustive options, and more attention needs to be given to a-security. Usually those who do not feel insecure do not self-consciously feel (or work on being) secure: they are more likely to be engaged in other matters' (Wæver 1998: 71). Furthermore, he notes that there is no sacrifice of narrow self-interests, and not an increasing attachment to new identities that weaken and undermine the old state/nation-based ones (but rather a reconfiguration and extending of the old ones across national lines of demarcation).

It appears, according to this line of argument, that the political space emerged in the Nordic case across the usual inside/outside divide, and it was *not* formulated as a security project. Instead, a different 'lens' was installed in viewing realities, and security was, in the new context that became visible, depicted as a basically irrelevant concern. The Nordic configuration thus had features of a by-product, one based on the displacement of the security argument rather than merely providing security-speak with a somewhat different twist.

This approach, one that pre-empted security concerns, then permitted stepping beyond the security dilemma that is assumed to be ever-present according to dominant theories. The move – one that in the light of the hegemonic theories stands out as naïve if not totally impossible – allowed for the viewing of Norden as a non-war community (one labelled by the absence of war rather than endeavours to increase security) and thereby able to steer free from securitisation in relations between the Nordics.

In essence, the national selves did not feel that there was a need for them to be protected from external threats in relation to their Nordic neighbours, these being capable of self-restraint. This, then, allowed the nations to abstain from requesting security-related services from their respective states. With the joint 'we' undermining efforts of placing the fellow-Nordics in a category of adversaries, and also allowing for the introduction of restraints as part of the prevailing self-understanding, the normal statist and security-related approaches were no longer credible, legitimate or applicable.

This is to argue that Nordic peace did not come about in a utilitarian manner or in terms of bargaining, reasoning and creating bonds of dependency. The communality created did not emerge in a project-like manner, but instead came into being as a kind of ontological revolt with regard to the standard views of interstate relations. It stood out as a move to downplay security in a manner that the various IR theories, including those of the late 1950s, have difficulties in accounting for, as they tend to approach security in a rather objectivist manner.

The Nordic outcome rested, in one of its aspects, on processes that were more bottom-up than top-down. One could speak of democratic or moral peace in the meaning that the nations and civil societies had considerable subjectivity in the process, thereby constraining the sovereignty of their respective states. The popular power of the Nordic nations was uniquely on a level with state power, although this does not, as such, underpin the claim that the Nordic countries would have been more outstanding and exemplary in terms of formal democracy than some other grouping of countries. Furthermore, as observed by Ole Wæver (1998: 68): 'There was no powerful programme for securing peace among the Nordic countries. Transactions, institutions and community feeling were mainly generated by other aspirations and contributed, as a side effect, to the creation and consolidation of a security community.' With enmity short of credibility, the endeavours of securitising failed in the sphere of inter-Nordic relations, with rather porous and cooperation-oriented intra-Nordic borderlines as a consequence.

In sum, the Nordic case was thus not built around overcoming war and aspiring for security; it was about other things. The absence of war became so self-evident, it seems, that there was no point in bringing up the issue in the first place. Nowadays it would almost sound like a joke if a major politician were to argue that further Nordic integration is required in order to avert the danger of intra-Nordic war. The argument would fall short of credibility. The problem of security in the ordinary statist and military sense has simply evaporated, and what has been left in terms of extra-Nordic relations has been handed over to the Nordic states to handle (there, full sovereignty and normal statist border-drawing prevails). As a form of political community that spurred the domestication of a previously international sphere, Scandinavianism/Nordicity has basically been about togetherness. It seems that the relationships became so amiable that there was no need for a gradual dismissal of the security argument. The nations restricted the options available for the states to such an extent that the latter were exempt from behaving – within an intra-Nordic context – in a power-political fashion. In order to become states that had the full approval of their respective nations, the Nordic ones had to assume a different – a Kantian and far more pacific – relationship to each other than the one assumed to prevail between statist actors in general in the context of a modern, sovereignty-related international system and the IR theories attached to it.

A more general critique

The failure to coin any broadly acceptable and durable explanation of Nordic peace appears to have a broader background, as the problem does not merely pertain to the Nordic case; it goes for non-war communities in general. As argued by Emanuel Adler and Michael Barnett (1998a: 5), there have been 'decades of neglect' concerning research on communality in International Relations and groups of states that have managed to settle their relations peacefully. Moreover, the debate has tended to contribute to naturalisation and objectification rather than problematisation and penetrating analysis. Interpretations concerning the Nordic case have also been held in check by dominant ways of thinking, as these grant very little subjectivity to such categories of political space. The mainstream interpretations have only recently turned friendlier vis-à-vis deviations such as Norden and rendered them open for alternative views and explanations.

Deutsch's work has, in this context, also been in focus of a broader discussion, one that includes both a critique and efforts to explore the central themes further. Adler and Barnett (1998b) have specially focused on the security community concept by claiming that it contained, once launched, various theoretical, conceptual and methodological problems that scared off future applications. Another reason for the security community project failing to generate a follow-up was, they argue, because scholars were beginning to adopt new theories and were concerning themselves with new research puzzles that shifted the ground away from it. Attention moved on to regional integration and international cooperation that used the vehicles of international interdependence, and later, international regimes.

Adler and Barnett also remark that any talk of a community of states, not to mention a security community, seemed hopelessly romantic and vividly discordant against the backdrop of the Cold War and the prospect of nuclear war. Deutsch's study was often cited but rarely emulated, they observe, as IR research quickly distanced itself from the sociological spirit of his line of enquiry. The discipline became enamoured with structural realism, rational choice methods and other approaches to political life that excluded identities and interests as phenomena requiring explanation (Adler and Barnett 1998a: 9).

However, in addition to presenting such a critique, they also aim at developing the security community concept further. Their programme is, in fact, one of resuscitation of the Deutschian departure. Adler and Barnett (1998b: 59) see it as basically viable in both empirical and theoretical terms. However, instead of just embarking on realist or neo-liberalist institutionalist approaches – which are perceived as being ill-equipped to entertain the possibility of community – they pursue a constructivist line of enquiry. At a deeper level, communality warrants, they argue, a paradigm shift in International Relations theory which 'involves the intellectual conjecture that violent conflict can be mitigated and even eliminated by the development of mutual identification among peoples and not through conventional practices such as balancing and collective security schemes'.

Working around states

One might also note that the idea of security community broke, if seen in an ontological perspective, with the realist, Hobbes-inspired conception of anarchy as the basic condition in the relations between states. In a way, by assuming a sociological and behaviouralist approach that led him to statistical instead of interpretative endeavours, Karl W. Deutsch expanded what was understood as the realm of the domestic beyond statist borders. A different, and less conflictual, set of inter-unit relations could possibly be created through domestic transformation. He thereby ignored the inside/outside division quite essential for dominant theories of International Relations, as transactional forces could, in his view, undermine the atomistic nature of interstate behaviour. They did so, Deutsch claimed, by working around states. This was important because for Deutsch, security communities were not just anomalies and oddities located somewhere at the fringes of International Relations. Rather to the contrary, they could expand with the spread of modern reason – one labelled by shared knowledge, ideational forces and a dense normative environment – and become increasingly significant. This could particularly occur, he thought, in the North Atlantic area.

The dominance of the realist paradigm certainly explains why the Deutschian view never succeeded in occupying any central stage in IR research. There might, however, also be flaws in the theory itself in the sense that the relationship between transactions, institutionalisation, security and we-ness appears to be somewhat muddled in the context of the Deutschian approach. Is security to be achieved through integration that brings about a certain identity, or is it identity that allows security to be addressed in different terms, thereby also paving the way for transactions and integration? The relationship is not all that clear. Adler and Barnett seem to suggest that there is the danger of a circular move present, as the 'sense of community' is also defined by Deutsch in terms of dependable expectations of non-war.

In their own scheme, one that aims at remedying the problem, they settled for states first looking in each other's direction due to factors such as joint external threats, then moving on to various processes pertaining to social learning and erecting joint institutions, and this finally bringing about trust, dependable expectations of peaceful change and collective identity. There are, in other words, 'precipitating conditions', 'process variables' (transactions, organisations and social learning) and 'structural variables' (power and knowledge), then to amount to 'mutual trust and joint identity' (Adler and Barnett 1998b: 37–40). Notably, we-ness is seen as an end product rather than part of the origins of the creation of security communities. The improvements introduced appear, mostly, to be well taken. However, the clarification presented also warrants, in the Nordic case in particular, questions about whether this really has been the order of things and whether Adler and Barnett catch the essence of the process.

A deviant Norden

Norden, for one, seems to harbour a background of its own. The way the non-war community came about differs from a number of other cases, as it seems to have evolved in a specific manner. It emerged, as argued by Wæver (1998: 69), 'in contrast to the expectations of most contemporary theorists of security communities, in having not been achieved by erecting common security structures or institutions, but primarily by processes of "desecuritisation", that is progressive marginalisation of mutual security concerns in favour of other issues.' In elevating identity-formation to a core question (thereby challenging the Adler–Barnett stage-model), he also claims that too straightforward approaches are not feasible in the Nordic case, or for that matter, in tackling Western Europe more generally.

It could be crudely stated that the Nordics took a path of their own, but there was, above all, a breach in the discourse on International Relations, with 'Europe' being comprehended as the scene of power politics. In the process of nation-state building, the Scandinavian/Nordic nations had a comparatively strong standing. This became evident particularly after 1864 (and the Danish defeat in the Schleswig–Holstein war, which marked the end of the political integrationist Scandinavianism and created space for a more cultural Nordicity). They could influence the terms of the emerging nation-state relationship by blurring borders and extending identities beyond the modern way of constructing political space.

The condition laid on the states was that they should reduce their participation, if not abstain altogether from interfering in European power politics. This endeavour of staying aloof originated with the costs levelled upon the respective populations in the context of previous engagement in European struggles (cf. af Malmborg 2001: 88–99). The endeavour of opting out also allowed the Nordic nations to mentally reach beyond their borders and break with the statist inside/outside divide, this Nordic bond of solidarity then creating a political space broader than and different from that of the respective nation-states. The past was left behind by leaning on factors such as a shared Protestant culture, support for pacifism and neutrality, common history as well as romantic myths of joint origin. Memories of previous clashes were not provided with a constitutive role – as has been the case in the context of the European Union (Williams 2001: 540–2; Wæver 1998: 81–7). Instead, the Nordics seem to have nullified their warlike past. They refrained from turning it into an explicit endeavour of overcoming – by instrumental means – various fears and feelings of mistrust.

This is to say that the EU and Norden are quite different. In the Union's case, the overcoming of the past stands out as an integral part of the very project. The basic constitutive move consists of trying to prevent the past experiences from also governing the future. There is, in order not to slip back into power politics, a constant process of integration, communication and identity-building. Communality is produced by constantly keeping out various security-infused lines of argumentation.

This is something different from the Nordic configuration, as there was no need for such an endeavour among the Nordics. The warlike past had, in their case, already lost relevance, and security thus turned into an irrelevant concern. Some voices might have remained with security as a core issue, but they were not strong enough to carry the day. Borders and various barriers preventing communality from emerging and extending beyond statist lines of demarcation were easier to counteract as peace, and a joint 'we', was already understood to be there. The different relationship to security could be outlined by stating that Norden has been about asecurity (with the absence of the very argument). Nordic peace has been about utilising such a state of affairs, whereas the EU aims at gradual and constant desecuritisation (the security argument has remained rather central and constitutive of communality), i.e. in the end bringing about a state of affairs that the Nordics think they have already achieved by dropping the lens of security.

It hence appears that the modern process of nation-state building took a rather uncommon turn in northern Europe in resulting in a kind of second, Nordic nationhood. This then implied that the restrictions concerning the waging of war with other Scandinavian countries became formidable. The series of non-wars that have long been labelled intra-Nordic relations may, as such, provide reason to think of Norden as a security community along Deutschian lines. There are good grounds for 'dependable expectations of peaceful change'. However, a more detailed examination of the nature and background of such a state of affairs tends to indicate that Norden contains a number of features that run almost opposite to the Deutschian, rather security-geared, ontology.

Concluding remarks

Despite a variety of critical voices, the dominant view is still that of Karl W. Deutsch casting Norden in the format of a 'security community'. The Nordic configuration has, by and large, been left outside the more recent discussion and research on 'liberal' peace and 'democratic peace'. Norden, although often idealised and seen as exemplary in modernity, has remained somewhat unrecognised as a theoretically interesting case by itself. It has rather been viewed, as is the case with Deutsch, as a configuration that is interesting to include when exploring the prospects of peace in a North Atlantic context. The question thus emerges of what could account for this relative lack of interest in the Nordic case.

One way of pondering this would be to argue that the Nordic *states* lost their ability to control the discourse, with the logic of the *nations* – and in this sense democratic peace – becoming strong enough to quell the ordinary sovereignty-geared and security-related logic of the states. The Nordic nations did not just offer a different selection of friends and foes. They used their exceptional subjectivity by refraining from the option of articulating themselves and constructing identities through the ordinary depiction of the other Nordic nations as threats. In other words, they broke the barriers of modern inter-state discourse. They impacted, in going beyond the established limits and projecting part of themselves and their core values into a sphere beyond their own states, the underlying, constitutive aspects of the Nordic constellation by turning what used to be seen as the outside into an inside. The intra-Nordic sphere hence became exempt from the logic of security and categorical otherness. Given that identity-building is always a boundary-drawing process, an attempt to define something, to give it meaning and to establish an order of knowledge, the borders of sameness were drawn in a rather broad manner. Meaning was made in the Nordic case out of border-transcending sameness rather than difference. Exempted from the category of those to be excluded,

estranged or alienated, fellow Nordics were not to be depicted as a political challenge located outside the borders of the community to be securitised. Identities could be formed without a resort to arguments about
security. Notably, Nordicity rested on togetherness outside the ordinary
sphere of securitisation in the process of identity-building, i.e. there was
difference but it did not turn into radical otherness.

It could hence be argued, against this background, that research has
failed to follow suit. It has missed this liberating move and ontological
reversal that resides in the logic of the nations, perhaps because the theories applied have not been sufficiently dynamic in order to account for the
rather radical change. Research has managed to account for the obvious
results – i.e. the prevailing of peace – but not the essence of the constitutive and identity-related processes that brought it about. Above all, the
shift in the logic that underlined the changes that turned a previous
outside to an inside, a sphere no longer governed by the ordinary statist
logic, has remained in the dark. The approaches applied in the endeavours of explanation have resonated too closely, it seems, with state-centric
ways of thinking, and nations have been treated as given entities with a
stable and unchanging self-articulation. Moreover, security has been seen
as something that remains present also in the relations between the
Nordics, although it has been turned into a unifying factor and seen as
setting the ground for the construction of community. To categorise the
outcome as a 'security community' is fully in line with this, and only with
the recent introduction of constructivist perspectives has it been possible
to shed some doubt on security being the core argument in the constitution of Nordic communality.

A deeper understanding of the Nordic case might well involve – as recommended by Adler and Barnett (1998a: 424–5) – a further inquiry into
the links between liberalism, democracy and peace, including the question of recognition. However, they also conclude with a second recommendation of exploring in more detail the relationship between
knowledge and power in the social construction of security relations. The
latter appears at least as relevant as the former if viewed against the background of the Nordic case, one that has long cried for a more penetrating
theory and explanation in the case that appears to pertain to placing
oneself outside the security-related discourse. The Nordic configuration is
there in a rather stable manner, but does not rest comfortably with the
dominant endeavours of explaining occurrences of non-war. It was not, to
start with, exceedingly democratic. It remains difficult to grasp applying
the logics of sovereignty and state-centredness or by operating with tight
divisions of inside/outside and domestic/foreign, as it seems to constitute
a form in between.

The Nordic case rests, in this sense, on a breach of the dominant discourse. Security has been seen as redundant rather than elevated to a core
argument in the construction of communality. The identity coined was *not*

based on endeavours of creating a common sphere premised on improved security. Instead, the understanding was – premised on the democratic reason of the nations rather than that of the respective states – that it was wrong to cast fellow Nordics in a security perspective in the first place. Security was taken to label 'Europe' at large, and consequently the concept was not to impact on the relations between the Nordics themselves. Security-talk was actually something to be left aside. It should not be allowed to become part of Nordic communality, a set of relations that aimed at something qualitatively quite different, a kind of anti-power political Europe. This background then also implies that, in exploring the workings of Nordic peace, a vocabulary different from 'security community' is required, and it is, above all, the Nordics themselves that need it in order to develop a better self-understanding.

References

Adler, Emanuel and Michael Barnett (1998a) 'Security communities in theoretical perspective', in Emanuel Adler and Michael Barnett (eds), *Security Communities*, Cambridge: Cambridge University Press: 3–28.

—— (1998b) 'A framework for the study of security communities', in Emanuel Adler and Michael Barnett (eds), *Security Communities*, Cambridge: Cambridge University Press: 29–68.

Archer, Clive (1996) 'The Nordic area as a zone of peace', *Journal of Peace Research* 33 (4): 451–67.

—— and Pertti Joenniemi (eds) (2003) *Nordic Peace: Challenges on the Road to a Security Community*, Aldershot: Ashgate.

Deutsch, Karl *et al.* (1957) *Political Community and the North Atlantic Area: International Organization in the Light of Historical Experience*, Princeton, NJ: Princeton University Press.

af Malmborg, Mikael (2001) *Neutrality and State-building in Sweden*, Wiltshire: Palgrave.

Wæver, Ole (1998) 'Insecurity, security, and asecurity in the West European non-war community', in Emanuel Adler and Michael Barnett (eds), *Security Communities*, Cambridge: Cambridge University Press: 69–118.

Wallensteen, Peter *et al.* (1994) *Towards a Security Community in the Baltic Region*, Uppsala: The Baltic University.

Wiberg, Håkan (1993) 'Scandinavia', in Richard Dean Burns (ed.), *Encyclopedia of Arms Control and Disarmament*, vol. I, New York, NY: Charles Scriber's Sons: 209–26.

—— (2000) 'Security communities. Emanuel Adler, Michael Barnett and anomalous northerners', *Cooperation and Conflict* 35 (3): 289–98.

Williams, Michael C. (2001) 'The discipline of the Democratic Peace: Kant, liberalism and the social construction of security communities', *European Journal of International Relations* 7 (4): 525–53.

13 Initiating a security community

General theory, history and prospects for Baltic–Russian relations[1]

Hans Mouritzen

A key issue in North European security debates since the end of the Cold War has been whether a security community could be at least *initiated* on the eastern shore of the Baltic Sea. Should a full-fledged community prove unrealistic in this geographical area, it might be hoped, at any rate, that good cooperative patterns could develop. Such are hardly prevalent along Russia's borders today.

Since states, unlike molecules in a gas or consumers in a market, are mutually non-mobile, they must live with essentially the same neighbours – sometimes for centuries (Mouritzen 1998). This makes the soil fertile for 'special relationships' of various kinds, including enduring rivalries. Pakistan or India cannot 'sail' out into the Indian Ocean in order to get a break from their mutual conflict, for instance. The special relationships not only encompass governments, but also one or more layers of public opinion; mutual images, often derived from dramatic events in the past, sediment here, and years or generations later they may exert a restriction on governmental relations, preventing drastic changes of course (for instance a sudden peace settlement with the 'hereditary enemy').

A 'security community' is such a special relationship. It means that a sense of community, a 'we-feeling' – not excluding competition and mutual jealousies – has developed at the popular level so as to make war unthinkable between the states concerned (Adler and Barnett 1998; Deutsch *et al.* 1957). Regarding the mother of all security communities, the Nordic one, a series of 'non-wars' during the twentieth century can be counted, during which conflicting interests between pairs of the participating countries have frequently led to war in other contexts, but where a peaceful solution was found (Wiberg 2000).

A security community on the eastern shore of the Baltic Sea[2] could be imagined as an enlargement either of the Nordic or the EU security community. This is more than an academic alternative. The point is, as we shall see, that Norden and the EU represent widely different, almost paradigmatic, cases of how to initiate a security community. Of course, in their *current* functioning there is no essential difference between the two cases. Once the process towards such a community gains momentum, it is much akin to snowball rolling – it becomes self-reinforcing. As the countries involved can convince each other and the world around them that they indeed form a security community, the incentive to retain this peaceful and prestigious state of affairs the next time a conflict of interest emerges is all the more important.

However, when the practical and intellectual task is to *initiate* a security community, there is every reason to distinguish between a Nordic method ('bottom-up') and the EU method ('top-down'), and then see which one best suits the circumstances in the region in question. 'Bottom-up' means that mutual sympathies and transnational ties develop spontaneously over a long time-span at the popular level; for instance, NGOs, 'grassroots' and professional organisations establish ties, or perhaps even umbrella organisations. In this way, top decision-makers in the states concerned find themselves deprived of the option of mutual war. In other words, the community is created *inadvertently*. In the Nordic case, it is my view that intra-Swedish developments during the nineteenth century made Sweden the generous core power, which, combined with transnational ties and the ideology of Scandinavianism, laid the ground for a security community during the twentieth century.

The 'top-down' method, on the other hand, starts out with common institutions and a common project with security visions from above (like Jean Monnet and others in the EC case: 'never more a Franco-German war'). Only gradually do peaceful expectations come to encompass the popular level. The Nordic Council, by contrast, did not cause Scandinavianism and a Nordic security community; instead, it was the other way round. This is evident, for one thing, from the temporal sequence: Scandinavianism and the favourable intra-Swedish developments described below (pp. 155–7) date back to the middle and late nineteenth century, the security community emerged about 1905, whereas the Nordic Council was not created until 1952.

In the next two sections, I shall analyse in more detail the initiation of the Nordic and the EC/EU security communities, respectively. Only then can we proceed to the issue of whether 'top-down' or 'bottom-up' is best suited to initiate a security community on the eastern shore of the Baltic Sea.

Sweden: the generous core of Norden

The security community literature neglects the fact that somebody formed the Nordic security community 'snowball' in the first place. My assertion here is that this 'somebody' was Sweden. This may be slightly taboo, since it is an inherent part of Nordistic rhetoric not to emphasise a particular nation-state among them. This is politically sensitive, and it has to some degree spilled over into the scholarly field. However, it seems to me from the non-wars and other evidence that Sweden was the initiating generous core of the community, the sine qua non for the process starting out. The party being critical for a non-war to occur is, evidently, the non-war 'loser', if it can credibly wage war and thereby gain tangible benefits. Sweden has never been on the winning side in the series of non-wars referred to, and – most importantly – it was a loser in the vital first two non-wars to occur. Had war broken out in any of these cases, the snowball would have melted and the whole idea would have become obsolete for a couple of generations. The first precarious and paradigmatic instance of the security community in function was Norway's secession from the Swedish–Norwegian Union in 1905 (Vedung 1971). Norway got what it wanted, whereas Sweden 'lost Norway', as it was commonly regarded in Sweden. Still, Sweden did not use its marked military superiority to prevent it. This step was seriously considered, but eventually the Swedish King and government decided against it: it was not for Nordic 'brethren' to fight each other. In the words of King Oscar II, 'the Union is not worth anything if it is to be upheld by force' (Archer 1996). Since issues related to secessions, territory and sovereignty normally have a strong tendency to cause military action, a peaceful secession from a neighbouring state, as in this case, is indeed a rare phenomenon (Wiberg 2000); its only parallel prior to the 1990s was Singapore leaving Malaysia in 1963 (a somewhat special case).

Correspondingly, Sweden was a loser in the strife with Finland over the Åland Islands after the First World War. A total of 90 per cent of the Ålanders had voted to join Sweden in a popular referendum, and the islands located adjacent to the Stockholm archipelago were of significant strategic importance to Sweden, to say the least (a great power occupation of the islands in a crisis situation was described as a 'pistol in the back' of Sweden). Still, Sweden acquiesced in the decision of the Council of the League of Nations to give Finland sovereignty over the islands (though with preconditions safeguarding the Swedish language, for instance). The Åland population (approximately 25,000) is the largest one that has had its fate decided by an international court after a dispute between two states (Wiberg 2000).

Why was Sweden so generous? There is no reason to believe that Swedes should be any more peaceful than Norwegians or Finns, for instance. However, there were certain seemingly domestic reasons for the Swedish peacefulness. Sweden had not been allotted the injections of nationalist adrenalin that Denmark, Norway and Finland had experienced during the second half of the nineteenth century. Political dependence and wars, whether won or lost, produce popular nationalist sentiment.[3] Denmark had got its injections in connection with the wars of 1848–51 and 1864, leading to an inward-oriented, defensive type of nationalism. Norway had mobilised nationalism continuously as an underdog in relation to Sweden from 1814, and correspondingly with Finland as part of the Russian empire, in particular during the 'years of oppression' from about 1890. In contrast to these experiences, Sweden had lived a geopolitically insulated life, protected as the core of Norden by the Finnish and Norwegian flanks and by Denmark to her south-west. Sweden has not been at war since the Napoleonic wars.[4] This has provided barren soil for nationalism, but fruitful soil for the kind of internationalist/idealist opinion favouring a security community.[5] In addition to this fundamental factor, it is likely that some additional factors have also played a role in favour of Swedish internationalism. In the climate of opinion permitted by geopolitical fundamentals, there were niches for the 'free churches', the workers' movement and for a rationalistic impulse in public opinion.[6]

The free churches got a foothold in Sweden during the second half of the nineteenth century that was unparalleled in the other Nordic countries. This made for a more moralistic climate of debate in Sweden than, notably, in Denmark.[7] In other words, this difference diffused from the religious sector to public debate in general. Second, Sweden developed a stronger workers' movement than the other Nordic countries. Internationalism was a marked and integral part of the ideology of workers' movements at the time. Moreover, the religious and ideological peace orientations got their rationalistic, scientific counterpart through the Nobel prizes, including the Peace Prize awarded in Oslo.

Sweden made a deed out of its geopolitically conditioned need to keep apart from great power conflicts by giving 'neutrality' a special peace-loving implication. Even more, after the Second World War, Sweden had a vested interest in playing the role as 'world conscience'. In other words, what was permitted, perhaps even beneficial, for geopolitical reasons had its domestic underpinning in the virtue of religious life, the workers' movement and the institutionalisation of rationalism in not least the Nobel Prize.

Even though all the beneficial effects displayed in the course of the twentieth century could not be clearly seen in 1905 or 1921, it was seen as better to play the 'good guy' than to go for short-sighted military gains in what later came to be seen as the first vital test cases of a Nordic security community. Denmark, Norway and Finland, preoccupied with more immediate concerns of their own – licking their wounds or striving for full independence – could not at the outset cultivate the 'luxury interests' that Sweden could afford.[8] In other words, Sweden formed the initial snowball and was thereby the sine qua non for the process getting started.[9]

The emergence of another security community

The Nordic security community no longer exists in splendid isolation. In the course of the Cold War, the EC/EU developed into a security community (e.g. Wæver 1998). War had become unthinkable between EC/EU members, even between Germany and France, the two 'hereditary enemies'. They now had a common enemy in the form of the Soviet Union and a common ally in the form of the United States – an ally that was so superior in strength to both Germany and France that rivalry between the two for alliance leadership was altogether redundant. Under these geopolitically optimal conditions, there was time for the establishment of a security community ('stable peace *because of* community and identity') (Adler and Barnett 1998). Common coal and steel production made war virtually impossible in the short run, and with strong common institutions and deepened integration, war would simply be too costly for all parties concerned. Without drawing the parallel too far, West Germany (BRD) as a generous actor – like Sweden in the Nordic context – was probably a catalyst for European integration to take momentum in the post-war period. Germany having lost the war – and shifted regime – had to be the 'nice guy', paying the bill of the Community at critical moments in the process.

With war no longer a practical option, there was some trickling-down of elite 'we-feeling' to civil society. Although there is much less 'we-feeling' among the European peoples than among the elites, there is judged to be enough of this commodity for a community to apply, although no time demarcation, opinion poll or series of non-wars has been offered (Wæver 1998: 101). As the geopolitically optimal conditions for stable peace disappeared with the Soviet Union in 1991, the community faced its real test – a test that was apparently passed. People had stopped thinking how and why the Community got started; mutual peace now seemed a 'natural' thing.

Even though the Nordic and the EC/EU security communities were initiated according to different models, it is noteworthy that geopolitical background conditions were probably necessary for their emergence in the first place: the strengthening of Prussia (facilitating Scandinavianism) and Sweden's protected location in the former case, and the US–Soviet connection in the latter.

A security community on the Baltic eastern shore: 'bottom-up' or 'top-down'?

The question now is which of these two starting methods – 'bottom-up' or 'top-down' – are the most appropriate for the eastern shore of the Baltic Sea. Generally, the odds for a security community here are quite unfavourable, due not least to the overdoses of adrenalin (nationalism) that all parties concerned have experienced during the twentieth century. Also, while the Nordic countries had civil societies and extensive transnational ties between these, and the pre-EC European countries had civil societies (with modest transnational ties), this third group of countries with their socialist pasts started out in 1991 with *no* independent civil societies in the first place.

If we were talking about the three Baltic states only, it is dubious whether they form a security community today. The fact that they have never been engaged in mutual war is no proof that they form such a community. Their mutual differences, more significant than perceived from outside, the absence of a 'generous core power', the absence of historic transnational ties and any analogy to Scandinavianism speaks against an affirmative answer. Still, there seems to exist, after all, a fragile 'we-feeling', so it cannot be ruled out that the EU/Norden-induced process, which started after the Cold War, will lead to a security community. We need not go further into this question here, however, since intra-Baltic conflicts have always been overlaid by the Baltic–Russian conflict (Buzan 1992). That is to say: any intra-Baltic conflicts have been secondary to the Baltic–Russian conflict; the 'common enemy' has caused a degree of cohesion among the Balts, depending on the degree of Baltic–Russian tension at any given time. The latter has never 'allowed' intra-Baltic conflicts to develop in a serious direction.[10]

The conflict of practical interest, therefore, is the Baltic–Russian one. Is a Russian–Baltic security community realistic, and if so from a 'bottom-up' or 'top-down' starting point? One thing is granted: such a community does not exist today, and never has. Quite to the contrary: Stalin's incorporation of the Baltic states into the Soviet Union 1939–40, and again in 1944, his subsequent deportations of Balts to Siberia, and the Soviet Union's suppression of Baltic freedom 1944–91 has had far-reaching implications for the Balts' perception of Russia. Russia is seen as the 'empire of evil'. Whereas many Russians tend to interpret themselves as the Balts' co-victims in relation to the Soviet Union, the Balts look back on the Soviet Union as the imperialist tool of Russia. So not only is there an absence of the 'Nordic' attributes mentioned earlier in the chapter, there are also the traumatic experiences of the past virtually forbidding any 'bottom-up' development in the direction of a security community. Therefore the Nordic way of starting such a community is unrealistic, to say the least. But what about the EU method?

It may sound naïve, but since the EU 'top-down' method could create a security community between the French and German 'arch-enemies', it is not unlikely that it can do so also in the case of Russia and the Balts. There may be legitimate objections, of course: first that Russia and the Balts do not share a common enemy and, second, that Russia will never become an EU member. The first objection is probably valid. Terrorism, in the form of the Al-Qaeda network in the wake of 11 September 2001, may be too volatile as a common enemy; in any case, Baltic sympathies with the Chechnian cause and that of other small peoples tend to make Baltic and Russian perceptions of 'terrorism' quite different. A compensation for the lack of a common enemy could be huge common *problems*, for instance of an environmental nature – 'huge' and 'common', that is, so that only a common, concerted effort could solve them (cf. below, p. 162).[11]

Turning to the second objection, it is probably also correct that Russia will never join the EU, since the country's size alone seems forbidding.

However, there are a number of other mechanisms, more or less related to the EU, that may also be instrumental towards creating a security community in the long run. There are the disciplining effects of EU/NATO-norms on would-be EU/NATO members (Friis 1999; Mouritzen 1998: 103–8). This is basically due to the unipolar power structure in Europe, where the EU/US is the one and only pole – a pole of attraction. In order to qualify for membership, candidates must live up to EU/NATO norms in a number of respects. For instance, they should not have unsettled border issues, and they should not have conflicts internally with minorities of 'foreign' nationalities. These norms – whose 'stability projection' has also been seen in Central and Eastern Europe – have caused the Baltic would-be members not only to settle their mutual border issues, but also to reach border agreements with Russia (although not all are ratified). The Russian minorities in Estonia and Latvia have gained improved conditions, probably due to the same logic. All these developments have obviously been steps towards improved Baltic–Russian relations (e.g. Herd 1999).

In the absence of Russian EU membership, Russian NATO membership – and its prospects – could be a factor improving Baltic–Russian relations. Even though the latter may be seen by some as even more far-fetched than the former, the emergence of terrorism as a common enemy to Russia and the USA means that Russian NATO membership is far from unthinkable (Krickus 2002), albeit hardly in the near future.[12] Baltic–Russian relations would undoubtedly improve within a NATO framework. However, as the case of Greece–Turkey should remind us, the NATO framework may well prevent outright war, but it does not in itself promote good neighbourly relations or, even less, a security community between the parties. Should a Russian membership materialise, it would be a stabilising framework around Baltic–Russian relations that, nonetheless, would have to be supplemented by other types of cooperation, to which we shall now turn.

Various types of cooperation can be subsumed under the codeword *Einbindung* (binding): instead of trying to deter a presumed threatening actor (here: Russia), one binds it into a web of commitments, over time socialising the actor and oneself to mutual trust and the non-use of force. The EU–Russia relations are an example as subsumed under the heading 'EU Northern Dimension' (Archer 2000; Mazur-Baranska 2000). This originally Finnish idea is to develop EU political and economic relations towards its northern adjacent areas, in particular north-west Russia. Such fields as transport, investment, environment (including nuclear safety), organised crime and illegal immigration are covered.

There are also other types of socialising cooperation, such as the Council of Baltic Sea States (CBSS). As distinct from its substantial tasks such as democracy and minority issues, environment, education, crime fighting and so on, the high politics significance of the CBSS is inherent in the very fact that Russians and Balts sit around the same table (they also do so in the UN and the OSCE, but not in such a relatively narrow and intimate circle). Also, multilateral diplomacy makes possible bilateral meetings that might be difficult to arrange as state visits, for domestic political reasons in both countries (in the cases of Russia–Estonia or Russia–Latvia). Given the similarity of substance between the EU and CBSS agendas, and given that four CBSS states are EU members and four are coming members (and the EU Commission is represented in the CBSS as well), the CBSS has become something of a forum for EU enlargement discussions or discussions of EU relations to non-members (e.g. the EU–Russian partnership). It is increasingly obvious that the high politics role of the CBSS is to add to the blurring of NATO and EU external 'borders' in Europe.[13]

This is in no way the Balts' 'cup of tea'; they wish a clear dividing line. The attitude eastwards follows the formula '*we* belong to Europe, and Europe ends *here*' (Wiberg 1996: 48). Therefore, the Baltic engagement in the CBSS has been lukewarm, at best. The Baltic countries have feared that regional forums would be exploited by Western countries to disclaim 'responsibility' for the Baltic countries' security. However, now that major NATO and EU enlargement decisions have been taken for the foreseeable future, the Baltic countries should be less reluctant towards regional forums than they used to be, even one like the CBSS where Russia is a member.

NATO may be instrumental towards binding through its 'Partnership for Peace' (PfP). PfP has been referred to as a 'geopolitical eraser', removing or weakening sharp dividing lines between NATO members and non-members (Heurlin 1998). Whereas the Baltic countries have participated eagerly and with increasing efficiency in PfP (because they have seen it as a road towards NATO membership), PfP cooperation with Russia has been modest and frozen temporarily as a consequence of the NATO enlargement, the Kosovo war and the Chechnian uprising in Russia. However, with the Balts as NATO members from 2002 and the Russians as possible *future* members, it may be that PfP cooperation will be strengthened in this region to include Russia on a more regular basis. This presupposes, of course, that the Baltic countries, instead of turning their backs on Russia, manage to improve their self-confidence as a result of NATO membership, and therefore will be willing to go into active cooperation eastwards.[14]

Kaliningrad: a golden opportunity

With the competitive relationship among the Baltic countries, the most realistic strategy for improved Baltic–Russian relations is probably that one Baltic country functions as a forerunner; the two others will then follow. The forerunner seems to be Lithuania,[15] and for no strange reasons:

although sharing the traumatic past of Estonian–Russian and Latvian–Russian relations, Lithuanian–Russian relations are built on more stable foundations – no tense border region like in Estonia, and a minor and more integrated Russian population than in Estonia and Latvia. Lithuania has two paradigmatic options for its Russia-relations upon EU membership: the Greece–Turkey option and the Finland–Russia option. Whereas Greece very much sought to use the EC/EU as an instrument in its eastward conflict, Finland has worked energetically for good EU–Russia relations upon joining the EU (the Northern Dimension Initiative being the best example of this). Whether Lithuania will select the Greek or the Finnish example upon entering the EU remains to be seen, but there are already signs now – also required by the EU – that Lithuania will come much closer to the Finnish than to the Greek example (e.g. Usackas 2000).

Also – paradoxical as it may sound – Lithuania and Russia have the kind of tangible, clearly delimited, 'huge common problem' in the form of Kaliningrad that was called for above. 'Huge' needs no further justification (environmental problems, not least), and 'common' is simply due to Kaliningrad's geopolitical and geo-economic situation in the middle of a future enlarged EU: a source of regional instability. In other words, Kaliningrad is far from a zero-sum problem; quite to the contrary, benefits to Kaliningrad are also benefits to Russia and to Lithuania (as well as to Poland to the south). Moreover, Kaliningrad has already attracted the interest of the EU by being incorporated in the EU Northern Dimension. In other words, powerful external catalysts in the form of the EU and EU member countries are available (Usackas 2000). Of course, would-be Russian suspicions of a Western plan to bring about Kaliningrad's secession from Russia should not be nourished. However, as long as Moscow is not circumvented and EU–Russia relations remain stable, this should not be a problem.

Security communities' enlargement potential

Whereas the 'bottom-up' method of initiating a security community *may* be relevant to intra-Baltic relations, it is unrealistic to Baltic–Russian relations. The Nordic prescription says: 'do like us: nominate a generous core power, create a transnational ideology, develop transnational ties, "let the thousand flowers bloom" – and wait from fifty to one hundred years.' With such a prescription, the *enlargement potential* of the Nordic community is modest. By contrast, the EU security community has a significant enlargement potential: due to the EU–US unipolar power structure in Europe, there is one core, a pole of attraction, from which power and influence radiate. Power and influence are applied 'top-down' on relations and regions to be 'conquered'. The EU prescription says: 'if you don't follow our norms and rules, you will be deprived of future benefits, and/or the option of EU membership will vanish.' This is a much more effective pre-scription than the Nordic one.

There is also an intermediate method between these two: 'top-down' *without* power projection. An example could be the Organisation for Security and Cooperation in Europe (OSCE), covering an area 'from Van-couver to Vladivostok'. The security community potential of the OSCE has been discussed by Adler (1998). Being an intergovernmental organisation, its principles and consensus (minus-one) decisions (based on the lowest common denominator between mutually heterogeneous states) are trans-mitted 'top-down' to crisis situations. However, they are not supported by a corresponding power structure (e.g. the inside/outside logic) – as are the EU and NATO norms. Therefore, the OSCE authority *eo ipso* is modest (although, for instance, NATO has gone far in emulating OSCE prac-tices). Other intergovernmental organisations like the CBSS also belong to this intermediate category; however, the CBSS is more closely tied to the EU, and therefore it can to some extent lean on its power structure.

In the context of Baltic–Russian relations, a 'top-down' method of gov-ernmental binding based on the European power structure seems to be the only way ahead – notably if huge common problems require con-certed efforts. Apart from Russian NATO membership – that is hardly an option for the near future – the EU Northern Dimension, the CBSS and NATO PfP cooperation have been mentioned as strivings in this direction. In all of these forums, Nordic states have taken on rather active roles as co-binders. This seems to be Norden's most useful security role on the eastern shore of the Baltic Sea – rather than functioning as a model of its own.

It might be objected by some that EU/NATO stability projection is a Western 'hegemonic project'. Following such a logic, however, the EC/EU project as such is actually an American/French hegemonic project, since both the USA and France, more or less intentionally, had the upper hand in the initiation of post-war European cooperation (not least the European Coal and Steel Community and the European Eco-nomic Community). It is necessary in these matters, however, to distin-guish sharply between origin and (peace) validity, i.e. between the very initiation of a security community and its subsequent functioning. Accord-ing to the well-supported general principle of 'unintended consequences' of social behaviour (Popper 1966, Chapter 14), good consequences may result from 'dubious' intentions, and vice versa. In other words, one should judge a security community on its current merits, not on its initia-tion, i.e. whether its alleged motives are more or less conforming to one's ideological or other preferences.

Notes

1 The present chapter is a significantly revised version of the same author's 'Security Communities Around the Baltic Sea: Real and Imagined', *Security Dialogue*, 32, 3, September 2001, pp. 297–311, with the kind permission of the editors and SAGE Publications Ltd.

2 That is, encompassing relations between the Baltic states and and, more importantly, relations between the Baltic states and Russia. Neither Finnish–Russian relations nor relations involving Beylo-Russia or Poland are included in the analysis.

3 Unless, of course, the regime in question breaks down in the process, as for instance did Nazi Germany 1945. Then a counter-reaction is likely to take place that makes nationalism and national self-assertion politically incorrect (e.g. Mouritzen 1997; Snyder 1993).

4 The pattern described here has been exacerbated by twentieth-century events. Finland fought two wars with the Soviet Union, 1939–40 and 1941–4, and persisted afterwards somewhat in the shadow of Soviet power. Norway and Denmark were occupied by Germany 1940–5.

5 During the seventeenth century, Sweden was at war for sixty-six years; during the eighteenth century the corresponding figure was thirty-four years; during the nineteenth century, four years; and during the twentieth century, 0 years (figures provided by the Swedish historian Sverker Oredsson).

6 On my view of the interplay between domestic and external (geopolitical) factors in conditioning foreign policy, cf. Mouritzen, 1998, Chapter 6. An *allowance model* of the interplay is presented: external factors may allow – or forbid – the effects of domestic factors. In this book I have formulated my general conception of IR and international politics.

7 Instrumental in this regard was also the influential temperance movement.

8 It is noteworthy in the Danish case, though, that hostilities southwards during the nineteenth century not only created an inward-oriented nationalism, but *also* made Scandinavianism and the formation of transnational ties northwards more attractive.

9 I shall add one example of a Nordic non-war from a Second World War context that has so far not been mentioned in the security community literature. When Germany at midsummer 1941 demanded from the Swedish government that the 'Engelbrecht division' should be allowed passage through Sweden from Norway to Finland, Swedish decision-makers considered arguments for and against permission (Björkman 1971). One argument – which played an important role – was that if Sweden said 'no', Germany would declare war on Sweden and Sweden would end up as a Western/Soviet ally. This in itself might be all right. However, the fact that Sweden and Finland would be involved on *different* sides in such a war scenario was considered 'unthinkable' by ministers in cabinet; this was simply not allowed to happen. Even if there were other reasons as well for the Swedish decision to acquiesce in the German demand, it is telling to see which importance was ascribed to the retaining of the Nordic security community among Swedish decision-makers.

10 Wallensteen *et al.* (1995) evaluate the security community prospects for twelve relations among the littoral Baltic states. Few of the relations, though, are of practical relevance in the area today, due to various forms of overlay.

11 Think of the earthquakes in Greece and Turkey (1999, 2000), creating at least an embryo of goodwill and cooperation between the two countries. No party could justifiably suspect the other of having orchestrated the earthquakes, and the usual zero-sum assumption between the two countries (i.e. that the gain of

one party means a corresponding loss of the other) was invalid for this delimited field.

12 The *general* pros and cons in this connection fall beyond our purpose here, of course.

13 On the Baltic Sea rim space as a future grey zone, interpreted as a positive scenario through its blurring of sharp dividing lines, cf. Archer, 1998. On the beneficial, often unintended, consequences flowing from the sheer existence of international organisations, cf. Mouritzen, 1998, pp. 126–30.

14 The Russia–North Atlantic Council of 2002 represents a high-level *Einbindung* of Russia, as Russia is given the status enjoyed by officials from the nineteen member countries – short of a veto – in deciding how to address common security problems. Its practical functioning, though, remains to be seen.

15 *Lithuanian Foreign Policy Review*, 2000/2, special issue.

References

Adler, Emanuel (1998) 'Seeds of peaceful change: the OSCE's security community-building model', in Emanuel Adler and Michael Barnett (eds), *Security Communities*, Cambridge: Cambridge University Press: 119–60.

—— and Michael Barnett (1998) 'A framework for the study of security communities', in Emanuel Adler and Michael Barnett (eds), *Security Communities*, Cambridge: Cambridge University Press: 29–66.

Archer, Clive (1996) 'The Nordic area as a "zone of peace"', *Journal of Peace Research* 33 (4): 451–67.

—— (1998) 'Prospects for Europe's Baltic Rim', in Hans Mouritzen (ed.), *Bordering Russia: Theory and Prospects for Europe's Baltic Rim*, Aldershot: Ashgate: 259–81.

—— (2000) 'Security aspects of the EU's northern dimension', in Lars Hedegaard and Bjarne Lindström (eds), *The NEBI Yearbook 2000*, Berlin: Springer: 315–27.

Björkman, Leif (1971) *Sverige inför Operation Barbarossa*, Stockholm: Allmänna Förlaget.

Buzan, Barry (1992) *People, States and Fear: An Agenda for International Security Studies in the post-Cold War Era*, Hemel Hempstead: Harvester Wheatsheaf.

Deutsch, Karl W. *et al.* (1957) *Political Community and the North Atlantic Area: International Organisation in the Light of Historical Experience*, Princeton, NJ: Princeton University Press.

Friis, Lykke (ed.) (1999) *An Ever Larger Union? EU Enlargement and European Integration*, Copenhagen: DUPI.

Herd, Graeme P. (1999) 'Russia's Baltic policy after the meltdown', *Security Dialogue* 30 (2): 197–212.

Heurlin, Bertel (1998) 'Military command structures in the Baltic Sea area', in Lars Hedegaard and Bjarne Lindström (eds), *The NEBI Yearbook 1998*, Berlin: Springer: 405–22.

Krickus, Richard J. (2002) *Russia in NATO: Thinking about the Unthinkable*, Copenhagen: DUPI.

Mazur-Baranska, Agnieszka (2000) 'The northern dimension of the EU', *The Polish Quarterly of International Affairs* 9 (2): 31–44.

Mouritzen, Hans (1997) *External Danger and Democracy. Old Nordic Lessons and New European Challenges*, Aldershot: Ashgate.

—— (1998) *Theory and Reality of International Politics*, Aldershot: Ashgate.

Popper, Karl R. (1966) *The Open Society and its Enemies*, vol. 2, London: Routledge.

Snyder, Jack (1993) 'Nationalism and the crisis of the post-Soviet state', *Survival* 35 (1): 5–26.

Usackas, Vygaudas (2000) 'Lithuania and Russia: knowing the past, building genuine partnership for the future', *Lithuanian Foreign Policy Review* 2: 9–26.

Vedung, Evert (1971) *Unionsdebatten 1905: En jämförelse mellan argumenteringen i Sverige och Norge*, Stockholm: Almqvist & Wiksell.

Wæver, Ole (1998) 'Insecurity, security and asecurity in the West European non-war community', in Emanuel Adler and Michael Barnett (eds), *Security Communities*, Cambridge: Cambridge University Press: 69–118.

Wallensteen, Peter *et al.* (1995) *Towards a Security Community in the Baltic Region*, Uppsala: The Baltic University.

Wiberg, Håkan (1996), 'Adaptive patterns and their deep roots: a European overview', in Hans Mouritzen, Ole Wæver and Håkan Wiberg (eds), *European Integration and National Adaptations*, New York: Nova Science Publishers: 43–63.

—— (2000) 'The Nordic security community: past, present, future', in Bertel Heurlin and Hans Mouritzen (eds), *Danish Foreign Policy Yearbook 2000*, Copenhagen: DUPI: 121–37.

14 The EU as a foreign policy actor
The limitations of territorial sovereignty

Christopher S. Browning

Introduction: a neomedieval/Westphalian configuration

The question of just what kind of entity the European Union is or aspires
to be has been a point of debate since the inception of the European
project in the 1950s. Whilst descriptive metaphors abound, perhaps the
most evocative and prevalent are those depicting the EU either as a *neomedieval* or *Westphalian* entity. Although it is easy to see these metaphors as
directly opposed, this chapter starts from the premise that they point to a
paradox at the heart of EU debates, with both capturing a part of current
developments.

When the spotlight is focused on the internal social, political and economic organisation of the EU, arguments that the European Union is
developing into the world's first postmodern/neomedieval political entity
appear rather convincing (Ruggie 1993). Characteristic of this postmodern neomedievalism is the undermining of territorial sovereignty as the
foundational principle of political order. Therefore, whilst nation-states
remain important, it is pointed out that, through such things as the sub-
sidiarity principle and processes of debordering and globalisation, governance within the Union has actually become characterised by overlapping
spaces of authority, networks, decentralisation and the fostering of multiple identities.

Externally the picture is less clear. On the one hand, debordering,
decentralisation and the development of overlapping networks and spaces
find a place in the promotion of liberal democratic norms and structures
beyond its borders as a part of the EU's origins as a peace project. This is,
of course, a central motivation behind the enlargement process, but is
also apparent in such things as the Northern Dimension Initiative and the
Barcelona Process, which aim at disseminating EU values to countries that
have little hope or desire of joining the EU in the future. However, the
EU has also been seen to have clear aspirations to be a very traditional
unitary actor, the archetype of a modernist Westphalian nation-state
(Ginsberg 1999). This appears clear in the goal to provide the Union with
a unified international subjectivity through such things as the Common

Foreign and Security Policy (CFSP) and the common European Security and Defence Identity (ESDI). It is also clear in the creation of a post for an EU foreign minister and in the Schengen border regime, which aims at preserving and re-instituting the territorial sovereignty of the Union vis-à-vis its neighbours.

This chapter focuses on this external level and argues that the post-modern elements of the EU peace mission are presently being marginalised by more modernist concerns, a development that will have potentially negative effects. More particularly, it is argued that the Union is in danger of becoming trapped in a modernist discourse that argues that to have a voice in international affairs, to be an effective international actor, one needs to be a sovereign territorial entity with clearly defined boundaries. As will be pointed out, such entrapment is unnecessary since there is no essential link between 'actorness' and territorial sovereignty.

First, the chapter will seek to explain why, in its external relations, the EU frequently remains preoccupied with modernist questions that see the world and political space as clearly divided between exclusive political units. This will entail looking back at the origins of the EC project and some of the contradictions evident in the philosophical heritage of EU ideals. Second, the chapter will highlight that being stuck in modernist discourse entails a number of consequences. In particular, this results in a desire for exclusive territorial borders and the tendency to construct self–other divisions in negative terms. In short, the Union's external relations policy is frequently reduced to the demands of re-inscribing and reasserting the Union's modern subjectivity. As a result, the central questions of EU external relations often become centred on concerns over the Union's security, concerns that should not be seen as objectively identifiable in the external environment but which are largely constituted by the very frame of reference. Through examples drawn from EU policy in northern Europe, the chapter will argue that this, in turn, severely limits the options available for the EU in tackling the problems it faces.

The EU as a modern actor

The difference between the EU's neomedieval internal configurations and aspirations and those of its current Westphalian external form largely derives from the origins of the European project in the 1950s. Building on ideas of functionalist spillover and the power of interdependence to foster cooperation and a democratic security community, the European Community emerged as a peace project to overcome the divisions that had led to the Second World War. Central to this has been the desire to break down the borders existing between the member states, to facilitate the growth of cross-border networks and regions, and to foster the emergence of multiple overlapping local, regional and European identities to meliorate the exclusionary nationalisms of the past. Internally, therefore, the peace project has tended to promote the 'postmodernisation' of the Union.

Externally, however, the peace project has produced tension and paradox. On the one hand, it is often considered vital that the peace project should be continually extended beyond the Union's borders if the EU is to live up to its identity as an agent of peace. As noted, such identity-based motivations clearly exist as a driving force behind the enlargement process. On the other hand, however, the Union's peace-project origins also promote the construction of the EU in rather modernist Westphalian form. As Wæver has argued, understood as a peace *project*, the continued extension of the Union's *internal* integration has widely become considered essential to the very survival of the EU and European *security*. As such, the EU's continued integration and development into a unified social, economic, political and military actor is considered good in and of itself to preserve peace. 'Fragmentation', in contrast, is viewed negatively as 'a self-propelling process that by definition will destroy "Europe" as a process' (Wæver 1996: 123; see also 121–5). Indeed, the fear that if the integration process stops moving forward Europe will fragment, and possibly even 'Balkanise', is evident in the rhetoric of many European leaders (e.g. Chirac 2001: 21; *International Herald Tribune* 16 October 2001).

This tendency to project the EU as a unitary actor in international politics is also promoted by the *functionalist unitarism* that constitutes the philosophical heart of the EU and EU integration studies. As Parker argues, underlying the functionalist approaches to European integration that have dominated the agenda ever since 1957 is an implicit presumption that Europe is (or at least should be) a cultural, economic and political unity. In this respect, the common-sense (though illogical) view of functionalism is that Europe's common political or governmental problems necessarily entail common solutions, which in turn will necessarily support the further process of European integration, which ultimately will lead to a unified European government akin to a territorial sovereign state (Parker 2000: 18). Particularly important about this functionalist heritage is that, despite its implicit challenge to the sovereignty of states, functionalism does not challenge the 'modern' idea that political legitimacy and agency requires a centralised authority premised on territorial sovereignty (Kelstrup and Williams 2000: 8). In short, therefore, as long as functionalist unitarism constitutes the philosophical background of discussion in the EU, then its construction into a unified global actor will remain the implicit goal.

The preoccupation with constituting the EU as a territorially sovereign global actor can also be understood with recourse to the modern philosophical understanding of subjectivity that underlies most theoretical approaches to International Relations and the world more generally. As Williams argues, prevalent theoretical understandings of international politics are founded on the claims of contractarian philosophers like

Hobbes and Rousseau, who argued that, in order to get out of the insecurity of the state of nature, individuals would need to agree to a social contract establishing the sovereign state as the authority with the responsibility to enforce the contractual obligations of its members. Thus, concomitantly the state became seen as not only the prerequisite for community and security, but also the limit of political life and order (Williams 2000: 90–1). Typically, therefore, International Relations theory operates with a limited understanding that restricts the world of international politics to the realm of unified sovereign states, with state units depicted as interacting with each other on the basis of purely strategic (contractual) considerations. However, the problem with this narrow definition of international politics is that it 'risks both replicating modernist structures of violence, and obstructs [sic] the emergence of new conceptions of political order' (Williams 2000: 91). Put another way, in confining international politics to the world of states, for the EU to have a voice in international affairs the conclusion is easily drawn that it too must assume the characteristics of modern statehood. In this respect, one might note the comment of Kenneth Waltz, the founding father of neorealist IR theory, that for the EU ever to amount to much in the 'international structure', it would have to take on the form of a unified state (Waltz, cited in Ruggie 1993: 140).

Although there is nothing self-evident in the link drawn in modernist thinking between actorness and territorial sovereignty, that the EU has accepted this conflation has become clear since the end of the Cold War. The EU has constructed a post-Cold War discourse that contends that, in order to cope with post-Cold War challenges (regional political instability, immigration, ecological imbalances, globalisation), the EU must develop into an international actor with a defined role and ability for political action (Larsen 2000: 222–3). For example, the 2001 EU White Paper on Governance is unequivocal on the need for the EU 'to speak more with a single voice' if it is to become a powerful actor on the world stage (Commission of the European Communities 2001a). In part, this desire for the Union to develop into a more coherent actor in world politics reflects ideas of the EU as a peace project that therefore has responsibilities in ordering the post-Cold War situation. However, the EU also seems to be driven by the more traditional interest-based concerns of power politics. In particular, the EU appears to be responding to the classic criticism that the EU lags far 'behind' traditional geopolitical actors like the USA and Russia. Whilst being an economic giant, politically and militarily the EU is lamented as being a dwarf and a soft touch that is incapable of dealing with the 'hard realities' of world politics (Aalto 2002: 143–4) and that is frequently in danger of being 'taken for a ride' (Valtasaari 1999) by others.

When drawing on such conflictual interest-based notions, the post-Cold War EU is drawn into a modern discourse that promotes its future development in terms of the achievement of traditional geopolitical subjectivity and in turn marginalises contending discourses of de-centralisation. In this world, the EU is defined as a geopolitical subject with clear sovereign borders of territory and governance differentiating the inside from the outside. In this respect, the further integration of the EU into a state-like actor is securitised (i.e. it has become of existential importance) for the reason that without this it is feared Europe will be open to easy exploitation by others. Notably, the discourse of the Commission is replete with prognoses of an emerging multipolar world order in which each regional pole will need to be strong (politically, economically, militarily) if it is to be effective in the global competition over resources and interests (Larsen 2000: 224). To summarise, however, what this section illustrates is the extent to which the EU, in its external relations, has become stuck in what John Agnew has termed the 'Territorial Trap', the preoccupation with thinking that the world is necessarily made up of a patchwork of territorially sovereign political units (Agnew 1998: 51).

From the Territorial Trap to the internal/external security paradox

Importantly, certain consequences flow from the modernist thinking that underpins the territorial trap. At a general level, Campbell has argued that one consequence of modern Hobbesian accounts of subjectivity, which establish the state as the Leviathan and provider of security, is that the external environment, the realm of International Relations and other states, tends to be depicted as threatening. Consequently, foreign policy is often reduced to a discourse of danger in which the self needs to protect itself from external threats (Campbell 1992: chapters 3–4). As Paasi notes, in this quintessentially modern discourse, boundaries between self and otherness are given highly positive connotations as central to maintaining internal security and unity (Paasi 2003).

Moreover, as this section tries to show, the 'Territorial Trap' runs the risk of precluding a wider political vision. There is a tendency that the Union's external relations become little more than an exercise in re-inscribing and re-asserting the modern subjectivity of the Union. This pre-empts a more courageous approach to issues that raise the prospect of the de-centralisation of the conduct of its external relations. In this respect, the EU's approach to the problems facing the Russian exclave of Kaliningrad, sandwiched between Lithuania and Poland on the Baltic coast, illustrates the constraining aspects of the EU's modernist framework particularly well.

Kaliningrad first appeared on the EU radar towards the end of the 1990s in connection with the Union's future enlargement to Poland and Lithuania, which will leave Kaliningrad surrounded on its land borders by EU states. As a number of commentators (not least the Kaliningraders themselves) have pointed out, enlargement threatens to exacerbate the problems of this already impoverished and marginalised region. The most widely documented issue concerns the impact of the Schengen visa regime that applicant countries must impose to qualify for membership. This has provoked fears amongst the many Kaliningraders who make a living out of border trade that the new visa regime will undermine their livelihoods (Trenin 2000: 35). More controversial is that Kaliningraders wanting to travel to 'big Russia' by land will now have to acquire a visa before they will be allowed to visit their homeland – all, of course, assuming European visa officials approve their application (Fairlie 2001: 12). Kaliningrad also faces other problems. Particularly notable is that, whilst Lithuania and Poland have benefited from large EU funding programmes to assist them in developing their infrastructure up to EU standards, assistance to Kaliningrad has been minimal in comparison. This is exacerbating regional imbalances and threatening to lock Kaliningrad into a vicious circle of social and economic poverty and exclusion.[1]

To a certain extent, of course, these problems are explicitly territorially driven, with Kaliningrad's geographical isolation from the Russian motherland problematising aspects of EU enlargement in a way that the extension of the EU to Russia's borders, with Finland's membership in 1995, did not. However, the EU's prioritisation of modernist perceptual frames that emphasise territory in exclusive sovereign terms has made the issue doubly problematic. In particular, for the most part modernist discourse has tended to deflect EU attention away from the problems facing Kaliningraders (and local border populations in Lithuania and Poland) as a result of the negative effects of enlargement and, rather, has re-constituted the Kaliningrad issue in terms of the questions Kaliningrad's forthcoming position as an EU enclave raises about the Union's own security and the nature of EU subjectivity. Crucial here is the fact that, with Kaliningrad's enclosure within its geographical borders, previously distinct borders separating the inside and outside of the EU will become visibly blurred. In turn, this framework has limited the solutions the EU perceives to be available in tackling the Kaliningrad issue, and continues to do so.

Of course, it would be wrong to suggest that the EU is totally blind to the problems facing Kaliningraders as a result of EU enlargement. Notably, in 2001 the Commission (Commission of the European Communities 2001b) felt compelled to issue a specific, if somewhat dismissive, report on Kaliningrad, which in turn also highlights how the Kaliningrad question actually encapsulates the tension between modernist and postmodern perceptual frames in the EU's external relations.

The dominance of modernist discourses is, however, evident. This is clearest in the fact that, for the EU, the Kaliningrad question is generally framed in terms of the threats Kaliningrad poses to the EU's own security and its development as an international actor, both understood in terms of the preservation of territorial sovereignty. Indeed, it has become common to frame the Kaliningrad question as a paradox between the internal and external security needs of the Union. On the one hand, *internal security* is seen to require a strict border regime with Kaliningrad in order to prevent the infiltration of crime, disease and illegal immigration from the Russian exclave. On the other hand, the negative effects of EU enlargement on Kaliningrad threaten to destabilise EU–Russian relations. In this respect, it is argued that in order to foster external security and preserve the EU–Russian relationship, the border with Kaliningrad needs to be open and porous with the semi-integration of Kaliningrad into the EU. In this reading, however, preserving *external security* through opening up the Union's external border is seen to undermine internal societal security; whilst maintaining a strict border regime in the interests of internal security, in turn, is seen to undermine external security. In this context, the Kaliningrad question is one of how best to balance these contradictory demands, with critics of the Schengen regime essentially arguing the balance has fallen too far in favour of internal security (e.g. Fairlie 2001; Huisman 2002: 6–7).

Kaliningrad has thus become inscribed into the discourse as being a potential 'soft security' threat to the Union that, in the opinion of the European Parliament, might need to be 'contained' through 'isolating' it (European Parliament 2000: 13–15). When framed in these terms the Kaliningrad question becomes one of how best to manage the boundary with others, not how to overcome it as the EU remains concerned to clearly differentiate itself from others. The justification and rationalisation of Schengen is occurring through the characterisation of Kaliningrad and Kaliningraders in highly negative terms as a site of pollution, illegal immigration, disease, criminality and prostitution, i.e. in the terms of External Affairs Commissioner, Chris Patten, Kaliningrad is the northernmost part of 'an arc of danger and instability' that rings Europe (Patten 2001).

This discourse of threat establishes a clear hierarchical distinction between 'us' (the EU) and 'them' (Kaliningraders/Russians). In characterising Kaliningrad as a region of chaos and crime, pollution and disease, the EU in turn is reified as a site of order and health. In Campbellian terms, identifying the 'threat' becomes a central way of constituting EU identity.

In more political terms, this move in itself becomes constitutive of some of the problems raised by the Kaliningrad issue, whilst at the same time it also tends to limit the political solutions that become conceivable. Trapped in a discourse of danger, with Kaliningrad understood as a threat to its security, the EU has been rather unwilling to treat Kaliningrad as a special case that somehow blurs the borders between the EU's inside and outside. Therefore, instead of looking for the local or regional-based solutions that the EU tends to promote in its internal affairs and that foster the emergence of overlapping regional spaces, in the Kaliningrad case the

EU approach has tended to be quite opposite. Indeed, the reliance on strategies that reaffirm the unity of the EU and the sanctity of its borders has been the norm. This has been no more apparent than in the EU's almost dogmatic insistence on the instigation of the common Schengen regime. This reached a crux in May and June 2002 with the EU's sharp refusal to even consider Russian proposals for the creation of two transit corridors through Lithuania to Belarus that would enable the continuation of visa free travel and for the right of Russians to travel visa free on non-stop trains through Lithuania. Whilst the proposal for transit corridors was not the most historically sensitive idea given unhappy memories of the 'Polish corridor' of the inter-war period, the categorical nature of the refusal considerably soured the EU's relations with Russia (Smirnyagin 2002), but was one driven by the frame of the internal/external security paradox that has developed as a result of aspirations for modern subjectivity. Similarly, although subsequently the EU has made an attempt to explore the flexibility that may be allowed in the Schengen regime, the application of Schengen has not been in question (Commission of the European Communities 2002). Consequently, the transit agreement signed at the November 2002 EU-Russia summit appears to be one largely dictated by the EU. Thus, all Russians travelling between Kaliningrad and mainland Russia through Lithuania will require a Facilitated Transit Document (essentially a multi-entry visa by another name) (Tenth EU-Russia Summit 2002). This means that EU visa officials will, ultimately, be able to prevent Russian citizens from travelling to and from Kaliningrad by certain means. At the same time, the fact that all Russian citizens who wish/need to travel by train or car will have to ask permission from a foreign power is something that remains antagonistic to many Russians (Acher and Grajewski 2002). Moreover, although Russian proposals for a non-stop visa-free train have been noted, the EU has only agreed to conducting a feasibility study. The fact that in essential respects Schengen appears not to be open to any significant renegotiation tends to re-enforce an impression amongst outsiders that there are first (EU members), second (candidate countries) and third (non-applicants) class European states in Brussels' view.

Similarly, this inflexibility on the part of the EU is further reflected in the cautious attitude the EU has adopted to regional organisations such as the Council of Baltic Sea States (CBSS) and its inability to fully embrace proposals such as the Lithuanian–Russian 'Nida initiative' and the EU's own Northern Dimension Initiative, both of which open the way for overlapping spaces of governance. Also illustrative, though, is that the Kaliningrad question, for the most part, continues to be dealt with through the EU–Russia Partnership and Cooperation Agreement (which came into force in 1997) or through the EU's Common Strategy on Russia (1999). As Joenniemi *et al.* (2000: 19–20) note, both the PCA and CSR treat Russia (and also the EU) as a homogeneous whole making no allowance for the specificity of Kaliningrad.[2]

To summarise, therefore, caught in the modernist discourse of the internal/external security paradox, the EU continues to conflate subjectivity and actorness with the need for territorial sovereignty and clearly defined borders. In this thinking, the Union's borders are inscribed as sites of fear that need to be strengthened in order to prevent contamination. The consequence, however, is that these 'traditional statist and territorially geared concerns leave little room for new challenges of integration, and Kaliningrad thus tends to be locked in to the old agenda of security, exclusion, borders, territorial disputes and more generally classical power political rivalry' (Joenniemi *et al.* 2000: 23–4). All this is not to say that *security* is not an issue; it is, but *whose* security is the issue. In EU discourse it is the security of EU citizens, and more particularly the preservation of the EU's territorial sovereignty, that is prioritised over the security of outsiders, a rhetorical move that at one and the same time shifts the referent object of security from people to the Union as an institution and fails to recognise the way in which the security of insiders and outsiders can never be divorced from each other. Not only does this discourse result in a focus on bilateral approaches, thereby restricting the Union's ability to capitalise on the expertise of the applicant countries in conducting relations with the EU's near abroad, but it also raises significant questions about the EU's ability to live up to its *raison d'être* as the peace project of Europe. The point is that the modernist discourse of security is, in fact, only likely to perpetuate insecurity through re-affirming self–other divisions in negative terms, as the outside remains seen as potentially threatening. In short, what this illustrates is the Union's inability to think in truly regional terms, as the Union fails to treat all people in the European north as equal: rather, Kaliningraders can ultimately be sacrificed to the needs of the Union as a whole.

Conclusion

In conclusion, two points will be made. First, despite internal neomedievalism and the centrality of the peace project to EU identity, it has been argued that, in its external relations, the EU often remains trapped in modernist frames of reference that not only undermine the effectiveness of the Union's approaches, but also become constitutive of some of the challenges it faces. Central to the problems of modernist conceptual frames is the conflation of actorness/subjectivity with the need for territorial sovereignty, a conflation which in turn is seen to require uniform, stable borders clearly demarcating the inside from the outside. Such assumptions, however, are mistaken. As Paasi puts it, ' "identity" does not inevitably need to be based on a bounded experience' (Paasi 2001: 22). Likewise, borders should not be seen as impermeable edges of a

pre-defined subjectivity, but actually as sites of interaction where subjectivity is negotiated.

These conceptual problems are compounded and become particularly
visible at a material level. This can be seen in the case of Kaliningrad,
where the modernist assumptions underpinning the EU discourse of the
internal/external security paradox are making it very difficult for the EU
to embrace the interdependence and regionality that *de facto* already
exists, not only precisely because of Kaliningrad's geographical location,
but also increasingly as a result of processes of globalisation. In many
respects, therefore, the questions of borders and governance raised by
Kaliningrad elude the logic of the modernist framework through which
the EU has addressed the issue to date, and consequently erecting the
Schengen wall can only be a partial solution at best. This is to say that the
problems of Kaliningrad are not particularly modernist in nature and as
such indicate that the principle of territorial sovereignty as an organisational principle of governance is no longer always applicable, let alone
always an adequate description of world politics (see Joenniemi 2001: 56).

Therefore, this chapter stands as an encouragement for the EU to
adopt different perceptual lenses in its external relations that will enable
it to deal with the problems it faces more effectively. In particular, the
neomedieval character of the EU's internal organisation provides a
particularly successful example of the way in which borders can be recon-
ceptualised as zones of opportunity and interaction, rather than simply
understood as sites of fear. Likewise, the decentralisation the EU
embraces internally need not necessarily be feared in its external relations, where it is often understood as undermining the EU's achievement
of international subjectivity. To the contrary, such modernist fears thereby
largely preclude the Union from capitalising on the expertise of its
margins (Lithuania and Poland in the case of Kaliningrad) and of engaging in international politics more fruitfully (Aalto 2002: 162; Huisman
2002: 41). As both Parker and Hartnell point out, the margins and
borders are actually sites where 'bold innovation and nimble action are
possible' (Hartnell 2000: 29–30; Parker 2000).

To turn to the second concluding point, essentially at issue in these
debates is the future construction, identity and subjectivity of the EU and
what it means to be European. Advocating more neomedieval frames of reference is arguably a way to reclaim and prioritise some of the heritage of
the European Union as a peace project in its broadest sense. The issue of
enlargement is central here. In the context of modernist discourses,
enlargement assumes the appearance of a divisive project with those left
outside relegated to negative threatening positions in the discourses constructing European identity. Notably, the idea that the current enlargement
process is only pushing the border separating East and West further eastwards, rather than overcoming this divide, remains popular (Grabbe 2000;
Huisman 2002: 6). In contrast, by breaking the tight link between the con-

cepts of territory, sovereignty and identity in modernist discourse, neome-dieval frames offer the potential to circumvent these problems, with enlargement being a process that opens towards those not presently included, rather than discriminating against them. Notably, the EU's own Northern Dimension Initiative, which stemmed from a Finnish proposal in 1997, but which has generally been side-lined by the Union, is a prime example of the type of perceptual framework advocated here (for an overview, see Browning 2001). Of course, such a development entails a con-siderable re-envisaging of just what type of configuration, actor and subject the EU is, or professes to be. Instead of aspirations to be a sovereign territor-ial subject with hard divisive borders excluding those left on the outside from European space, this is rather a vision of a softer Europe of multiple networks, overlapping spaces, decentralised patterns of governance and with borders understood as inviting interaction, not discouraging it.

Notes

1 For example, between 2000–6 Poland will be eligible for up to 1.1 billion euro in EU assistance funds *per year*. For Lithuania the figure is about 180 million a year. In contrast, through the Tacis programme, Kaliningrad only receives around 4–5 million a year (Dewar 2001: 102). For a general overview of the problems facing Kaliningrad, see Baxendale *et al.* (2000).
2 In the case of Russia/Kaliningrad, the reluctance to let local actors in on the game and the desire to highlight unified approaches is probably also related to the historical (and continuing) negative positioning of Russia as a defining other of Europe. This may further explain why the EU appears to be less insis-tent on speaking with a single voice in its relations with other neighbours, such as Norway.

References

Aalto, Pami (2002) 'A European geopolitical subject in the making? EU, Russia and the Kaliningrad question', *Geopolitics* 7 (3): 143–74.
Acher, John and Marcin Grajewski (2002) 'Tension rises in EU–Russia dispute over Kaliningrad', *Reuters*, 27 September. Online, available at: http://virtual.finland.fi/reuters/00000002.bsk/_rl2002092701386.htm.
Agnew, John (1998) *Geopolitics: Re-Envisioning World Politics*, London: Routledge.
Baxendale, James, Stephen Dewar and David Gowan (eds) (2000) *The EU and Kaliningrad: Kaliningrad and the Impact of EU Enlargement*, London: Federal Trust.
Browning, Christopher S. (2001) 'The construction of Europe in the northern dimension', Copenhagen: COPRI Working Papers 39/2001.
Campbell, David (1992) *Writing Security: United States Foreign Policy and the Politics of Identity*, Manchester: Manchester University Press.
Chirac, Jacques (2001) 'The common foreign and security policy of the European Union', *Defence Europe* (Les Dossiers de L'Abécédaire parlementaire, No. 8, 2nd trimestre): 20–1.
Commission of the European Communities (2001a) *European Governance: A White Paper*, Brussels, 25 July 2001, COM (2001) 428 final.

——— (2001b) *The EU and Kaliningrad*, Brussels, 17 January 2001, COM (2001) 26 final.

——— (2002) *Kaliningrad: Transit*, Brussels, 19 September 2002, COM (2002) 510 final.

Dewar, Stephen (2001) 'Kaliningrad needs a special development fund', *Kaliningrad – Isolation or Co-operation?* Helsinki: The Finnish Committee for European Security, STETE: 99–107.

European Parliament (2000) *Report on Lithuania's Membership Application to the European Union and the State of Negotiations*, 15 September. FINAL A5 – 0240/2000.

Fairlie, Lyndelle D. (2001) 'Kaliningrad borders in regional context', in Lyndelle D. Fairlie and Alexander Sergounin (eds), *Are Borders Barriers? EU Enlargement and the Russian Region of Kaliningrad*, Kauhava: Ulkopoliittinen instituutti and Institut für Europäische Politik: 9–138.

Ginsberg, Ray H. (1999) 'Conceptualizing the European Union as an international actor: narrowing the theoretical capability–expectations gap', *Journal of Common Market Studies* 37 (3): 429–54.

Grabbe, Heather (2000) 'The sharp edges of Europe: extending Schengen eastwards', *International Affairs (London)* 76 (3): 519–36.

Hartnell, Helen E. (2000) 'European integration through the kaleidoscope: the view from the central and east European margins', in Noel Parker and Bill Armstrong (eds), *Margins in European Integration*, Houndmills: Macmillan: 28–52.

Huisman, Sander (2002) *A new European Union policy for Kaliningrad*, Paris: European Union Institute for Security Studies, Occasional Papers 33.

International Herald Tribune (2001) 'EU losing momentum, senior leaders warn', 16 October.

Joenniemi, Pertti (2001) 'Kaliningrad – a pioneer for the new global era', *Kaliningrad – Isolation or Co-operation?*, Helsinki: The Finnish Committee for European Security, STETE: 56–60.

———, Stephen Dewar and Lyndelle D. Fairlie (2000) *The Kaliningrad Puzzle – A Russian Region within the European Union*, Karlskrona: The Baltic Institute of Sweden and the Åland Islands Peace Institute.

Kelstrup, Morten and Michael C. Williams (2000) 'Introduction: integration and the politics of community in the New Europe', in Morten Kelstrup and Michael C. Williams (eds), *International Relations Theory and the Politics of European Integration: Power, Security and Community*, London: Routledge: 1–13.

Larsen, Henrik (2000) 'The discourse on the EU's role in the world', in Birthe Hansen and Bertel Heurlin (eds), *The New World Order: Contrasting Theories*, Houndmills: Palgrave Macmillan: 217–44.

Paasi, Anssi (2001) 'Europe as a social process and discourse: considerations of place, boundaries and identity', *European Urban and Regional Studies* 8 (1): 7–28.

——— (2003) 'Space, boundaries and the social construction of territorial identities', in Sanjay Chaturvedi and Madan Mohan Puri (eds), *Rethinking Boundaries: Geopolitics, Identities and Sustainability*, New Delhi: Manohar Publishers.

Parker, Noel (2000) 'Integrated Europe and its "margins": action and reaction', in Noel Parker and Bill Armstrong (eds), *Margins in European Integration*, Houndmills: Macmillan: 3–27.

Patten, Chris (2001) 'EU policy in the Balkans', speech to the International Crisis Group, 10 July. Online, available at: http://www.zeit.de/reden/Europapolitik/20132_patten.html.

Ruggie, John Gerard (1993) 'Territoriality and beyond: problematizing modernity in international relations', *International Organization* 47 (1): 139–74.

Smirnyagin, Leonid (2002) 'The Kaliningrad issue: the sensation that need not have been', Moscow: Carnegie Moscow Center, Briefings Papers Issue 5 May. Online, available at: http://pubs.carnegie.ru/english/briefings/2002/issue02–05.asp.

Tenth EU–Russia Summit (2002) *Conclusions, Joint Statement on Transit between the Kaliningrad Region and the Rest of the Russian Federation,* Brussels, 11 November. Online, available at: http://europa.eu.int/comm/external_relations/russia/summit_11_02/js_kalin.htm.

Trenin, Dmitri (2000) 'Security cooperation in north-eastern Europe: a Russian perspective', in Dmitri Trenin and Peter van Ham (eds), *Russia and the United States in Northern European Security,* Kauhava: Ulkopoliittinen instituutti and Institut für Europäische Politik: 15–54.

Valtasaari, Jukka (1999) Secretary of State, 'Finland and the EU Presidency: an agenda for the new millennium', remarks at the Nordic Policy Studies Centre, London School of Economics, 4 May. Online, available at: http://virtual.finland.fi/news.

Wæver, Ole (1996) 'European security identities', *Journal of Common Market Studies* 34 (1): 103–32.

Williams, Michael C. (2000) 'Modernity, postmodernity and the new world order', in Birthe Hansen and Bertel Heurlin (eds), *The New World Order: Contrasting Theories,* Houndmills: Palgrave Macmillan: 81–111.

15 Fears into fences

The isolationist pitfall of European federalism

Jaap H. de Wilde

On 28 February 2002, the former French president Valéry Giscard d'Estaing, at the age of eighty-one, opened the 'European Convention' in three out of eleven official EU languages. This one-year conference is to do what Heads of State and Government had failed to do during the Inter-Governmental Conferences (IGCs) of Amsterdam (1997), Nice (2000) and Laken (2001): prepare the EU for enlargement, enhance its democratic structure and create the basis for a coherent role in world politics. The initiative itself fits neatly into the long row of steps that have created an institutionalised waiting room, in which the countries of the former Warsaw Treaty Organisation, with the exception of the GDR, have patiently been sitting since 1989 – waiting for the West to open its side of the wall to the East. The purpose of the European Convention is institutional change.

The stakes are noble: more democracy, more transparency, an EU constitution, and procedures that allow for about twenty-five member states. As many as sixty issues have been put on the agenda. MEP Hanja Maij-Weggen, one of the fifteen representatives of the European Parliament in the Convention, cynically noted that even during adolescence her children didn't dare to raise that many questions at one time (*Staatscourant*, 1 March 2002: 5). Drowning in good intentions? The Convention presented a comprehensive 'Constitution for Europe' on 18 July 2003, to be debated at the next IGC, in 2004. The EU seems ready for the twenty-first century.

A successful Convention, however, may be worse than its failure. It may reinforce the ideal of federalism. Judging from a wide range of media reports, policy statements and academic EU studies, federalism is back on the agenda as a horizon of European integration.[1] This chapter will argue that this ideal is outdated and dangerous. The new horizon reflects a past political world.

The present arguments for federalising the EU further are twofold. First of all, the EU needs to enhance its executive powers. This argument has an external focus and two normative connotations: indecision creates serious damage (for example the unintended contribution of the EU and its member states to the civil wars in former Yugoslavia), and lack of power undermines diplomatic credibility (for example the marginal role

of the EU in the Middle East). The plea for increased EU power is concentrated on the making of a European Security and Defence Policy
(ESDP). At the Helsinki Summit it was decided that the EU should have
60,000 operational troops in 2003. Obviously, such a decision triggers a
functionalist logic: command and control require effective leadership,
i.e. centralisation of military decision-making power and political
responsibility, as well as the abolition of the veto power of member states,
presently implied by their sovereignty. Federalisation is the widely perceived answer. The EU needs to speak with one voice. The EU needs to
act upon its words.

Second, the EU needs to democratise. This argument has an internal
focus. The people need to get closer to Brussels. The European Parliament has insufficient supervising and corrective powers; national parlia-
ments still treat European politics as secondary; the media are still unable
to cover news from Brussels in an appealing way; and public commitment
is nil. Here too, federalisation is expected to show the way out.

This chapter focuses on the external aspects. Treatment of internal
democratisation requires a separate analysis. Here it suffices to say that the
problem of a democratic deficit is more complicated than the one that
confronts the EU. The crisis of Western nineteenth-century democracies is
of a general nature. Transparency, accountability and control in a world
economy characterised by fragmented national and transnational, ethnic,
ideological and religious polities cannot be achieved through administrative blueprints for governmental organisations. The main direct effect of
federalising the EU will probably be increased bureaucracy: more rules,
procedures and agents in the turbid policy process.

Worse than increased bureaucracy are the potential negative effects of
increasing the EU's power along federal lines. It may lead to a return of
traditional power politics, a return to an international structure dominated by great-power rivalry and endemic interstate warfare: Mearsheimer's
'back to the future' scenario, not as a result of European fragmentation,
but as a result of federalisation. In order to develop this argument, it is
necessary to understand the unique structure of contemporary Europe on
which its political stability and economic prosperity rests.

Three good old paradigms

The strength of Europe is its uniqueness. It can't be described correctly
within our existing academic vocabulary. Any analysis that relies on existing metaphors, ideas and theories misses the point. My way to circumvent
this problem is to combine three dominant views on Europe:

1   a story about the echo of the traditional power political structure:
    Europe's geopolitical relations or, in English-School vocabulary,
    Europe as an international subsystem;

2   a story about the power political structure of international organisations in Europe: Europe as a subset in international society; and
3   a story about the power-political consequences of globalisation: Europe as a subset in world society.

The three stories reflect three of the dominant paradigms in IR: Realism – shorthand for state-centric thinking that allows an important regulatory role for coercive power, the military and the police; Pluralism – shorthand for the intertwining of public and private structures that allows an important regulatory role for market forces and international organisations; and Radicalism – shorthand for centre–periphery models that highlight the reverse side of the world economy, dominated by the economic, political and military power elites.

It is fruitless to choose between these worldviews. In every corner, authors can be found who have made impressive analyses. But they cannot be simply fused together (though the English-School revival and some IPE variants come close). They appear to be complementary, yet they exclude one another. Their sum comes closest to the 'impossible triangle' (cf. Figure 15.1), used so often by M.C. Escher.

It is possible to merge the corners to some degree for three reasons. First, it is very hard to find literature that focuses on just one of the corners. Hence, the corners are exaggerations of normative characteristics in IR literature. It is possible, however, to operationalise the corners and trace their characteristics, lines of argumentation and so on in IR literature. A book like Morgenthau's *Politics Among Nations* (1948), for

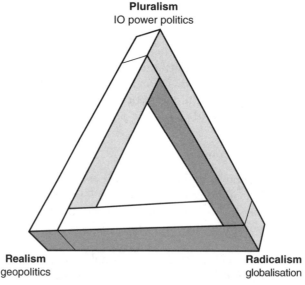

Figure 15.1 Three main perspectives on IR (the impossible triangle).

example, will not just score in the Realist's corner, but also in the Plural-ist's corner when it comes to his hopes for the UN system. Here the trian-gle helps to trace inconsistencies. Second, the three 'schools of thought' have entered many courses and textbooks on IR. They provide a helpful instrument to present a kaleidoscope of theories, ideologies and ideas floating around in the rich world of IR (see, for example, Baylis and Smith 2001). Third, thanks to social constructivism, IR may have found a way to make sense of paradigmatic differences. These differences occur within a single academic discourse, called IR, organised by academic journals and publishers, and domed by professional umbrella organisations. The impossible triangle exists as a social fact. It represents the core thinking that has constructed IR since the 1940s (Weber 2001).[2] Below, the current state of affairs in Europe is described from each of the three perspectives in order to highlight the normative policy choices they imply, and to make clear why federalism is the wrong choice.

The geopolitical echo: concentrations of power and conflict

Despite globalisation, it is still relevant to do an old-fashioned state-centric analysis of Europe in terms of traditional military–political power politics. The parameters of such an analysis are those of Waltzian and Buzanian Neorealism. Such an analysis begins by identifying the global superpowers and other great powers – states, of course. They set the boundary con-ditions for variations in regional subsystems like Europe. I accept Barry Buzan and Ole Wæver's analysis that we presently face a $1 + 4$ Structure (Buzan and Wæver, 2003). There is one superpower, the United States of America, and there are four great powers that play a global role: the Russian Federation, China, Japan and the France–Germany/EU-combina-tion. The *hit and run* hegemon, the USA, always plays a role in power-polit-ical considerations the world over, either as an active player or as a joker in the pack of cards. They can always show up. Moreover, the willingness to intervene, not only militarily, but also with diplomatic means, is suffi-ciently clear to uphold the image of a superpower. Its control in space goes unchallenged.

Within Europe, the traditional power-political structure is simple. Germany, France and Russia are dominant, followed by the United Kingdom, Italy and Turkey.[3] Obviously, the USA also plays a strong role. Crucial, however, for the dynamics in Europe is the Paris–Berlin axis. If it is stuck, there is a problem: European integration stagnates and the outside world does not know where 'Europe' stands. If it runs smoothly, there is also a problem: their consensus dictates the 'common' policies.

Additionally, a realist analysis of Europe's power political structure requires an inventory of latent and manifest armed conflicts in and close to the region: the civil wars in former Yugoslavia, Algeria and Chechnya; the instability of Turkey; and the world's powder keg, the Middle East.

'Europe' can choose its level of involvement, except for the spillover. Political extremism and terrorism in the Basque region, Corsica and Northern Ireland deserve a place on this agenda at times as well. As a result, there is a Realist call that 'we' have to put a halt to these threats; united we stand. It will be my claim that this Realist call, and not the attempt to overcome power politics, underlies much of the "strong voice" motive behind present-day pushes for federalisation.

IO power politics

The assessment of the concentrations of power and conflict is open to debate. However, it is striking that none of the conflicts are created by European states. There is no aggressor. Failed states, civil wars, domestic turmoil and the spillover from the Middle East – these are the problems. The powers of Europe do not pose any serious military threat towards each other. Even the Russian Federation has become a NATO partner in peace.

The role of international organisations (IOs) is crucial in explaining the essence of the dominance of peace in Europe. War and terrorism are not absent, but the structure of the subsystem is such that interstate rivalry has been demilitarised. There are still interstate military conflicts, most notably the recent short war of the NATO members against the Yugoslav Republic over Kosovo, and the latent risk of escalation between Greece and Turkey. There is terrorism in Spain and Turkey, and there are minor troubles throughout Europe, but their meaning is marginal to the dominant power-political discourse. That discourse is about integration. The Convention on the EU's institutional future is among the most recent steps. Historically this is unique. The change of discourse can be explained with a number of variables: the 'never again' reading of the thirty years war (1914–45); American benign hegemony, including the Marshall aid plan; the political receptiveness of David Mitrany's functionalist integration theory, leading to the Schuman Plan (1951); Western cohesion in the face of the Cold War; decolonisation, which brought Europe's global powers back to the continent; and last but not least, the gradual development of international administrative structures. The integration discourse they triggered has 'tamed' anarchy. IOs have been pivotal in this development.

Quantitatively and qualitatively, the meaning of international organisation has grown constantly since the late nineteenth century. They are unique works of diplomatic art. People who do not speak each other's language, who do not understand each other's customs and who contest each other's authority somehow manage to institutionalise a common approach of issues they cannot master unilaterally at the same level of quality. They are unique too, because of the paradox inherent to their existence: they help to improve the functioning of the system of sovereign states by undermining it. Governments accept international commitments that bind their successors. International secretariats, staffed by loyal bureaucrats, administer this inheritance. States bind themselves and give up specific sovereignty rights, but as a result they perform better.

Still, states keep their sovereign status; the anarchy continues. International organisations have not ended or replaced the sovereignty discourse, but have led it into a new round (Werner and de Wilde 2001). The self-imposed constraints fit the state's eternal struggle against its own image: how can the 'effective authority over the population on a given territory' ascribed to the state be achieved? Various scholars have argued that European integration should be interpreted as a new phase in an age-old process of state formation (Koch 2001; Moravcsik 1999). In spite of their administrative beauty, international organisations have not ended the struggle for power that characterises interstate politics; they have themselves become a bureaucratic and a diplomatic battleground. The three-piece suit as a uniform, legal rules as daggers and bureaucratic procedures as trenches.

The richness of this development is twofold. First of all, international organisations create a new theatre for traditional interstate competition. This is reflected by the position of intergovernmentalists within European Studies, like Alan Milward (1992) and Andrew Moravcsik (1999). Second, the institutionalised nature of IOs stimulates continuous consultation between the permanent representatives and other delegations of their member states and observer states. This reflects the position of those who point out the emergence of multilevel governance within the European Union, like Beate Kohler-Koch *et al.* (1998) and Liesbet Hooghe and Gary Marks (2001). Moreover, the administrative loyalty of a growing number of officials and bureaucrats shifts towards the interests of the international organisation. Even if they do not work directly for an IO, their agendas, and often their wallets too, are filled by them. The result is a kind of 'bureaucratic patriotism' (Delanty 1995: 141) on the national and European level, which probably contributes to the taming of the anarchy.

The Realism–Pluralism rib

If we combine the two stories told so far, we end up with a Europe of concentric circles based on the two most powerful international organisations, the EU and NATO (cf. Wæver 1995). Core Europe consists of a collection of EU institutions, NATO institutions, the bureaucracies of the member states' capitals and the Paris–Berlin axis. More passively, all of the Euro-countries belong to the core.

The first circle is populated with the more sceptical EU and/or NATO member states, in particular the United Kingdom and the Nordic countries. Strikingly, this ring consists of states that consciously keep a distance to the core. They fear a core-Europe as presented, for example, by Joschka

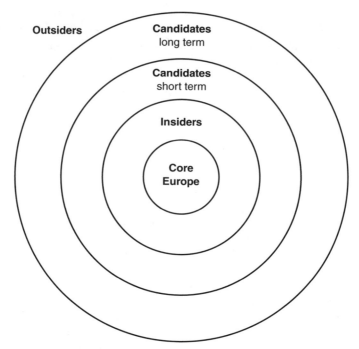

Figure 15.2 A Europe of concentric circles.

Fischer (2000): a kind of Carolingian empire under French–German reign. Switzerland, Liechtenstein, Monaco and other economic free-rider states in Europe also belong to this ring. Obviously, the Vatican too.

The second and third circles host the EU candidate states. Originally, the so-called Copenhagen criteria (membership requires democratisation, economic liberalisation and implementation of the *acquis communautaire*) helped to split this group into two: short-term and long-term candidates. But for political reasons the composition of these groups is variable. Meanwhile, the enthusiasm of the would-be insiders is declining, due to increasing Western demands over the past decade and decreasing expectations of EU subsidies. However, as long as politically feasible alternatives are absent, the candidates are kept under the EU's thumb. Moreover, NATO enlargement (not as costly) keeps the candle burning.

Finally, there is the fourth ring, with the outsiders: Ukraine, Belarus, Moldova, Turkey and the Balkan countries. The fear of 'Balkanisation' is often mentioned as a key motive for federalising the EU. The Balkans (from which Slovenia has escaped), however, are in a position of overlay. NATO and the UN Security Council rule; the EU tries hard to join them; the OSCE is present too. Overall, the West took over Tito's role. Belarus and, to a lesser extent, Moldova have given up any expectations of EU or NATO membership. They acquiesce in the geopolitical fate that ties them to Moscow. The Ukraine, however, offers resistance. Joining the West figures high on its security agenda (de Wilde 2001). Turkey finds itself in the most interesting position. The country can hardly be called democratic, but its societal pluralism is impressive. In that respect, it looks like Russia. Both countries struggle with democratisation of their administrative centres and with a civil war at their periphery. Both countries are member states of the Council of Europe and have signed the European Convention for the Protection of Human Rights and Fundamental Freedoms. Still Turkey is closer to Europe than Russia: it is, strategically speaking, Europe's most important NATO member, and many Turks live, often with dual nationality, in the countries of core Europe. Nevertheless it is an outsider: knocking at the door but repelled time and again.

The Russian Federation is in a different situation. It does not belong to any of the circles. Economically, Russia fits the outer ring, but politically and militarily its size it too big for the EU, and it is at best a partner for NATO. They choose the global option: the G–8, the UN Security Council and bilateral relations with the USA, Japan and China. As long as the Russian Federation is active on this global chessboard, Moscow is the core of an independent sphere of influence. Russia's agenda in many respects stands apart from EU/NATO's European agenda, and vice versa.

The beauty of concentric circles is that 'Europe' has no sharp eastern border. Brussels' Europe fades away towards the Urals and Asia Minor, while Moscow's Europe fades away in the opposite direction. The Council of Europe, the OSCE, the NATO's Partnership for Peace programmes and the Russian–NATO Council encompass both, thereby providing useful fender functions.

Towards the south, the situation is much more worrisome. North Africa (the Maghreb countries) hardly participates in the power-political arenas of the European IOs. There are no concentric circles, but a hard borderline. Its hardness showed in 1992, when the EU and its member states closed their eyes after the military coup that ended democratisation in Algeria. Apparently, this is not Europe's backyard. Although a Common Strategy for the Mediterranean has been developed, Europe towards the south lacks a second and third circle. Malta and Cyprus are candidates, but too small to form a ring. Despite Association Treaties, none of the Maghreb countries are candidates for EU or NATO membership. Worse: the OSCE and the Council of Europe do not play a role either. Insiders and outsiders stand in direct confrontation on both sides of the Strait of Gibraltar – a cemetery for illegal migrants. Here, the victims of globalisation drown. Federalism will create a similar border in the east.

Securitisation of the global village

This leads us to the third story: the power-political consequences of globalisation, highlighted in terms of Radicalism. Since 11 September 2001, it is hardly necessary to explain the essence and importance of this dimension. The attacks on New York and Washington have overshadowed other recent manifestations of the dark side of globalisation.

In July 2001, the first antiglobalist was killed during demonstrations and riots in Genua. It is telling that the meetings of international organisations, the WTO, the G–8 and the EU are the butt of their protest. Apparently, the value of these organisations has grown. The G–8 hardly possesses power, but as a club of the richest states it symbolises the asymmetries of the world. The World Bank (IBRD 2001) has calculated that two billion people – a third of the world population – do not profit from globalisation. Way back in the 1960s, Johan Galtung (1969) emphasised these problems of structural violence. A new generation of mainly Western activists demanded that transnational corporations and capitalist governments release their suffocating grip on much of the Third World. Another concerned part of Western societies expresses its discontent with globalisation in the opposite direction: in xenophobia. Globalisation threatens their petit bourgeois way of life. Debates about multicultural societies, in particular its edges, reinforce step-by-step a discourse in which it becomes self-evident that ethnic groups constitute the basic variables in analyses of societal stability.

Antiglobalism and xenophobia are but two of the side-effects of globalisation that confront Europe. Europe's security agenda shows other issues, varying in salience and scale: old and new dimensions of terrorism (often linked to ethnic, ideological and religious social conflict); old and new proliferation risks of nuclear, biological and chemical weapons; the new dangers of cyberspace (including its vulnerability); old and new dimensions of organised crime (trade in human beings, trade in illicit goods, illegal arms trade, corruption and fraud of officials and companies); the increased proliferation of small arms; the continued risks of environmental crises; the spread of new and old diseases.

For two reasons global issues are crucial for understanding political developments in Europe. First, they colour the daily news. Suddenly there is a wave of migrants, an environmental disaster, a computer virus or a terrorist attack, and politics has to respond instantly. Second, they alter societal structures. The speculators on the local stock markets in Copenhagen, Frankfurt, Tokyo and New York have more in common with each other than with the homeless person who tries to sell them the *Street News* on the doorstep of their design-styled offices. State borders may have disappeared; the walls inside of society are on the rise again. Globalisation reintroduces Dickensian conditions to some parts of the world. Domestic estrangement and alienation create new barriers between insiders and outsiders.

Moreover, from a power-political perspective it is important to notice that the present phase of globalisation creates a new balance between the private and the public sectors of life. Europe's security issues are caused by the behaviour of private actors: the environmental polluters are companies and individual households, organised crime rests on private groups, just like terrorism (even when state-sponsored), corruption means the incorporation of private interests in public life, migrants are seldom sent by their governments. This part of Europe's security agenda follows the logic of domestic security policies rather than the logic of interstate rivalry.

In the 1970s, scholars were already pointing at a *Weltinnenpolitik* (Czempiel and Rosenau 1992). Europe's security concerns have more to do with combating crime and arresting offenders than with arms races and deterrence policies. Traditional aggressors nowadays are called 'rogue states', and their number can be counted on the fingers of one hand. Failed states pose a much larger threat: the domestic public orders have failed; the globalised world fears spillover effects. Military deterrence does not work in these circumstances. In most cases restoration of a legitimate sovereign authority is paramount.

The *World Conflict and Human Rights Map, 2001/2002* shows 277 armed conflicts (Jongman 2002). Only 21 cases are directly between sovereign states. These are not among the bloodiest ones. In all other cases the conflicts involve weak states: dictatorships, kleptocracies, quasi-states or failed states. Europe's security agenda derives from the mismanagement and misbehaviour of governments and armed private groups, both in the direct vicinity and in all corners of the world. This is the agenda that needs to be answered. Can federalism show the way?

Europe's uneasiness

There is a threat that the responses to the problems caused by globalisation may have reverse effects. Integrationists favoured federalisation in times when this was a remote and utopian horizon. Before, during and after the Thirty Years World War (1914–45) federalism was a progressive ideal meant to overcome the dominant threats to political stability at that time: interstate warfare within a weak and unreliable alliance structure. European integration, however, took a different track. It developed a structure of overlapping authorities and competing competences, i.e. a new realm for power politics, without closing the traditional realm. In the original ideal, a European federation was a means of overcoming traditional power politics. The goal has been achieved without the means.

Confronted with the new (and often old) threats of globalisation, European federalism is again offered as a way out. At face value this seems a logical continuation of the old discourse. But this time, federalisation is strengthening traditional geopolitics rather than IO politics. Hence, federalisation moves Europe towards the power-political dynamics that belong to the Realist corner. A European Federation is weakening international society. It destroys the richness of concentric circles and erects border controls: it turns the EU into a state.

IO politics emphasises the importance of the overall complexity of international organisation. Integration politics, first of all, needs to be linked to those of NATO, OSCE, Council of Europe and the European Court for Human Rights and, second, to those of the UN Security Council, the OECD, the WTO, the World Bank, UNDP and the other UN specialised agencies. Third, integration politics needs to focus on the main organisational effects of globalisation: the new balance between transnationalised public and private sectors. In the face of flaming headlines about globalisation's flipside, subtle power politics does not score well in public. Immediate and decisive action is asked for, and promised by popular politicians. This is not new.

Historically, the confrontation with the growing complexity of policy-making contexts has produced stereotypical reactions. First of all, it has produced isolationism, an attempt to withdraw from the complexity of the changed political environment. Next, when this strategy fails, imperialism emerges: an attempt to reduce complexity by creating superior power. Finally, when this strategy has also shown its flaws, interdependence is accepted: a willingness to structural negotiation and a willingness to accept mutually binding international agreements emerges (de Wilde 1991). Apparently, the new generation of political leaders has to go through these phases. EU Europe is in the first phase, the USA is in the second. There is a tendency to restrict European politics, and Western politics at large, to its geopolitical dimension and its traditional power political reasoning.

America's isolationism is well known: North America has to become an invulnerable aircraft carrier, superior in military technology, dominating the world economy by military means. This impracticable isolationist policy was painfully illustrated by the attacks on the Twin Towers, the Pentagon and the White House (the latter failed) with civilian airplanes from domestic territory on '9/11'. The USA immediately shifted to the second, imperialist mode. In foreign policy, the terrorist problem is simplified to interstate proportions: attack Afghanistan and, if necessary, the entire 'Axis of Evil'. Given the Egyptian and Saudi Arabian background of the terrorists, it may be hoped the impracticability of the second response is understood in time.

The isolationist course of European politicians is less evident, because the integration discourse breathes an atmosphere of international brotherhood. But EU adherents behave imperialistically towards the other European organisations: in spite of the Council of Europe, they want their own catalogue of fundamental rights; in spite of NATO they want their own army; in spite of the OSCE they want their own conflict prevention mechanism; and they are courting the idea of a directly elected president. In short, they want to put an end to the unique complexity of Europe's multilevel structure of national and international interlocking institutions. Moreover, there is a tendency to solidify the EU's common borders.

Poland's border with the Ukraine and Belarus is a major concern in the membership negotiations. Brussels aims to harden them. Hence, they will come to look like Europe's borders in the Mediterranean. This will not only be ineffective (compare the US–Mexican border), but it will also make politics more xenophobic (Andreas and Snyder 2000).

EU Europe is translating fear into fences. There is fear of further Balkanisation of the outer ring, fear of growing organised crime and fear of uncontrolled waves of migrants. Despite the association treaties with Tunisia, Morocco, Israel and the Palestine Authorities, the EU member states are barricading their doors by raising the criteria for asylum-seekers and regular migrants, while installing infrared cameras to prevent illegals from crossing the border. Traditional threats have disappeared; traditional answers have not. The Realist analysis of European power politics still makes sense. This makes it tempting to say the same about its inherent policy advice. The effects of globalisation, however, cannot be controlled territorially. Instead of hardening the borders, it seems more reasonable to cultivate Europe's current practice of its gradually fading influence towards the east and south-east. This implies investments in cooperation with states and societies in North Africa. It also implies investments in cooperation across the new eastern borders as soon as the Central European and Baltic states have entered the EU and/or NATO. An ever-closer union with Romania, Bulgaria, Belarus, Moldova, Ukraine, Kaliningrad, St Petersburg and Turkey is needed. Borderlines do not work; border regions stand a better chance.

The European Convention is symptomatic for the equivocal nature of European integration: in the interest of Europe, the Convention should fail to build a federation, but it should be successful enough to keep the integration discourse alive, and to open up less isolationist ways to answer the perceived perils of globalisation.

Notes

1 For various political views on 'Europe', see http://europ.eu.int/futurum. See also Guttman (2001, especially Chapters 17 and 18); and Farrel et al. (2002).

2 It is beyond the scope of this chapter, but it is easy to relate other schools of thought in IR to the triangle. IPE, for example, combines elements of all three corners in an uneasy balance. Neoliberal institutionalism lies on the rib between Realism–Pluralism. The English School mainly operates on the same rib, but also tries to make sense of the third corner by developing the notion of a world society. Radicalism and Realism share the centrality of power relations in their analyses. On the rib between Radicalism and Pluralism, issue-specific approaches can be located, like gender studies, development studies, environmental studies, etc.

3 The criteria are those developed by Hans J. Morgenthau (1948) and other classical Realists, most recently John J. Mearsheimer (2001). They form a mixture of demographical, economic, military and political factors.

References

Andreas, Peter and Timothy Snyder (eds) (2000) *The Wall Around the West: State Borders and Immigration Controls in North America and Europe*, London: Rowman & Littlefield.

Baylis, John and Steve Smith (eds) (2001) *The Globalization of World Politics: An Introduction to International Relations*, Oxford: Oxford University Press.

Buzan, Barry and Ole Wæver (2003) *Regions and Powers: The Structure of International Security*, Cambridge: Cambridge University Press.

Czempiel, E. Otto and James N. Rosenau (eds) (1992) *Governance Without Government: Order and Change in World Politics*, Cambridge: Cambridge University Press.

Delanty, Gerard (1995) *Inventing Europe: Idea, Identity, Reality*, New York, NY: St. Martin's Press.

Farrell, Mary, Stefano Fella and Michael Newman (eds) (2002) *European Integration in the 21st Century: Unity in Diversity?* London: Sage.

Fischer, Joschka (2000) 'From confederacy to federation: thoughts on the finality of European integration', Humboldt Universität, Berlin. Online, available at: www.auswaertiges-amt.de.

Galtung, Johan (1975) *Peace: Research – Education – Action. Essays in Peace Research. Volume One*, Copenhagen: Christian Ejlers.

Guttman, Robert J. (ed.) (2001) *Europe in the New Century: Visions of an Emerging Superpower*, Boulder, CO: Lynne Rienner.

Hooghe, Liesbet and Gary Marks (2001) *Multi-Level Governance and European Integration*, Lanham, MD: Rowman & Littlefield.

IBRD (2001) *Globalisation: Growth and Poverty*, New York, NY: World Bank.

Jongman, Berto (2002) *World Conflict & Human Rights Map 2001/2002*, Leiden: PIOOM.

Koch, Koen (2001) 'Het alledaagse wonder van Europa, of Europese integratie als voortzetting van Europese statenconcurrentie', *Vrede en Veiligheid*, 30 (2): 209–20.

Kohler-Koch, Beate *et al.* (1998) *Interaktive Politik in Europa: Regionen im Netzwerk der Integration*, Opladen: Leske und Budrich.

Mearsheimer, John J. (2001) *The Tragedy of Great Power Politics*, New York, NY: W.W. Norton.

Milward, Alan S. (1992) *The European Rescue of the Nation State*, Berkeley, CA: University of California Press.

Moravcsik, Andrew (1999) *The Choice for Europe: Social Purpose and State Power From Rome to Maastricht*, Ithaca, NY: Cornell University Press.

Morgenthau, Hans J. (1948) *Politics Among Nations: The Struggle for Power and Peace*, New York, NY: Alfred Knopf.

Wæver, Ole (1995) 'Identity, integration and security: solving the sovereignty puzzle in EU studies', *Journal of International Affairs* 48 (2): 389–431.

Weber, Cynthia (2001) *International Relations Theory: A Critical Introduction*, London, New York, NY: Routledge.

Werner, Wouter G. and Jaap H. de Wilde (2001) 'The endurance of sovereignty', *European Journal of International Relations* 7 (3): 283–313.

Wilde, Jaap H. de (1991) *Saved from Oblivion: Interdependence Theory in the First Half of the 20th Century*, Aldershot: Dartmouth.

—— (2001) 'New threats on the security agenda', in Margriet Drent, David Greenwood and Peter Volten (eds), *Towards Shared Security: 7–Nation Perspectives*, Groningen: CESS Harmonie Papers: 91–116.

16 The new NATO

Europe's continued security crisis

Sten Rynning

Western Europe – in the shape of the EU and the WEU – has, through the 1990s, developed the ambition to manage crises on the peripheries of Europe. The ambition is not new. Discomfort with an excessive reliance on nuclear deterrence during the Cold War inspired ideas of détente, mediation and conflict resolution throughout Europe. The prospect that the ambition may be realised, however, is new. The end of the Cold War led the WEU to adopt its crisis management 'Petersberg' declaration in June 1992, which has since been taken over by the EU within the framework of its European Security and Defence Policy (ESDP). This chapter assesses the likelihood of Western Europe becoming a crisis manager.

The analysis focuses on NATO because this security organisation must change – or even wither – for a new European 'pillar' to emerge. I conclude that, in spite of ESDP advances, the European ambition is in crisis. Western Europe may build on ideas that are distinct from American and Russian ideas, but Western Europe is not well enough organised to make its voice heard.[1]

The Kosovo intervention of 1999, as well as the 2001–2 war in Afghanistan, demonstrated that the European countries are far from capable of operating militarily with American forces, much less provide military power on the same scale, whether for purposes of active intervention or diplomatic deterrence. The European allies may have invoked NATO's Article 5 for the first time in the history of the Alliance – declaring the terrorist attack of 11 September 2001 to be an attack on all allies – but all military operations have been run almost exclusively by the USA. In fact, of all the allies contributing to the American effort, only Great Britain has been allowed physical access to the American military headquarters in Tampa, Florida.

Europe is becoming a regional appendix in the global American security design, its main task being the maintenance of regional stability and the provision of diplomatic support for US-led operations. This trend will be enhanced as Russia establishes a closer relationship with the USA, which will also result in a renewed partnership with NATO. NATO will become a 'soft' organisation whose security guarantees, once vital, are now fading in importance, and the European vision of crisis management will be hard pressed to gain influence.

This chapter reaches these conclusions in four steps. The following section examines the strategic and political evolution of NATO as it adapted to new threats through the 1990s. Distinct US, Western European and Russian perspectives are emphasised. The second section analyses the apparent success of the ESDP, developed from 1999, and argues that the terrorist attack of 11 September undermined much of its inner dynamism. The third section investigates NATO's relationship with Russia and argues that a new deal, although in many ways fragile, is being made due to converging American and Russian interests. The final section turns then to Western Europe to assess the way in which cohesion and unity are challenged.

NATO's grand bargain

The end of the Cold War and the critical question of redefining its purpose naturally challenged NATO. A grand bargain of 1997–9 testifies to the fact that NATO embraced several distinct purposes, and that all parties involved, including the advocates of greater European crisis management, could find grounds for optimism.

I distinguish between American, European and Russian positions and begin by examining the first two. Transatlantic allies have since 1990–1 debated the way in which NATO could be decentralised in order to let 'Europe' – in one shape or another – assume greater security responsibilities. Pushed and shoved by warfare in the former Yugoslavia and the parallel evolution of the European Union (EU), NATO allies grappled with a burden-sharing debate that in many ways reflected old positions. Europeans argued that they could pick up new challenges only if the USA actually devolved responsibility. The USA responded that responsibility had to follow capability.

European disorganisation frustrated both Europeans, who were particularly unhappy with the aloofness of American policy in Bosnia, and Americans, who realised that European weakness would end up forcing the USA to become involved. President Clinton thus engaged the USA behind the Dayton peace process in 1995 only after his advisers, notably Richard Holbrooke, made clear that the USA would have to move in on the ground, if nothing else in order to get the Europeans out. Stronger support for NATO's European Security and Defence Identity (ESDI) was henceforth forthcoming, and NATO accelerated its effort to make its integrated command structure slimmer and more flexible.[2] The prospect of greater Europeanisation was notably articulated in Berlin in June 1996, just seven months subsequent to the Dayton agreement (NATO 1996).

Europeanisation entailed a reconsideration of the strategic concept NATO had defined in November 1991 in light of the break-up of the

Warsaw Pact. NATO had articulated four 'fundamental tasks' (NATO 1991, paragraph 20):

- to provide an indispensable foundation for stability in Europe,
- to serve as a transatlantic forum for consultation on security issues,
- to deter and defend against threats to members' territories,
- to preserve the strategic balance within Europe.

Tasks number two and three were simply rewrites of Articles 4 and 5 of the NATO treaty. Task number four was aimed at the Soviet Union, which, however, disappeared just one month after the NATO summit. Task one was therefore the crucial new task, namely to make NATO a cornerstone of any new European security architecture. Europeanisation in the mid-1990s invited further reflection on this architecture, and NATO announced in 1997 that the strategic concept would be rewritten at the fiftieth anniversary summit in Washington in April 1999.

The European agenda at this stage was to use NATO as an instrument of external crisis management. To do so, NATO would need to operate 'out-of-area', which is to say outside the area covered by Article 6 of the Treaty (the national territories north of the Tropic of Cancer). NATO had declared itself willing to operate 'out-of-area' in 1992, on behalf of UN mandates, but now the Europeans wanted this decision written into the strategic concept.

The traditional lack of European unity was belied by the French–British rapprochement born in the former Yugoslavia. Britain found France to be a closer ally than the USA. France found that it needed to embrace NATO, always a British priority, and therefore sought to return fully to the integrated command in 1995–7. In the end, France did not return fully, but it is now fully part of all NATO non-Article 5 (out-of-area) work.

The ambitious US agenda for a broader and globalised NATO also made a contribution to European unity in 1997–8. US policy-makers effectively argued in this period that the price for US engagement in Europe was European support in the battle against global terrorism, weapons' proliferation, and rogue regimes and politics. In February 1998, Senator John Warner directly linked US support for NATO to European support for the war on Iraq (*Washington Post*, 22 February 1998). Stimulated by subsequent terrorist bombings of American embassies in Kenya and Tanzania, as well as North Korean missile tests in August 1998, and a renewed air war over Iraq in October 1998, the allied debate heated towards the end of the year. In December 1998, Secretary of State Albright demanded that NATO should respond to any global threat that affects member states' vital interests. European allies – France, Great Britain and Germany notable among them – responded that NATO was primarily North Atlantic, as opposed to global, and designed primarily for military rather than all threats (*Daily Telegraph* and *New York Times*, 9 December 1998).

A compromise was hammered out for the Washington summit, April 1999. NATO deleted the fourth 'fundamental task' of 1991 – maintaining the strategic balance – but kept the first three. NATO then added two new fundamental tasks intended to 'enhance the security and stability of the Euro-Atlantic area' (NATO 1999b, paragraph 10):

- to stand ready, case-by-case and by consensus, in conformity with Article 7 of the Washington Treaty, to contribute to effective conflict prevention and to engage actively in crisis management.
- to promote wide-ranging partnership, cooperation and dialogue with other countries in the Euro-Atlantic area, with the aim of increasing transparency, mutual confidence and the capacity for joint action with the Alliance.

Although some Europeans worried that crisis management in time would overshadow Article 5 operations, all Europeans could be satisfied that with this strategic concept NATO remained focused on their 'Euro-Atlantic area'.

The American agenda is found in that part of the Strategic Concept that deals with 'perspectives' (paragraphs 20–4) – as opposed to the 'fundamental tasks' (paragraph 10). As a perspective, NATO declares that 'Any armed attack on the territory of the Allies, from whatever direction, would be covered by Articles 5 and 6 of the Washington Treaty.' Moreover, threats include 'acts of terrorism, sabotage and organised crime'.

The events of 11 September effectively turned the Strategic Concept on its head. The prospect of global terrorism revealed itself to be a very real threat, and the Europeans accepted this with their Article 5 declaration of 12 September. Terrorism had thus been explicitly recognised as an Article 5 situation, a status to which crisis management in the Euro-Atlantic area cannot aspire, since it does not concern threats to territories.

We should not forget that a third perspective was making its presence felt through these negotiations, namely the Russian one. Russia was formally in a weak position, considering its political and economic turbulence, but NATO had a natural interest in ensuring Russia's (partial) satisfaction with the new security order, especially in light of NATO's eastward expansion.

Russia's new relationship with NATO began in 1993–4, when Russia became one of NATO's Partners for Peace (PfP).[3] The agreement was signed in June 1994. Russia had insisted on obtaining a special status vis-à-vis NATO, but NATO agreed only to attach a one-page, unsigned declaration of intent to the general PfP agreement. Russia's obtaining a special status in the May 1994 'contact group' of great powers, which emerged to handle the Yugoslav situation, quite possibly facilitated its acceptance of NATO's meagre PfP offer in June.

The ensuing optimistic vision of a new security order reaching from

'Vancouver to Vladivostok' was put under pressure by subsequent events. In 1994–5, NATO decided to move ahead with the process of eastward enlargement at a time when Russia felt increasingly marginalised in the Dayton peace settlement. Naturally, Russia could not prevent NATO's enlargement (announced in the summer of 1997 and completed in April 1999). As compensation, it once again obtained a kind of special status, in 1997, in the shape of a NATO–Russia 'Founding Act', which was intended to invoke the image of great-power collusion. For this purpose a 'Joint Partnership Council' (JPC) was established, also in 1997.

Russia maintained a critical attitude, however, because the JPC represented much less than the 'truly pan-European security system' that Russian leaders had called for ever since Gorbachev outlined his vision of a fully integrated 'European house'. In the spring of 1997, Russian President Yeltsin thus reacted to the incipient NATO enlargement decision with a series of menacing statements.

The grand bargain of 1997–9 is therefore best interpreted as 'an uneasy compromise among a variety of competing objectives' (Carpenter 2000: 7). Inevitably, NATO's Strategic Concept was host to contradictions and tensions. Enlarging its reach towards Russia's near abroad, NATO wanted to be Russia's partner. Focusing on the Euro-Atlantic area, NATO entertained global perspectives. Promoting a stronger European pillar, NATO sought to preserve American leadership.

From Kosovo to the World Trade Center

The Kosovo intervention of 1999 appeared momentarily to act as a catalyst for strengthening NATO's crisis management policy, not least because this European focus was underscored by the conflict itself and the fact that the allies adopted NATO's new Strategic Concept in the midst of the intervention.

European momentum can be said to have picked up in mid-1998, when the situation in Kosovo worsened. NATO went so far as adopting an executive order of action (ACTORD) in October 1998, which authorises military authorities to use force within 96 hours unless the situation improves – a unique step in the history of the Alliance (Clark 2001: 144–5). Kosovo problems nourished the reform agenda of Tony Blair that led to the ESDP initiatives of late 1998 and 1999. Blair had already signed off on a national Strategic Defence Review in the summer of 1998, which emphasised force projection and expeditionary warfare. In the following months he cast a more critical eye on the political context and endorsed the view that the EU should be able to act 'autonomously' – of the USA and NATO. Once Britain and France reached a preliminary political agreement in St Malo in December 1998, the process continued. The EU decided in mid-1999 to absorb most of the WEU and thus became the only 'European pillar' in defence affairs. In December 1999 in Helsinki, the EU countries then defined the Headline Goal of becoming able to deploy up to 60,000 soldiers in a hostile area and maintain them in operation for up to one year.[4]

The Helsinki Headline Goal has become a primary and tangible target for subsequent European defence efforts. Inspired by another British proposal of mid-1999, now launched with Italy, the EU countries decided to initiate a 'convergence criteria' process in the defence area akin to the process that led to the common currency, the euro. Thus, the EU now has a force catalogue comprising some 100,000 soldiers, 100 ships and 400 planes for their emerging 'reaction force', and, moreover, they have identified a range of necessary investments. While new investments are made on a wholly voluntary basis (like in NATO), the result is that the EU now has a force planning mechanism.

The apparent vigour of the ESDP soon became a cause of American concern. The USA had supported European defence cooperation with NATO's 'Berlin Plus' agreement of April 1999, but only because it was linked to NATO. Secretary of State Albright underscored that the USA would not accept 'de-coupling, discrimination, or duplication'. Strobe Talbott, Deputy Secretary of State, warned in October 1999 against the perspective that the European defence capability 'comes into being first *within* NATO but then grows *out of* NATO and finally grows *away from* NATO' (Talbott 1999). And Senator McCain declared in February 2001 that the Europeans, with the Helsinki process, were causing 'unnecessary discord' within NATO (*International Herald Tribune*, 8 February 2001).

McCain voiced his concerns at a moment in time when a compromise was emerging. The preceding period had clarified that the Europeans did not want to exclude NATO from crisis management and, in fact, only sought autonomy in the case that 'NATO as a whole' would not be engaged. US President George W. Bush (sworn in on 20 January 2001) appeared to sympathise with this European effort as a quid pro quo for the American policy of building a missile defence. This bargain captured the headlines of Tony Blair's February 2001 visit to Washington, and in many ways the bargain was reasonable. The USA would focus on the global picture, the Europeans on the regional one, and the new bargain would ensure that cooperation prevailed over discord.

However, the energy behind the ESDP is fading. Part of the reason is found in Europe itself, where governments have moved from fairly painless political decisions and institutional adaptation to the difficult questions of budgetary prioritisation and rationalisation. Part of the reason is found in the events of 11 September and the way in which they added credibility to the previous American security agenda.

The events of 11 September changed the European perception of the American concern with terrorism and its manifestations in the World Trade Center in 1993 and later in Yemen, Saudi Arabia and Kenya. The immediate European decision to declare the 11 September attack an 'attack on all allies' was decisive (NATO 2001a). Not only did NATO for the first time invoke its Article 5, but it had accepted that the 'Perspectives' of its Strategic Concept were more real than one of its 'Fundamental Tasks' – crisis management – which is not covered by Article 5. The fight against global terrorism has become a new, fundamental task for NATO, while the previous fundamental task of crisis management declines in priority.

The American security agenda within NATO is thus gaining in weight, and the grand compromise of 1997–9 has consequently altered. Two developments accelerate the process: Russian policy towards the USA, and European weakness.

Russia and the USA

Elected Russian president in January 2000, Vladimir Putin has sought to rebuild relations with the West in order to strengthen the Russian state and its ability to act as a vehicle of modernisation within Russian society. The USA naturally figures prominently in Russian security policy, and Russia has repeatedly objected to what it perceived as bullying behaviour. Russia was against the 1999 Kosovo intervention, not least because it occurred in spite of Russia's permanent seat on the UN Security Council.[5] Russia also repeatedly criticised the American plans for building a missile defence that erodes the established policy of mutual deterrence.

However, the relationship has changed in the wake of 11 September. President Putin was the first foreign leader to get in touch with President Bush in the wake of the terrorist attack – using their 'hot line' – and Russia has agreed to a very strong American military presence in Central Asia in connection with the war in Afghanistan. Russia also reacted with remarkable pragmatism to the American December 2001 announcement that it will draw from the Anti-Ballistic Missile Treaty in June 2002. Moreover, in May 2002 Russia agreed to a nuclear arms reduction agreement with the USA that for all intents and purposes was suited to reinforce the new American nuclear posture.

These are significant changes: the USA is questioning the political foundation of Russia's nuclear role and is physically establishing itself on former Soviet territory. Putin and a number of his advisers – the role of the military forces per se remains less clear – have thus clearly decided to bet on a tighter partnership with the USA.

The gains for Russia are quite tangible in the short run: a more stable Afghanistan and thus a decreased threat from fundamentalism against Russia's southern border; and a greater Western understanding of Russia's own war in Chechnya. The gains become bigger, but also more potential, in the long run: to become a fully accepted security actor in the European architecture. Russia will again emphasise its vision of one pan-European security system and plead for its full, rather than partial, association with NATO.

NATO took a first step in this latter direction in December 2001 when the allies declared that they would reform the PJC.

> We have decided to give new impetus and substance to our partnership, with the goal of creating a new council bringing together NATO member states and Russia to identify and pursue opportunities for joint action at 20.
>
> (NATO 2001b)

This new NATO–Russia Council was finally agreed on 28 May 2002 in Rome. It involves 'joint action at 20' in a limited number of areas in which Russia will be accepted as an equal in deliberations and no longer face one position already agreed to by the full NATO members.

One should caution against excessive optimism in the 'new' US–Russia relationship. Russia may be betting on a new partnership and its rewards, but it may not be satisfied with its outcomes. Russia's entry into the NAC, even though it is a limited entry, is truly unprecedented. However, NATO preserves the right to pull issues out of the new Council and thus take charge of policy, just like it has excluded issues such as territorial defence from the new Council. NATO thus remains able to maintain full control of all issue areas, although cooperation with Russia naturally is the goal. This formula may satisfy the Russian government and its expectation of a deal different from the damage-limitation that lay behind the JPC in 1997,[6] but the Council is an empty vessel that has yet to be filled.

Still, US policy-makers seem to have moved far beyond the perception of Russia as a threat, and they will probably be increasingly willing to let Russia 'associate' with NATO, which, as an alliance, is becoming less militarily relevant to the USA. The USA itself will need to continue to cultivate Russian relations in order to achieve its goals of non-proliferation of weapons of mass destruction, fighting international terrorism and gaining international support for a limited US missile defence.

European centre or periphery?

NATO will continue to be politically important to the USA. A strong NATO will ensure a US voice in European affairs and incite NATO allies to support US diplomacy outside of Europe. But driven by European military weakness and the American necessity of garnishing Russian support, NATO is becoming a regional stabiliser, a forum for political–military cooperation and peacekeeping, that is removed from US military strategy.[7]

The Western European pillar in the European security architecture is so weak, or rather poorly organised, that it may be marginalised. Pressure on this pillar emerges not only from the new US–Russian relationship in the context of NATO, but also from the fact that the organisational infrastructure – both the EU and NATO – is about to be enlarged. With enlargement into Central and Eastern Europe, the institutional home for *Western* European cooperation will disappear. In spite of measures to 'deepen' cooperation before 'widening' it, security cooperation will be case-by-case and erratic unless the USA is called on to act as a leader. Most actors in most cases may desire US leadership, but the point worth emphasising is that Western Europe will not harbour a cohesive political vision that enable European policy-makers to enter into a meaningful dialogue with US policy-makers.

The enlargement of both the EU and NATO is proceeding. The EU appears set to invite up to ten countries to join it by 2004, or at least soon thereafter. NATO promised in April 1999 that enlargement was a continuing process, and in Prague in November 2002 NATO will make a decision on a second round, which is likely to be of a significant size.[8]

The current Western European pillar is, in addition, under great pressure to deliver new capabilities. The ESDP of the EU has gone through its first 'easy' stages of declaratory policy and institutional engineering, and now challenges of policy implementation and resource allocation emerge. The EU countries have gathered their existing forces in ESDP catalogues, they have identified investment priorities, but so far they have not produced any new capability (Centre for Defence Studies 2001). To do so, the countries must allocate more defence money and rationalise their defence infrastructures. The fewer the defence resources, the greater the need for rationalisation.

Rationalisation across political borders raises questions that are very difficult to solve to everyone's satisfaction. For instance, it may be rational for Western Europe to maintain just three training facilities for fighter pilots, but in what countries should they be located? Should future fighter pilots fly the British–German–Italian–Spanish Eurofighter, the French Rafale or the American Joint Strike Fighter? Moreover, once the model is (or several models are) chosen, how does one prevent countries from making individual adaptations to the fighter crafts that create diverse training needs and thus undermine the joint training facilities? The list of difficult questions continues, not least because industrial and strategic interests tend to get confused. Why should Western European countries build their own airlift craft (the Airbus A400M) when it is cheaper to buy American crafts that can be owned and operated by Europeans?

The Western European pillar is therefore under pressure not only from Russian and American security perspectives but also its own inability to move ahead with force planning and thus the basis of security and defence policy. Some observers may at this stage object that the new security threat – terrorism – is best fought with political and economic means, while military forces are becoming less and less relevant. Moreover, the EU has a great range of such political and economic instruments that could sustain a stronger policy.

However, the argument tends to overlook the role military force has indeed played in the current fight against terrorism in Afghanistan and also the fact that European forces participate both in combat and peace-keeping operations. Moreover, terrorism may not be the only security challenge. Crisis management may be necessary in, for example, Macedonia or Montenegro, and it may be that the USA will not be happy to take the military lead. In that case, it is up to the Europeans to demonstrate better organisation, including a deterring military muscle, than during Bosnia and Kosovo.

A new initiative is needed in order to arrive at the architecture of 'tripo-larity' that David Calleo has outlined (2001). This new initiative would respond to EU and NATO enlargement by re-constructing a forum for Western European cooperation. This is likely to happen only in the long run. Europe is currently engulfed in a constitutional debate, intimately linked to the EU's enlargement, that will result in a 'founding treaty' or 'constitution' in 2004, which must then be debated and submitted to ref-erenda and ratified. This constitutional process is not only complex, but also inflames the political differences that arguably exist between the three major countries of the Western European core: Germany, France and Britain.

Germany is more federalist than the others, and France and Britain dis-agree on the future ties across the Atlantic. Germany has no recent mili-tary tradition to build on and seems engulfed in the articulation of a political design that can take into account its central role between Western and Eastern Europe. Britain continues to emphasise the ESDP as a means to enhance transatlantic cooperation and has yet to articulate a coherent European vision that might flow from its embrace of European defence cooperation. France seeks to reconcile the ideas of federalism and nation-states and quite clearly lacks a vision for its new role in a new Europe and for how the Franco-German link can be renewed.

Conclusion

NATO is changing and is in crisis. The USA and Russia drive change; the crisis is predominantly Western European. This is a new challenge for Western Europe, which appeared to be making strong progress in the imme-diate wake of the Kosovo intervention with the elaboration of the ESDP.

This apparent European dynamism emerged against the background of a NATO compromise that reflected the interests and visions of the three security pillars – Western Europe, Russia and the USA. Western Europe sought to turn NATO into an instrument of regional crisis management, while upholding the Article 5 commitment; the USA promoted a global agenda focused on terrorism, rogue regimes and weapons of mass destruc-tion; and Russia urged the creation of a pan-European order. The com-promise, reflected in NATO's Strategic Concept of 1999 and the JPC, proved inadequate in Kosovo, however, and for a while it seemed that Western Europe with the ESDP and its Helsinki force planning process had taken the political lead in a further process of change.

The core of Western Europe may not be able to continue this drive, however. The core is under external pressure and lacks the inner coherence to push force planning and policy through its most difficult phases. It is likely that NATO will become a forum for peacekeeping planning and operations, as well as a forum for pan-European security dialogue. The USA will dominate this new NATO, just as they did previously, but they will strive to keep Russia satisfied. NATO will not be a vehicle for American military operations, and European countries will likely be incited to graft onto American operations bilaterally – depending on their areas of specialisation. Multilateral cooperation through NATO may become relevant once crisis management moves into its peacekeeping phase. This, then, appears to be the future political and organisational context for the European ambition to promote political mediation and crisis management policies.

Notes

1 For the argument that the European security architecture builds on three distinct 'pillars' (Western Europe, the USA and Russia), see Calleo (2001). As an extension of his argument, Calleo finds that a 'tripolar' architecture will be the most durable.

2 For this NATO will use a Combined Joint Task Force (CJTF), which is 'a multinational, multi-service deployable task force generated and tailored primarily, but not exclusively, for military operations not involving the defence of Alliance territory, such as humanitarian relief and peacekeeping' (NATO 1999a). To create CJTFs, individual allies must train and equip their troops for flexible engagements. Moreover, and at a collective level, the allies must create a more flexible command structure, which is to say headquarters that are mobile (during the Cold War they were stationary) and multinational.

3 The PfP consists of a series of bilateral agreements between NATO and former Warsaw Pact countries. NATO had previously, in 1991, constructed a grand forum, the North Atlantic Cooperation Council (NACC), for multilateral discussions.

4 The St Malo declaration and the Helsinki conclusions are available along with other key documents in a publication of the EU Institute for Security Studies (2001).

5 In the aftermath of the war, Russian forces from Bosnia moved ahead of NATO forces to capture the strategically important airport of Pristina. Russia then sought to reinforce its armed presence by air, but NATO was able to prevent this by having the air routes closed off.

6 The PJC did not live up to Russian expectations for a pan-European architecture. In June 2000, not least in light of the Kosovo intervention, Russia issued a Foreign Policy Concept that argued that 'The current political and military postures of NATO do not coincide with the security interests of the Russian Federation, and sometimes even run contrary to them' (Zagorski 2001: 26). However, as emphasised in the discussion, events in 2001–2 have led to a renewed, cooperative Russia–US relationship.

7 *The Economist* noted (6 April 2002) that NATO enlargement was predominantly about 'civic value' and not 'military readiness' because 'a functioning democracy and market economy, an absence of disputes with neighbours and respect for minorities now seem to be becoming just as important, maybe more so.' Likewise (9 April 2002) the *Washington Post* wrote in its editorial that 'The real benefit of NATO growing ... lies in the leverage it offers to shape the political and economic development of European countries where democracy and free markets are not yet taken for granted.'
8 The candidates are essentially all members of NATO's Membership Action Plan (MAP), of which there are ten. Only NATO partners (PfP) can become part of the MAP, which provides a framework for preparing countries to become full NATO members, although membership is not guaranteed.

References

Calleo, David P. (2001) *Rethinking Europe's Future*, Princeton, NJ: Princeton University Press.

Carpenter, Ted Galen (2000) 'NATO's new strategic concept: coherent blueprint or conceptual muddle?', *Journal of Strategic Studies* 23 (3): 7–28.

Clark, Wesley K. (2001) *Waging Modern War*, New York, NY: PublicAffairs.

Centre for Defence Studies (2001) 'Achieving the Helsinki headline goals', Discussion Paper, November.

EU Institute for Security Studies (2001) 'From St. Malo to Nice: European defense, core documents', Chaillot Paper 47, May. Online, available at: http://www.iss-eu.org.

NATO (1991) *The Alliance's Strategic Concept Agreed by the Heads of State and Government participating in the Meeting of the North Atlantic Council*, 7–8 November. Online, available at: http://www.nato.int/docu/basictxt/b911108a.htm.

—— (1996) *Final Communiqué of the Ministerial Meeting of the North Atlantic Council*, 3 June. Online, available at: http://www.nato.int/docu/pr/1996/p96–063e.htm.

—— (1999a) *Fact Sheet: The Combined Joint Forces Concept*. Online, available at: http://www.nato.int/docu/facts/2000/cjtf-con.htm.

—— (1999b) *The Alliance's Strategic Concept Approved by the Heads of State and Government Participating in the Meeting of the North Atlantic Council*, 23–4 April. Online, available at: http://www.nato.int/docu/pr/1999/p99–065e.htm.

—— (2001a) *NATO Press Release 2001–124*, 12 September. Online, available at: http://www.nato.int/docu/pr/2001/p01–124e.htm.

—— (2001b) *NATO–Russia Joint Statement issued on the Occasion of the Meeting of the Permanent Joint Council at the Level of Foreign Ministers in Brussels*, 7 December. Online, available at: http://www.nato.int/docu/pr/2001/p011207e.htm.

Talbott, Strobe (1999) 'America's stake in a strong Europe', remarks at a conference on the future of NATO, The Royal Institute of International Affairs, London, 7 October.

Zagorski, Andrei (2001), 'Great expectations', *NATO Review* 49 (1): 24–7.

17 Securitising European integration

Turkey and the EU[1]

Dietrich Jung

Turkey's national security syndrome

In August 2001, the leader of the Motherland Party (ANAP) and then Deputy Prime Minister, Mezut Yilmaz, stated that Turkey was suffering from a 'national security syndrome' and that national security issues were used to block democratic reforms that are necessary for Turkey's desire to become a full member of the European Union (EU). The harsh response to Yilmaz from both the military leadership and veteran politicians such as Prime Minister Ecevit and former President Süleyman Demirel indicated that the ANAP leader had indeed hit a sore point (*Turkish Daily News*, 9, 17 and 23 August 2001). In Turkey, the concept of national security is, at the same time, both narrow and wide. It is narrow in its strict military notion, having the integrity of the nation-state and its ruling elite as almost exclusive referents; and it is wide in the sense that it does not distinguish between external and internal threats, having the tendency to securitise any aspect of political, economic, cultural and social life. It is partly for this reason that the Turkish military acquired the power to draw the limits to politics in a much more general way (Candar 1999: 131).

Looked at from a historical perspective, this Turkish national security syndrome and its impact on Turkish–EU relations comes as no surprise. For centuries Turkey's relationship with Europe has been preoccupied with matters of military security, and Turkish nationalists have inherited the threat perception which the ruling elite of the Ottoman Empire built up during its destructive entanglement in the European power struggle. Ottoman–European relations were almost exclusively viewed in terms of military competition, and the so-called 'Eastern Question' of the nineteenth century, i.e. the dismantling of the Ottoman Empire, left the new republican elite a political atmosphere of outside conspiracy and inside betrayal. This historical legacy is still noticeable in some strains of the current relationship between Turkey and the EU. This is illustrated by the reportedly wide-spread suspicion among some Turks that the 'EU is not so much an ally closely identified with, but a hostile foe that has to be vanquished' (Gorvett 2001: 39).

Against this general background, this chapter will argue that the stalemate in Turkish politics is due to a paradoxical situation in which the country's Westernising elite itself represents a major obstacle to further Westernisation. In order to marshall evidence for this argument, I look at a particular aspect of the Turkish (national) security debate, more precisely, at the strategy of some circles that try to facilitate Turkey's EU accession by exploiting the country's geostrategic assets. Since the Helsinki decision (1999) to grant Turkey candidacy status, the attitude of 'EU-membership yes, but to our conditions' has become popular among some Turkish generals, politicians and academics – a strategy that seems to have gained further ground after the terror attacks of September 11, 2001. This strategy aims at a trade-off between the political standards of the Copenhagen Criteria[2] and the potential military benefits of Turkey's inclusion into the EU's Common European Security and Defence Policy (CESDP). Meltem Müftüler-Bac, for instance, explained the Helsinki decision in this sense and in relation to three Turkish assets for the EU's CESDP: Turkey's 'membership in NATO, its military capabilities, and its geostrategic position' (Müftüler-Bac 2000: 490). In the light of these military assets she comes to the conclusion that 'Turkey's incorporation into the EU becomes essential' and that this 'inclusion would enhance European military capabilities and allow the EU to exploit Turkey's geopolitical value' (Müftüler-Bac 2000: 492–3).

Taking this argument as its starting point, the following pages will examine the likelihood of such a security bargain between Turkey and the EU. More precisely, the chapter poses the question of whether it seems indeed possible to negotiate the non-negotiable: could Turkey become a full-member of the EU without living up to the standards demanded by the Copenhagen Criteria? The first section puts the alleged security bargain between Turkey and the EU into a critical, historical perspective, pointing at both the legacy and the continuity of viewing Turkish–European relations in geostrategic terms and terms of military security. The second step will briefly analyse the EU as a security community. This sketch claims that Müftüler-Bac's conclusion misses the essential transformation that the mere concept of security has undergone in the course of European integration. In looking more closely at Turkey's role in Europe's south-eastern periphery, the third section proposes that the country in its present condition could rather become an *in*security provider than a security partner from the perspective of EU policies. The chapter then concludes that the securitisation of European integration seems to be a blind alley. Instead of facilitating Turkey's EU accession, this attempted security bargain is, rather, another example of the paradoxical path that Turkey's Westernisation has taken.

Turkey and European security: a historical sketch

The strategy of selling Turkey's EU membership by stressing the country's role as a security provider is neither new nor very original. On the contrary, this strategy reflects the historical environment in which Turkish–Western relations have unfolded. After a short period of neutrality between the two World Wars, the emerging Cold War pushed the Turkish Republic back into a role comparable to that which the Ottoman Empire had played in the nineteenth century. Turkey inherited the Ottoman task of counterbalancing Russia's power in the eastern Mediterranean, and under Prime Minister Adnan Menderes (1950–60), the Turkish Republic assumed a key role in the US-containment policy against the USSR. For this reason, the country became an important regional player in promoting rather ill-fated British and American Middle Eastern defence schemes, such as the Baghdad Pact (1955), that had been designed according to Western security interests. Displaying the profile of a dedicated 'Cold War warrior' (Gözen 1995: 74), Menderes was able to acquire substantial Western aid and to establish a system of political patronage in order to strengthen domestically the position of his ruling Democratic Party.[3] In this way, Turkey's integration in NATO and other Western institutions was essentially based on the geostrategic assets that the country could offer in the light of Western security concerns. Under the impact of the Cold War, Turkey's foreign policy reflected the strategy of a political rent seeker whose bargaining chip was Western military security interests.

While Turkey's geostrategic position substantially changed with the end of the Cold War, its political elite has partly continued to follow this mode of interaction with the West. A case in point was President Turgut Özal's single-handed decision to join the anti-Iraq coalition in 1990. Coinciding with the end of the Cold War, the Iraqi occupation of Kuwait gave Özal a chance to show that Turkey could still play the role of a geostrategic heavyweight in US foreign policy. Demonstrating Turkey's continuing importance for Western interests in the region, Özal re-directed Turkish foreign policy and 'simply brushed aside Ankara's longstanding policy of non-interference in Middle East disputes' (Makovsky 1999: 92). At first critical of Özal's decisions, the Turkish armed forces and large parts of the Kemalist establishment soon adapted to this course. In shifting the threat perception of the Turkish security discourse from Communism to the perils of Turkey's regional environment, they are today themselves proponents of this new pattern of activism in Turkish foreign policy.

In addressing the National Defence University in 1997, the then Deputy Chief of Turkey's General Staff, General Cevik Bir, gave a fine example of this new security discourse. In accusing European politicians of having a 'fairly narrow-minded strategic concept' and a rather 'short-sighted approach when determining the new security borders of Europe', Bir pointed at the significant role that Turkey plays in the maintenance of peace and stability for Europe. In particular, the Turkish general stressed Turkey's geostrategic location at 'the epicenter of tension, unresolved conflicts and wars' of an area comprising the Balkans, the Caucasus and the Middle East (Bir 1998). In line with this view, Hikmet Cetin, a former foreign minister and speaker of Parliament, stated that 'Turkey is in the neighbourhood of the most unstable, uncertain and unpredictable region of the world' and that since the end of the Cold War the country 'has turned into a frontline state faced with multiple fronts' (Mufti 1998: 33). Even more drastic was the picture painted by Turkey's former Minister of Defence, Hikmet Sami Turk:

> In the midst of destruction and reconstruction, Turkey stood and continues to stand as an anchor of stability in its region. Geographic destiny placed Turkey in the virtual epicenter of a 'Bermuda Triangle' of post-Cold War volatility and uncertainty, with the Balkans, the Caucasus, and the Middle East encircling us.[4]

With its emphasis on military security, the previously mentioned analysis by Meltem Müftüler-Bac merely follows this trajectory. Like the Turkish generals and politicians, she presents Turkey as an indispensable security partner for the EU with a major role in Europe's south-eastern periphery. Yet the idea of exploiting the military capabilities and the geopolitical assets of a country in exchange for EU membership seems to miss the core rationale behind the process of European integration. Apparently, the proponents of this idea have not yet noticed that the mechanisms for establishing peace and security in Europe have drastically changed. They still view the EU through the classical lenses of an alliance of states, thereby echoing the military-focused security discourse that has characterised Turkish–European relations for so long. Moreover, the argument of a security bargain in the light of external threats simply reproduces the rent-seeking strategies that Turkish politics has pursued vis-à-vis the West since the end of the Second World War.

The EU as a security community

In order to discuss Turkey's role in EU security policies, it is first of all necessary to understand how the EU functions as a security community. There is a lively debate about the causal determinants behind the process of European integration. Realists, functionalists and constructivists disagree on the dominant motivations and structural determinants that provide a plausible explanation for the emergence of the EU. According to their respective readings, the dynamics driving European integration can either be found in '*realpolitik*' (Pedersen 1998: 2), in 'commercial motivations' (Moravcsik 1999: 373), or in the 'crucial variables of ideas and institutions' (Diez 1999: 359). However, although divided in their theoretical approaches, the overwhelming majority of them agree on the fact that, as a supranational phenomenon, the EU challenges classical reasoning about the formation of alliances and international organisations. Moreover, although the EU's most ambitious projects, the single market and the monetary union, are in the economic field, political and normative questions were visibly brought back onto the agenda by the Treaty of Amsterdam in October 1997. It is against this background that the general discussion about the Common Foreign and Security Policy (CFSP), so far the weakest pillar of EU policies, has gained a momentum that may enable the Union to develop a more effective CFSP (Cameron 1999: 110).

The notion of the relative weaknesses of European security and foreign policies is partly a result of the fact that, so far, CFSP has concerned only non-military aspects of security. As an international actor, the EU has provided a kind of 'soft security', 'but has not developed a credible military capability to support its diplomacy' (Cameron 1999: 13). The creation of a CESDP is a direct consequence of this fact, and right at this point the Turkish security bargain comes in. On the one hand, the Turkish establishment offers the country's strong military capabilities in exchange for its participation in the CESDP. Turkish politicians are at pains to emphasise the beneficial role that Turkey could play as an EU member because of its military power. On the other hand, some Turkish officials threaten to obstruct the CESDP, in particular the building-up of the so-called rapid action force, through the NATO Council in the case of Turkey's exclusion from the EU. Regarding the implementation of the EU's coming rapid action force, the Turkish Chief of General Staff, General Huseyin Kivrikoglu, reiterated that Turkey demands to 'take a place in the decision-making mechanism' (*Milliyet*, 13 September 2001).

Yet the indubitable difficulties of the EU to act as a military force on the international stage are not only a result of lacking capabilities and diverging interests among its member states. On the contrary, they are strongly bound to the collective identity of the Union as a security community whose internal security discourse largely builds on matters of non-military security and in which most 'security concerns were in post-sovereign patterns pushed towards referents other than state-to-state relations' (Wæver 1998a: 104). In this respect, European security has moved away from the classical meaning of security, i.e. 'the field where states threaten each other, challenge each other's sovereignty, try to impose their will on each other, defend their independence, and so on' (Wæver 1995: 50). In underrating this specific feature of the EU as a security community, any Turkish strategy to offer military security in exchange for full-membership is doomed to fail.

The historical logic of the emergence of the EU as a security community makes the incompatibility of this strategy with EU realities particularly apparent. In coining the term 'integration as security', Ole Wæver has convincingly argued that peace and stability in Europe is not the outcome, but the very process of European integration in itself (Wæver 1998b). In discursive terms, an effective process of desecuritisation among its members has accompanied the evolution of European institutions. Theoretically, securitisation is an extreme version of politicisation and it presents a discursive process through which an issue is transformed into an existential threat. To securitise an issue represents a move to require emergency measures and the application of extraordinary means. In contrast to this elevation of an issue to an existential threat, desecuritisation means 'to move issues out from the threat–defense discourse into the ordinary public sphere' (Buzan *et al.* 1998: 23–9).

Essential for this chapter's argument is the specific mechanism through which the EU not only produces security, but also transforms its very conceptual sense. In replacing a Europe of many centres with a Europe of a single centre, the EU not only acts 'as a magnet, pulling Europe's periphery toward its center, but it also induces the periphery to resolve preemptively issues that would otherwise be likely to produce security competition'. Consequently, the EU exercises a disciplining function in its periphery, 'without resort to the traditional instrument of security policy – the use (or threat of use) of military force' (Wæver 1998b: 55–6). In the EU context, security is built on internal affinities, as well as on shared norms and values, rather than on external threats, and it is this conceptual transformation of security that is reflected in the political demands of the Copenhagen Criteria. Contrary to the often-lamented weaknesses of military capacity and strategy in CFSP, the impact of this internal security logic of the EU on its periphery should actually be perceived as an asset. The disciplining function without military force is one of the features that make the EU particularly attractive as a cooperative partner. This not only applies to the candidates for full-membership, but also to Europe's southern and south-eastern periphery.

Turkey as an (in)security provider

The Barcelona Declaration of November 1995 provides a good example of the non-military disciplining function that the EU exerts on neighbouring regions.[5] In establishing a Euro-Mediterranean partnership with the EU, utterly authoritarian Arab states such as Algeria, Egypt, Morocco, Syria or Tunisia at least agreed in principle on the rule of law, human rights, freedom of thought, respect for diversity and pluralism, protection of minority rights, equality, self-determination and territorial integrity. In the Barcelona Process, the EU conducts foreign and security policies with a combination of economic incentives and the normative power of its own democratic principles. This promotion of 'soft security' reflects the EU's particular security concerns in its immediate periphery. In stark contrast to US Middle East policies, oriented towards military security and revolving around the two often contradictory key issues of energy supply and Israel, the EU is more concerned about migration, environmental issues and the spill-over of regional conflicts, such as those surrounding the Kurdish question. In the light of this divide of both Western interests and Western threat perceptions, Turkey's military stance is certainly able to support US strategies, but it could increasingly clash with European foreign policies.

In particular, Turkey's more assertive foreign policy towards the Middle East has a potential to contradict the Barcelona Process. Turkey's frequent military incursions in northern Iraq, its political tension with Armenia and Iran, as well as the Turkish–Syrian crisis of October 1998, are just some cases in point.[6] As a matter of fact, the demise of the Ottoman Empire left a legacy of territorial grievances, historic resentments, political tensions and mutual suspicions that neither Turkey nor its neighbours have so far overcome. Although the historical accuracy of Turkish and Arab narratives of mutual conspiracy and betrayal seems highly questionable (cf. Kayali 1997), they have been reinforced by the political experiences of the post-Second World War period. Therefore the negative Arab response to Turkish military support during the Second Gulf War was no surprise. While accepting the military assistance of countries such as the United States, Britain, France, Pakistan, Egypt and Syria, Saudi Arabia gave a cool reception to a similar offer from Turkey (Birand 1996: 172). Given the prevalent atmosphere of mutual suspicions between Arabs and Turks, the idea that Turkey can play the role of a peace promoter between Israel and the Arab world because of its military cooperation with Israel sounds almost grotesque (Müftüler-Bac 2000: 496–7). Since the collapse of the Oslo Process, the precarious character of the Turkish–Israeli alignment has become self-evident – even its Turkish architects have now realised that they subordinated Turkey's regional politics to the imponderabilities of the volatile Arab–Israeli relationship (Jung and Piccoli 2000).

A brief glance at Turkey's domestic problems and how they have become intertwined with regional inter-state disputes underlines that, in the 1990s, Turkey was more often a problem for, rather than an answer to, European security concerns. In particular the Kurdish issue renders as nonsensical the idea that Turkey in its current condition would be an ideal partner to 'help the EU to deal with such security challenges as ethnic conflict, the rise of political Islam, immigration, and instability in the Middle East' (Müftüler-Bac 2000: 497). Viewing the Kurdish reality almost exclusively as a problem of terrorism, Ankara's military solution created a major predicament for Turkey's society. According to US statistics, between 1984 and 1998 more than 34,000 people were killed, an estimated 3,000 villages depopulated, and between 350,000 and two million people forcibly evacuated from the war zone (US State Department 1999: 13). Fifteen years of war destroyed vast parts of south-eastern Anatolia, spurred waves of migration, shattered popular confidence in the

Turkish state, and aggravated religious and ethnic cleavages within the populace. The strategy of securing the integrity and sovereignty of the Turkish state by military means swung to the other extreme. In distributing arms among an estimated number of 70,000 village guards (Kilic 1998: 102), Kurdish loyalist vigilantes enrolled by Turkish authorities, the state partly passed on its monopoly of physical force to tribal leaders and kinship groups. These irregular forces, the PKK, and special security units (*özel tim*) – which had been raised to fight Kurdish separatism and fell under the control of Turkey's extreme right – entered into fierce competition about drug profits (Seufert 1998: 390).

In the aftermath of the 1980 military coup, a complex scenario of authoritarian rule, economic liberalism, guerrilla war, counter-insurgency, corruption and organised crime developed in Turkey. In this political climate, popular dissatisfaction with state institutions, as well as economic and political grievances, were increasingly articulated in Islamist and Kurdish nationalist terms. In sharp contrast to these findings, however, the Kemalist state elite has persistently denounced political Islam and Kurdish nationalism as being spurred by external forces. Attributing the Kurdish insurgency and the rise of religious parties to conspiracies from outside, it confuses domestic conflicts caused by social change with alleged attempts of foreign political interference. This has inevitably provoked stresses between Turkey and its immediate neighbours (for a more elaborate argumentation on this issue, see Jung with Piccoli 2001). During the 1990s, the Turkish sense of encirclement almost turned into a self-fulfilling prophecy. Kemalist policies of securitisation explain how perceived threats develop into real ones and even fields of possible cooperation turn into areas of conflict.

To be sure, Turkey is located in a volatile regional environment where military security cannot be disregarded. While EU security policies might increasingly rely on credible military deterrence, NATO will certainly also in future represent the major instrument of Western military security, in which Turkey continues to play an important role. From an EU perspective, there is then no necessity for Turkey to perform this military role from within the EU. On the contrary, it has been argued that Turkey as a 'security insulator' between the EU and the Middle East can perform this role best as a non-member state (Buzan and Diez 1999: 52). In stark contrast to Müftüler-Bac's arguments, the particular strategic interest that the EU has vis-à-vis Turkey could rather speak against Turkey's full-membership in the EU. In military terms, a classical alliance with the Turkish state, as already established in NATO, would perfectly serve European needs. Even more important, neither the narrow and nationalist notion in which Ankara conceives security nor its tendency to confuse internal and external conflicts suit the political realities of the Union. The Turkish discourse of securitisation essentially contradicts the internal logic and the cohesion of the EU as a 'postmodern' security community. Instead of being an 'anchor of stability', Turkey as an EU member-state in its present condition could rather turn into a pronounced *in*security provider.

Securitisation and Westernisation as a paradox

In the line of the arguments presented so far, the strategy to achieve the desired EU membership via a security bargain with Brussels contradicts the internal logic of European integration. If it is right that the dynamics of European integration were built largely on a process of gradual desecuritisation, attempts to securitise the membership aspirations of a particular candidate seem to be detrimental to the whole project. Indeed, to fully integrate a state whose political institutions are deeply moulded by authoritarianism and whose civil–military relations do not even live up to the principles of NATO enlargement would not only create a negative precedence, but a major predicament for the future of the EU.[7] Becoming a full member of the Union is essentially bound to the implementation of the Copenhagen Criteria in law and practice. In this regard, the constitutional amendments in the fields of human rights, judiciary, democratic institutions and fundamental freedoms that the Turkish Parliament passed in October 2001 and the three subsequent reform packages in February, March and August 2002 were necessary steps towards the corpus of shared norms and values that became the internal building blocks of European security. Nevertheless, in its general evaluation, the EU commission came to the conclusion that despite these 'significant steps', Turkey 'does not yet fully meet the Copenhagen Criteria'. In particular the issues of 'real enjoyment of cultural rights', the 'independence of the judiciary', corruption and Turkey's civil–military relationship remain matters of concern. Moreover, the EU will now turn its attention from formal changes to the effective implementation of the new legislation (EU Report 2002: 46–7).

In conclusion, the strategy to substitute democratic reform by providing military capabilities is doomed to fail. In the first place, this strategy is a legacy of the geostrategic emphasis that characterised Turkish–European relations until the end of the Cold War. Since then, however, not only has Turkey's geostrategic position changed, but also the security concerns of the EU and USA have been gradually drifting apart. In this environment of more fragmented Western security policies, the Turkish strategy is pleasing US interests rather than those of the EU. This applies in particular to the idea that Turkey could serve as a security provider in the Middle East. From an Arab point of view, Turkey's alignment with Israel has the quality of a strategic alliance. Seen from Cairo, Amman, Beirut or Damascus, Turkey does not play the role of a mediator between Arab states and the West, it is rather perceived as an instrument of US policies in the region. Revoking the historical experience of both late Ottoman policies of suppression and Turkey's role in the Baghdad Pact, the Turkish–Israeli alignment is clearly interpreted as directed against the Arab world.[8]

Yet it would be a mistake to analyse this strategy only through the historical and geostrategic lenses of international politics. The attempt to trade military security against democratic reform is not only a legacy of Turkey's International Relations, but also an expression of a state elite under siege which harbours 'a deep mistrust of the people' (Kinzer 2001: 16). In living up to the Copenhagen Criteria, the ruling elite would lose its instruments of societal control. In the light of Turkey's national security syndrome, both Turkish–European relations and Turkish state–society relations have been securitised in order to prevent major changes in the political power structure of the country. Turkey's Kemalist state elite have become hostage of its own politics of top-down Westernisation. In promoting European integration without wholeheartedly sharing the basic democratic and pluralistic values of European democracies, Turkey's ruling elite has turned into the enemy of those ideals that it gave life to (Kinzer 2001: 13). In this regard, the affair around Mezud Yilmaz' remarks highlighted the central paradox of Turkish politics that meanwhile the country's self-appointed Westernising elite represents one of the major obstacles to Turkey's Westernisation. The flawed strategy to achieve full EU membership via a security bargain is just another expression of this paradox.

Notes

1 This chapter is related to a larger research project that the author has conducted under the working title *The Future of Middle Eastern Security: Arab and Iranian Views on the New Turkish-Israeli Axis*. The author is grateful to a travel grant provided by the Carlsberg Foundation and the valuable comments of Ümit Cizre and Stefano Guzzini to a previous draft.

2 According to the decision of the Copenhagen European Council in June 1993, membership requires that candidates have achieved 'stability of institutions guaranteeing democracy, the rule of law, human rights and respect for and protection of minorities', see http//:www.europtr.org.tr.

3 According to Hale (2000: 152), Western economic assistance to Turkey in the 1960s was 'equivalent to over half of Turkey's foreign exchange earnings from trade and other sources'. The policies of US assistance to Turkey during the Menderes period are covered by Harris (1972).

4 Hikmet Sami Turk, in a speech given at the Washington Institute in March 1999, see http://www.washingtoninstitute.org/media/samiturk.htm.

5 I refer to the Final Version 2 Rev. 1 of the Barcelona Declaration from 27 and 28 November 1995 that can be found at: http://europa.eu.int/en/comm/dg1b/en/den-barc.htm.

6 According to official Turkish accounts, the Turkish army intervened during its war with the Kurdistan Workers Party (PKK) no less than 57 times in northern Iraq, see Gunter (1998: 40).

7 According to Chapter One (A.3) of the Study on NATO Enlargement, one of the purposes of enlargement is to enhance civilian and democratic control over the military in Europe. Furthermore, Chapter One (B.6) demands that member

states with ethnic conflicts have to settle them by peaceful means (http://www.nato.int/docu/basictxt/enl-9502.htm).
8 In the Arab press, the Turkish–Israeli agreements were named as *hilf istratiji, itifaq istratiji* or *ta' awun 'askeri* (cf. *al-Hayat*, 7 April 1996; *al-Arabi*, 28 May 1996; *al-Ahram*, 6 June 1996, *an-Nahar*, 10 September 1998 or *Anba' al-Kuwaitiyye*, June 1996). For a scholarly discussion see also Ma'ud (1998), Na'ama (1997), Tiyyar (1999).

References

Bir Cevik (1998) 'Turkey's role in the new world order', *Strategic Forum*, 135, February. Online, available at: http://www.ndu.edu./inss/strforum/disclaim/html.

Birand, Mehmet Ali (1996) 'Is there a new role for Turkey in the Middle East?' in Henry J. Barkey (ed.), *Reluctant Neighbor: Turkey's Role in the Middle East*, Washington, DC: United States Institute of Peace Press: 171–8.

Buzan, Barry and Thomas Diez (1999) 'The European Union and Turkey', *Survival* 41 (1): 41–57.

——, Ole Wæver and Jaap de Wilde (1998) *Security: A New Framework for Analysis*, Boulder, CO, London: Lynne Rienner.

Cameron, Fraser (1999) *The Foreign and Security Policy of the European Union: Past, Present and Future*, Sheffield: Sheffield Academic Press.

Candar, Cengiz (1999) 'Redefining Turkey's Political Center', *Journal of Democracy* 10 (4): 129–41.

Diez, Thomas (1999) 'Riding the AM-track through Europe; or, the pitfalls of a rationalist journey through European integration', *Millennium* 28 (2): 355–69.

EU Report (2002) *2002 Regular Report on Turkey's Progress Towards Accession*, Brussels. Online, available at: http://europa.eu.int/comm/enlargement/report2002/tu_en.pdf.

Gorvett, John (2001) A Berlin Wall at the Bosphorus', *The Middle East*, January: 38–9.

Gözen, Ramazan (1995) 'The Turkish–Iraqi relations: from cooperation to uncertainty', *Foreign Policy* (Ankara) 19 (3–4): 49–98.

Gunter, Michael (1998) 'Turkey and Iran face off in Kurdistan', *Middle East Quarterly* 5 (1): 33–40.

Hale, William (2000) *Turkish Foreign Policy, 1774–2000*, London: Frank Cass.

Harris, G.S. (1972), *Troubled Alliance: Turkish–American Problems in Historical Perspectives, 1945–1971*, Stanford, CT: Hoover Institutions Studies 33.

Jung, Dietrich and Wolfango Piccoli (2000) 'The Turkish–Israeli alignment: paranoia or pragmatism?', *Security Dialogue* 31 (1): 91–104.

Jung, Dietrich with Wolfango Piccoli (2001) *Turkey at the Crossroads: Ottoman Legacies and a Greater Middle East*, London: ZED Books.

Kayali, Hasan (1997) *Arabs and Young Turks: Ottomanism, Arabism and Islamism in the Ottoman Empire, 1908–1918*, Berkeley, CA, Los Angeles, CA: University of California Press.

Kilic, Ayse (1998) 'Democratization, human rights and ethnic policies in Turkey', *Journal of Muslim Minority Affairs* 18 (1): 91–110.

Kinzer, Stephen (2001) *Crescent and Star: Turkey Between Two Worlds*, New York, NY: Farrar, Straus and Giroux.

Makovsky, Alan (1999) 'The new activism in Turkish foreign policy', *SAIS Review* 19: 92–113.

Ma'ud, Jalal Abdallah (1998) 'at-ta'awun al-askeri at-turki – isra'ili' ('The Turkish–Israeli cooperation'), *Mustaqbal al-Arabi* 237: 6–30.

Moravcsik, Andrew (1999) 'The future of European integration studies: social science or social theory? *Millennium* 28 (2): 371–91.

Mufti, Malik (1998) 'Daring and caution in Turkish foreign policy', *Middle East Journal* 52 (1): 32–50.

Müftüler-Bac, Meltem (2000) 'Turkey's role in the EU's security and foreign policies', *Security Dialogue*, 31 (4): 489–502.

Na'ama, Kathim Hashim (1997) 'at-ta'awun at-turki – al-isra'ili: qira't fi ad-dauwafi' al-kharijiyye' ('The Turkish–Israeli co-operation: an interpretation of its foreign policy motives'), *Mustaqbal al-Arabi* 220: 4–17.

Pedersen, Thomas (1998) *Germany, France and the Integration of Europe: A Realist Interpretation*, London, New York, NY: Pinter.

Seufert, Werner (1998) 'Das Gewaltpotential im türkischen Kulturkampf', in Heiner Bielefeldt and Wilhelm Heitmeyer (eds), *Politisierte Religion*, Frankfurt am Main: Suhrkamp: 360–92.

Tiyar, Khalil Ibrahin (1999) 'at-ta'awun al-askeri at-turki – isra'ili wa mukhatiruhu 'ala al-amn al-qaumi al-'arabi' ('The Turkish–Israeli co-operation and its threat to Arab National Security'), *Shuun Arabiyye* 97: 38–46.

US State Department (1999) *Turkey Country Report on Human Rights Practices for 1998*, Washington, DC: Bureau of Democracy, Human Rights, and Labor.

Wæver, Ole (1995) 'Securitization and desecuritization', in Ronnie D. Lipschutz (ed.), *On Security*, New York, NY: Columbia University Press: 46–86.

—— (1998a) 'Insecurity, security, and asecurity in the west European non-war community', in Emanuel Adler and Michael Barnett (eds), *Security Communities*, Cambridge, New York, NY: Cambridge University Press: 69–118.

—— (1998b) 'Integration as security. Constructing a Europe at peace', in Charles A. Kupchan (ed.), *Atlantic Security. Contending Vision*, New York, NY: Council on Foreign Relations: 45–63.

18 Algeria

Securitisation of state/regime, nation and Islam

Ulla Holm

The year 2002 marked the tenth anniversary of a military-backed coup that halted the electoral process in Algeria, after a first round of voting had assured the *Front Islamique du Salut* (*FIS*) a huge majority in Parliament. In the name of safeguarding democracy from religious extremism, the new military rulers cancelled the second round of voting. Since then, approximately 150,000 people have been killed whilst thousands more have 'disappeared'. The peak of horror occurred in 1997 when hundreds of villagers were slaughtered in spite of the fact that military barracks were situated close to the place of the massacre. The outcome of the growing revolt against generalised violence was a societal request for knowing *'qui tue qui'* (who killed who). The political answer to the growing revolt was to call a presidential election in 1999, which was won by former Minister of Foreign Affairs, Abdelaziz Bouteflika. He was the first civilian to become president in the history of Algerian independence (in 1962). Since his coming to power, the annual rate of killings has decreased: 'only' 1,900 people were killed in 2001 (www.algeria-interface.com/new/article).

Many books analysing the reasons for violence in Algeria have been published since its outbreak in 1992. The explanations most often run along the following lines: either the Islamists are to blame, or the state/regime or, finally, both (Mahiou and Henry 2001: 15). This chapter will argue that one of the reasons why the violence is so ferocious is because the state/regime has 'securitised' the fusion of the concepts of state/regime, nation and Islam. This conceptual fusion is at the centre of all discourses with the exception of one. Whilst they define the content or the order of each concept in different ways, the fusion of the concepts is maintained. Thus, the discursive struggle is centred around who has the power to define the content and the order of the fusion. Whenever this fusion is contested by societal groups, there is a political fear of a complete break-up of the hitherto 'deep' construction of the state/regime, nation and Islam. This in turn leads to a quick 'securitisation' on behalf of the fusion, which legitimises the use of violence. First, I will analyse how the fusion of state/regime works. Second, I will look at how the fusion of state/regime and nation leads to securitisation. Then, I will make the argument that Islam is the most important variable with respect to the whole fusion. This in turn leads to the argument that the political battles are about *how* Islam is linked to the fusion of state/regime and nation. The conclusion, then, is that only if Islam – with all its interpretations – is 'desecuritised' will the possibility of violence be reduced.

The fusion of the state and the regime

Charles Tilly's famous statement that war makes states (Tilly 1984: 170) fits the foundation of the Algerian state perfectly. The independence war against France made the state. But the important question is, what kind of a state? Is it a successfully imported European/French state (Badie 1992) or is it a failed state (Snow 1996: 58)? In practice, it is neither of these; rather, it is a state which is still in a process of state building, i.e. 'which signifies a conscious effort at creating an apparatus of control' (Martinez 2000: 9). Although the state monopoly of legitimate violence has been seriously challenged ever since 1992, the military, administrative and educational institutions continue to function. The functional machinery of the state has survived the continuous violence.

Until 1988, when army and security forces killed about 500 demonstrators, it looked as if the state was strong. Internationally, the state appeared strong in the sense that it was recognised by other states as an important player. Domestically the state appeared strong because the state succeeded in eliminating all oppositions. But the strength of a state neither depends on, nor correlates with, power (Buzan 1983: 66). A strong state should not be recognised for deriving its strength from its military capacity, but for possessing a high level of political internal consensus centred around the idea of the state.

Since 1988, the domestic support for the idea of the state as a distributor of economic welfare and as a social entrepreneur broke down in the wake of the oil crisis in 1983–4, and because of the killings of demonstrators. The increasing impoverishment of the population resulted in a profound distrust of both the idea of the state, the functional state machinery and the regime/government. The *FLN* state[1] was severely shaken because the economic and social crisis laid bare the de facto fusion of the state and the particularistic interests of the regime. The corruption of the state/regime became evident and thousands of people demonstrated in the streets, thereby provoking violent reaction from the state/regime.

At a theoretical level, it has been argued that any appropriation of a neutral impersonal state apparatus by a particular power can encourage the quick resort to violence, with the use of force becoming a central rather than a peripheral feature of domestic political life (Buzan 1983: 60). In such instances, the *raison de régime* prevails over the *raison d'État*, and the praetorisation of the army is its natural consequence (Salamé 1994: 23). Whenever society protests against the policies of the state/regime, the latter is prone to perceive the protest or criticism as a threat to the survival, not only of the regime, but also the state. Any political change at the governmental level is therefore to be perceived as entailing the risk of the complete breakdown of the state. The regime therefore tends to cling to the armed status quo, which in turn will likely result in further erosion of legitimacy, bringing about further protests. The outcome of such a process will be a weak state/regime that permanently considers itself besieged by opposition of any kind, which has to be broken down at any cost. This obsession with state/regime security has been clear in Algeria but is by no means unique to it. All Third World nation-states are concerned with state/regime security (Ayoob 1995: 191). However, in contrast to many African states, the Algerian state/regime has succeeded in containing violence to an extent which does not break up the state institutions.

Securitisation of state/regime and nation

The intense violence that Algeria experiences appears to be built into and triggered by the fusion of the state with the regime with its attendant 'securitisation' of this fusion, as well as with the fusion with the nation.

The theory of 'securitisation' operates with 'security' being understood as a speech act through which a condition of insecurity is identified, threats are pointed out and an object of security is constructed. It is thus only from the moment when somebody (a securitising actor) claims that something or somebody (the referent object) which has an inherent right to survive is existentially threatened that an issue becomes a question of security concern (see Chapter 5). In order to cope with the exigencies of the situation, 'securitisation' requires extreme measures that by-pass the 'normal' rules of the political process. However, an instance of 'securitisation' is not met simply by situations where the breaking of the normal political rules occurs, or by the simple identification of existential threats. It also requires acceptance by a sufficiently large 'audience' that will tolerate violations of rules that would otherwise have to be obeyed (Buzan *et al.* 1998: 24–6).

The important question is what constitutes 'normal' politics in an authoritarian nation-state where all opposition has been suppressed and where the real power container, the army, remains highly secretive, the hidden puppeteer pulling the political strings. It is therefore not easy to analyse who is securitising what, or how successful 'securitisation' is. With regard to the latter problem, it is difficult, for example, to 'measure' the public support to 'securitisation' of the survival of the state/regime because elections have never been free or fair – with the possible exception of the election of President Zeroual in 1995. But even an authoritarian state/regime has to legitimise its use of extraordinary measures. The lack of legitimisation manifests itself, for example, in riots, demonstrations, lack of participation in elections and regime negotiations with armed guerrillas. Although it is nearly impossible to know who is acting in reality, it is possible to analyse how the logic and legitimisation of 'securitisation' works through analysing party programmes, party statements and the constitutions enacted since independence in 1962. Given considerations of space it is impossible to unfold this logic (Holm 2003). Instead, I will sketch out how the securitisation of the state/regime and nation work together.

Algeria's experience of politics under the 'normal rules' of the game has been limited to the period 1989–92. A new constitution (1989) established a pluralist democracy which allowed for the participation of multiple parties of different stripes. In 1992, however, a state of emergency was imposed. *FIS* was banned and the constitution was annulled with the suspension of parliamentary elections in 1992. The most recent constitution of 1996 permits a certain level of political pluralism. All parties that do not refer to a religious, regional or ethnic affiliation in the party name have the right to present themselves at all state and local elections. In fact, religious parties considered moderate by the regime and the Berber parties have participated in the various governments since 1996. Furthermore, since 1996, a relatively free press has existed (Mahiou 2001: 27).[2] At the same time, though, the state of emergency still exists and the anti-terrorist decree of October 1992 has been incorporated into the penal law that defines a terrorist as a criminal 'who is affiliated to armed groups or is in league with armed groups'. How to define 'affiliation' and being 'in league with' is entirely up to the judges who are appointed by the state/regime (www.hrw.org/reports98/algeria/ALGER). Hence, the survival of the state/regime is still considered existentially threatened, although a timid process of 'desecuritisation' has started since Bouteflika became president in 1999.

According to Wæver, it is necessary to distinguish between perceived threats to society (nation) and state, because the ultimate criterion for societal security is identity, whereas state security has sovereignty as its ultimate criterion. Both usages imply survival. A state that loses its sovereignty does not survive as a state; a society (nation) that loses its identity fears that it will no longer be able to live as itself (Wæver 1995: 67). An important problem of these definitions is that the society/nation is regarded as a whole, as constituting one identity. The Copenhagen School has therefore been criticised for fixing the notion of 'identity' and 'society/nation' (Albert 1998: 24–5; McSweeny 1996: 85). I will argue that one also has to recognise 'that any entity can be situated in more than one mental context' (Albert 1998: 24). Hence, this interaction between fluidity and fixation opens up an understanding of the various processes of securitisation that take place *in* a society/nation constituted by a multiplicity of identities. In a state like Algeria, the political elite's construction of the idea of the nation is highly contested by different societal factions. In the beginning of the 1980s, the Berbers revolted against the suppression of their culture, whilst the Islamists started their armed campaign against the state/regime in order to mobilise for the foundation of a Sharia-state (Meynier 2000: 208). These mobilisations have continued and have further fuelled the security dynamics. The more the Islamists gained influence, the more the representatives of the state/regime and the secularised francophone elite responded to their challenge by securitising the state/regime. This finally resulted in the suspension of the elections in 1992 and in the banning of the *FIS*. These events led to the outbreak of violence, which was represented by the state/regime and the secularists as a struggle against a Sharia-state, and by the Islamists as a struggle against the disenchantment of society and state/regime. The 'violisation'[3] of identities (Neumann 1998: 19) became so intense because the speech act on security of both sides was stated in terms of mutually exclusionary conceptualisations of the idea of the state/regime and nation.

The state and regime have fused. But the nation has also fused with the state/regime. The role of the *FLN* in this has been vital. Since its foundation in 1954, until its dismissal as *the* state/regime party in 1989, the *FLN* constructed the narrative of national identity around fusion of the state/regime and the nation. The *FLN* represented itself as the incarnation of the unified nation whose survival had to be guaranteed by an all-encompassing state represented by the *FLN* regime (Lamchichi 1991). The survival of national sovereignty, both in terms of recognition from the outside and territorial political unity inside, thus became the pivot on which all speeches on security have turned. In the terms of late president Boumedienne (1965–78). Boumedienne was thus obsessed by the foundation of a strong state/regime whose purpose was to prevent the territory from collapsing into numerous small entities which would have resulted in disappearance of Algeria as nation-state and as an internationally recognised actor (Balta 1990: 89–90).

Thus, one cannot speak about the state/regime without speaking about the nation. Logically, and as a result, whenever discourses on de-linking one of the elements of this fusion become manifest in riots in the streets or when they try to gain an audience in the political arena, the state/regime securitises itself and the nation either by means of violence or by law. All kinds of ethnic, religious and political opposition are excluded from the political arena. Only the representation of an undifferentiated and harmonious territorial nation-state is allowed at the political level. Even if this has occurred to a lesser extent during the reign of President Bouteflika, it is still the case that every societal demand for more cultural pluralism is considered a threat to the survival and identity of the state/regime and nation.

The deep structure of this dominant discourse is thus based on an exclusionary principle which results in the securitisation of all the elements of the basic structure. Whoever does not adhere to the fusion of the concepts is denoted a traitor. The 'radical Other' is created and this in turn leads quickly to violisation, i.e. violence on a massive scale. Of course, the construction of the 'radical Other' and the following resort to violence has been ever present on the Algerian agenda. Both before, during and since the independence war it has been 'normal' politics to eradicate whoever one represented as a traitor to the revolutionary cause. The famous writings of Frantz Fanon are a telling illustration of the glorification and need to use force against traitors, in this case the French soldiers and collaborators during the independence war. In order to be free, therefore, the subjugated population had first to purge their minds of the French culture (Crenshaw 1978). Carlier even speaks about an Algerian 'culture de violence' (1995: 393) due to deep-rooted historical memories of the relevance of the use of violence against whoever was perceived as a threat to the tribe, the family, the religion, the state. There has thus for many centuries been struggles for 'purifying' different territories of what were considered 'intruders'. This friend/foe–outside/inside dichotomy has framed the history of Algeria and has – since 1962 – been transferred to the violent struggle between those who were (and are) for/against a fusion of state/regime and nation.

The securitisation of the idea of the unified state/regime and nation excludes alternative representations of the construction of Algerian history. The narrative around war has constructed heroes that have acquired symbolic significance in the reproduction of national identity. The reference to the heroes or the martyrs[4] (*shouhada*) – as the dead freedom fighters are called in Algeria – is a constitutive part of storytelling about the construction of the nation-state. The preambles of the various constitutions, including the latest one from 1996, have inscribed that Algeria was born in 1962 upon the sacrifices of its sons and that 'November 1, 1954 was the height of its destiny. The current struggles are therefore firmly anchored in the glorious past of the nation' (preamble to the actual constitution, www.waac.org/library/documents/). Furthermore, Article 8 stipulates that it is forbidden to betray the ideals of the November Revolution. A consequence of the securitisation of the glorification of the Revolution is that the constitution of 1996 also requires that the president is able to prove his participation in the independence war if he was born before 1942. If born after, he has to prove that his parents did not collaborate with the French. Hence, the purpose of preserving presidential revolutionary purity is to guarantee that no traitor to the revolutionary ideals penetrates the national body. The memory of the war is thus considered the glue behind the fusion of the state/regime with the nation. The purification of the national territory from traitors, the glorification of martyrs, the story about one million dead in the war, the unification of all Algerians in the struggle against France and military victory over the French thus constitute the building blocks of national history writing. Contenders for power therefore come from among those who have participated or are descendants of freedom fighters, the *Mujahidin*. They are the watchdogs of the continuation of the revolutionary ideals with other stories necessarily being silenced. Notably, there exists no official history writing dealing with the internal killings and massacres of Algerians by the *FLN*. Neither are the *harkis*, who were Algerians that joined the French, dealt with in history even though 40,000 were killed just after the war by the *FLN* (Stora 1991). Nor is any history about the discussions inside the *FLN* concerning the construction of national identity and of the military's role allowed. Similarly, no history has been officially written, even though the future of the Berbers in a new nation-state was discussed in the 1940s–50s (Stora 1995). The state/regime possesses a monopoly on history writing and, due to the fact that it is obsessed with the break-down of the fusion of state/regime with the nation, it has consequently securitised history as an identity construct.

State/regime, nation, Islam and securitisation

What about the relationship between Islam and the state/regime and nation? Well, once again a fusion has been constructed. One cannot speak about the state/regime and nation without also linking Islam to these concepts. But how do they link together in the various discourses?

Islam is represented as *the* identity marker of the nation in all discourses, classic Arab becoming the other building block of the representation of the fused state/regime and nation. However, since the nation is fused with the state/regime, Islam is in turn also, logically, represented as fused with the state/regime and nation. Hence, Islam is held in check by the state/regime. In all of Algeria's constitutions (1963, 1976, 1989, 1996), it has been stated that *'Islam est la religion de l'État'* (Islam is the religion of the state) or *'Islam est religion d'État'* (Islam is state religion). But the two statements are not identical because the state and Islam are positioned in a different relationship. Islam as 'state religion' signifies that the state administers the religion, whereas 'Islam as religion of the state' indicates that Islam is either subordinated to the state or the state is subordinated to Islam (Babadji 2001: 56). In the former case, Islam puts its resources at the disposal of the legitimisation of a political project. In the latter, the state acts in conformity with the religious dogma.

The state/regime is not subordinated to Islam. It is Islam that is subordinated because the state/regime administers and instrumentalises Islam for a political purpose. Islam is represented as a social, moral and political public service system (Babadji 2001: 58), whose purpose has been the legitimisation of state-sponsored modernisation. Thus, until the 1989 constitution when references to socialism were deleted, Islam was linked to the socialist modernisation project in the *FLN* discourse. In particular, the egalitarian principle of Islam was represented as an underpinning of those of socialism. In Jean Leca and Jean-Claude Vatin's formulation: *'C'est bel et bien en tant qu' "idéologie", reflet d'une infrastructure sociale et économique, que l'Islam est considéré'* (Leca and Vatin 1975: 260). Alternative interpretations of Islam were more or less silenced. This especially goes for the marabou tradition and the Sufibrotherhoods, which are considered anti-modern especially because they are associated with small communities which the state/regime considers a hindrance to the concept of the modern and unified state/regime and nation.

The *harbous* (religious properties) which constituted religiously independent properties, thereby putting into question the power of the state as organiser of the whole territory, quickly became nationalised after independence. Furthermore, the construction of mosques was controlled by the state, which did not allow for 'free' mosques because they could be politically uncontrollable. Finally, a decree from 1969 stipulated that the Imams' status had to be identical to that of ordinary state employees. The Imams thus became politically and administratively subordinated to the state administration, which very often dictated the content of the Friday prayer (Lamchichi 1988). The political control of the Imams is still functioning and has even been strengthened. An amendment of June 2001 to the constitution curbed political speech in mosques by lengthening to five years the maximum sentence for delivering sermons 'capable of harming social cohesion' (www.algeria-watch.de/mrv/mrvrap).

This permanent control of the mosques and thereby also of the practice of faith, is due to the inherent tension between administration and subordination of Islam to the state, and the state as subordinated to Islam, that is, between 'Islam as the religion of the state' and 'Islam as state religion'. This has been increasingly evident since the weakening of references to socialism from the mid-1980s. One might argue that both the disappearance of the reference to socialism in 1989 and the fragile balance between 'Islam as religion of state' and 'Islam as state religion' has opened up discursive space for the political Islamism represented by the *FIS*. The disappearance of the concept of socialism has left references to the political egalitarian principle orphaned. Here, political Islam offers itself as a substitute by referring to an egalitarian concept of *umma* (the community of the believers).

The dominant state/regime discourse and that of the *FIS* share the concept of the fusion of the state/regime, nation and Islam, which does not allow for cultural and political pluralism. But they differ on one essential point: the FIS has turned upside down the order of the concepts of the state/regime, nation and Islam. The *FIS* discourse posits Islam as the transcendental sacral referent object: Allah. That is to say that Allah is the sovereign ultimate reference that justifies and legitimises earthly politics. Legitimisation of the state/regime and nation is thus derived from Islam. The state/regime discourse posits, by contrast, the sovereignty with the people, which in turn is incarnated in the immanent state/regime. Thus the immanent state/regime is the ultimate reference because it incarnates the people.

State/regime as the people and state/regime as expression of Allah's will are, in both discourses, represented as untouchable. Nobody is allowed to enter the 'sacralised' state space unless they prove that they are the true representatives either of the people or of Allah. The result is that both parts securitise the state/regime. This securitisation leads to killings either in the name of Allah being incarnated in the Sharia-state or in the name of the state of people.

In the political Islamist discourse, it is not only the Sharia-state that is securitised. It also goes for the faith itself. The way the political Islamists interpret the expressions of faith is securitised. Thus, all who do not adhere to their interpretation of faith are considered to be living in a state of 'impiety', of *djahilliyya* (ignorance). License for killing is therefore easily given. However, this killing undermines the legitimacy of the discourse of the political Islamists. The same goes for the state/regime discourse that securitises its version of Islam. It allows for killing of political Islamists.

The legitimisation of the massive facts of violence has been slowly undermined since the massacres in 1997. Therefore terms like 'negotiations', *'concorde civile'* and *'concorde nationale'* have been central in all political discourses, especially since Bouteflika became president in 1999.

Moves and battles in the current constellation

Violence is still evident in Algeria. For the present it appears that the state/regime has won the battle of the survival of the state as institution because it has succeeded in splintering the different Islamist groups who are now more concerned with struggling against each other. Furthermore, the *FIS* program for a Sharia-state has lost much of their support as a result of the violence they have carried out in the name of Allah. This, though, does not mean that the question of the position of Islam in relation to the state/regime and the nation has disappeared. There is still a discursive struggle going on concerning this issue. For its part, the state/regime maintains the discourse of the complete fusion of state/regime, nation and Islam. However, the content of Islam has been slightly changed. Now the state/regime discourse posits the spiritual/individual and moral values of Islam as the defining feature. Islam as a private matter or as a code of moral and social behaviour is competing in the discourse of the state/regime, thus paying tribute both to the francophone elite and the conservative Muslims. This is evident in the statements of the *High Islamic Council,* which was constitutionally established in 1996 (www.hci-dz.org/presentation). The banned *FIS,* however, still propagates its discourse on a Sharia-state. However, it dissociates itself from the use of violence. For its part, the *FFS* (*Front des Forces Socialistes*) adheres to a secularised version of Islam whilst another party, *RCD* (*Rassemblement pour la Culture et la Démocratie*) is an unconditional proponent of the separation of the state and Islam. Finally, *MSP* (*Mouvement de la Societé en Paix*), a party in government, is advocating a conservative version of Islam which traditionalises social behaviour in public spaces and within the family. All of these discourses are now ardent, and an intense struggle between them is going on. Only two of the discourses (*FFS* and *RCD*) permit change in the deep structure of the fusion of the state/regime, nation and Islam either by de-linking Islam from the state/regime (*RCD*) or by de-linking regime from state and thereby also Islam from regime (*FFS*). In contrast, the other ones 'only' reformulate the *content* of Islam

Another discursive struggle that is on the political agenda concerns the fusion of the state and regime. Increasing parts of the population, especially the Berbers, have begun to question this fusion, particularly in view of the violent clashes between the Berbers and the security forces in 2001. Societal demands for justice and transparency regarding the position of the army have increasingly come to the political fore. High-ranking officers have published books where they have related their role in the violence. The fusion of the state/regime is thus contested both from the inside of the state/regime and from society. But the state of emergency is still functioning and the *FIS* is still banned because of its message about a Sharia-state. So, although the state has survived as an institution, the regime, and thereby the army also, still has not given in to a de-linking of the regime from the state. The army still remains the only actor that defines the relationship between state/regime, nation and Islam.

The discourse on the fusion of the state/regime and the *nation* is also being challenged. The violent riots in the Berber region, Kabylia, in 2001 have resulted in a move of 'desecuritisation' of the fusion. As a result of the riots, Bouteflika made a concession to the Berbers in April 2002 where the Parliament amended the constitution in such a way that the Tamazight (Berber language) became the second language of Algeria (http://www.algeria-interface.com/new/article.php?article_id=594).[5] Hence a slow process of 'desecuritisation'[6] of the idea of the fused state/regime and nation is in the pipeline. But at any moment, this process can be stopped at random by the state/regime. The state of emergency is still functioning!

A deepening of the process of 'desecuritisation' will only be possible if state and regime are de-linked. As long as this is not the case, the state of emergency will exist, thus preventing a discussion of the role of the army in the securitisation of the fusion of the state/regime. If the future of Algeria is to be more bright that it has been for years, it is therefore necessary to terminate the state of emergency. Only this measure can open up for *political* struggles with regard to the question about 'who the Algerians are' and how the fusion of state/regime, nation and public interpretation of Islam might be 'desecuritised'.

Notes

1 *FLN* is the acronym for *Front de Libération nationale,* which launched the independence war in 1954 and which was the only legal party from 1962 to 1989.
2 But on May 16, 2001, the lower house of parliament – the National People's Assembly – approved new amendments to the Algerian Penal Code that prescribe imprisonment and heavy fines for individuals found guilty of defaming the President of the Republic or other state institutions such as the army or judiciary. The amendments were legitimised by officials as necessary to 'preserve the dignity of the state and to protect individual and collective freedoms' (www.algeria-watch.de/mrvrap/).
3 Neumann slots the *action* of violence, which he formulates as 'violisation', into the three categories of the Copenhagen School: non-politicised – politicised – securitised – violised. He does that in order to take into account the difference between securitisation as a speech act and violisation as the *act on a certain scale,* which might be the possible consequence of securitisation (Neumann 1998: 18). But even if this is done, the question remains why, in certain cases, a speech act on security is backed up by violisation. This is a case for empirical research.
4 After the extremely violent clashes between security forces and Berbers in spring 2001, the Berber coordination group published a list of demands to be fulfilled by the government. One of the demands concerned the status as martyr given to Berbers killed during the confrontation. This claim contested the hitherto right of the state/regime to define a martyr as one who died during the independence war against the French. In this case, the casuality is a Berber who contested the state/regime, who is now represented as an actor in line with the former French colonisers (*El Watan,* 15 June 2001).
5 After the riots in spring/summer 2001, the Berbers foremost claimed the withdrawal of the gendarmery and of the security forces from the Berber region, Kabylia, because they triggered the violence. The state/regime response was to offer Berber language identity and not withdrawal of armed forces.
6 In Buzan's and Wæver's formulation, 'desecuritisation' of a referent object means that it is taken out of the security problematique with the result that politics can return to its place (see Chapter 4).

References

Albert, Mathias (1998) 'Security as a boundary function: changing identities and "securitization" in world politics', *International Journal of Peace Studies* 3 (1): 23–47.

Ayoob, Mohammed (1995) *Third World Security Predicament: State Making, Regional Conflict and the International System,* Boulder, CO: Lynne Rienner.

Babadji, Ramdane (2001) 'De la religion comme instrument à l'identité comme sanctuaire: quelques remarques sur la constitution algérienne du 28 novembre 1996', in Ahmed Mahiou and Jean-Robert Henry (eds), *Où va l'Algérie?*, Paris, Aix-en-Provence: Karthala-IREMAM: 53–71.

Badie, Bertrand (1992) *L'État importé,* Paris: Fayard.

Balta, Paul (1990) *Le grand Maghreb. Des indépendances à l'an 2000,* Paris: La Découverte.

Buzan, Barry (1983) *People, States and Fear. The National Security Problem in International Relations,* Brighton: Wheatsheaf Books Ltd.

——, Ole Wæver and Jaap de Wilde (1998) *Security: A New Framework for Analysis,* Boulder, CO, London: Lynne Rienner.

Carlier, Omar (1995) *Entre Nation et Jihad. Histoire sociale des radicalismes algériens*, Paris: Presses de Sciences PO.

Crenshaw, Martha Hutchinson (1978) *Revolutionary Terrorism: The FLN in Algeria, 1954–62*, Stanford, CA: Hoover Institute Press.

Hibou, Béatrice (1996) *L'Afrique est-elle protectionniste?* Paris: Karthala.

Holm, Ulla (2003) *Algeriet: Vold og sikkerhed*, Copenhagen: Gyldendal.

Lamchichi, Abderrahim (1989) *Islam et contestation au Maghreb*, Paris: L'Harmattan.

—— (1991) *L'Algérie en crise*, Paris: L'Harmattan.

Leca, Jean and Jean-Claude Vatin (1975) *L'Algérie politique. Institutions et régime*, cahiers de la Fondation National des Sciences Politiques, No. 197, Paris: Presses de la Fondation Nationale des Sciences Politiques.

McSweeney, Bill (1996) 'Identity and security: Buzan and the Copenhagen School', *Review of International Studies* 22 (1): 81–93.

Mahiou, Ahmed (2001) 'Les contraintes et incertitudes du système politique', in Ahmed Maliou and Jean-Robert Henry (eds), *Où va l'Algérie?*, Paris, Aix-en-Provence: Karthala-IREMAM: 13–34.

—— and Jean-Robert Henry (eds) (2001) *Où va l'Algérie?* Paris, Aix-en-Provence: Karthala-IREMAM.

Martinez, Luiz (2000) *La guerre civile*, Paris: Karthala. (English version (2000) *The Algerian Civil War: 1990–1998*, London: Hurst & Company.)

Meynier, Gilbert (ed.) (2000) *L'Algérie contemporaine. Bilan et solutions pour sortir de la crise*, Paris: l'Harmattan.

Neumann, Iver B. (1998) 'Identity and the outbreak of war', *International Journal of Peace Studies* 3 (1): 7–23.

Salamé, Ghassan (1994) 'The Middle East: elusive security, indefinable region', *Security Dialogue* 25 (1) 17–37.

Snow, M. Donald (1996) *Uncivil Wars: International Security and the New Internal Conflicts*, Boulder, CO, London: Lynne Rienner.

Stora, Benjamin (1991) *La gangrène et l'oubli*, Paris: la Découverte.

—— (1995) *L'Algérie en 1995. La guerre, l'histoire, la politique*, Paris: Éditions Michalon.

Tilly, Charles (1984) 'War making and state making as organized crime', in Peter B. Evans, Dietrich Rueschmeyer and Theda Skocpol (eds), *Bringing the State Back*, Cambridge: Cambridge University Press: 169–91.

Wæver, Ole (1995) 'Securitization and desecuritization', in Ronnie D. Lipschutz (ed.), *On Security*, New York, NY: Columbia University Press: 46–86.

Håkan Wiberg
Selected bibliography

Compiled by Anita Elleby

2003

Wiberg, Håkan, 'The Hesselø Episode', in Clive Archer and Pertti Joenniemi (eds), *The Nordic Peace*, Aldershot: Ashgate: 105–11.

—— 'Neutralitet, EU, NATO och blockpolitik' ('Neutrality, EU, NATO and Bloc politics') in Jan Øberg (ed.), (Volume on EU). 11 pages.

—— and Biljana Vankovska, *Between Past and Future: Civil–Military Relations in the Post-Communist Balkans*, London: I.B. Tauris.

—— and Johan Galtung (eds), *Democracy Works: People, Experts and the Future*, special issue of *Futures* 35 (2): 99–187.

—— 'Introduction': *Democracy Works: People Thinking About Futures*, ibid.: 99–106..

—— 'Peace, security and South Eastern Europe', in Anton Grizold (ed.), *Security and Cooperation in South Eastern Europe*, Ljubljana: Faculty of Social Sciences: 21–47.

—— 'Roles of peace research', in Unto Vesa (ed.), *Maailman tutkimisesta ja muuttamisesta/ Studying the World and Changing It/Per studia mundus explicatur et mutatur*, Festschrift for Jyrki Käkönen, Tampere: TAPRI: 109–19.

—— 'Reconciliation in Northern and South Eastern Europe', in Biljana Vankovska (ed.), *The Challenges of Post-Conflict Reconciliation and Peacebuilding in Macedonia*, Geneva: Center for Democratic Control of Armed Forces; Skopje: Institute for Defence and Peace Studies.

—— 'The Hesselø episode', in Clive Archer and Pertti Joenniemi (eds), *The Nordic Peace*, Aldershot: Ashgate: 105–11.

2002

Wiberg, Håkan, 'Review of Maria Ericson, *Reconciliation and the Search for a Moral Landscape. An Exploration Based on a Study of Northern Ireland and South Africa*', *Svensk Teologisk Kvartalstidskrift* 78 (2): 93–5.

—— 'Johan Galtung in Raum und Zeit' ('JG in space and time'), in Hajo Schmidt and Uwe Trittmann (eds), *Kultur und Konflikt/Dialog mit Johan Galtung*, Münster: agenda: 276–8.

2001

Wiberg, Håkan and Katsuya Kodama (eds), *Shinhassou no Boueiron: Hikougekiteki Bouei Tenkai* (*New Thinking of Defence Policy: Development of Non-Offensive Defence*), Okayama: Daigakukyouiku Shuppan.

—— 'Non-offensive defence in the wider context of security policy' (in Japanese), ibid.: 61–82.

—— 'Peace in the Balkans – obstacles and how to overcome them', in Georgi Efremov, Georgi Stardelov and Milan Gurcinov (eds), *The Balkans in the New Millennium*, Skopje: Macedonian Academy of Art and Sciences: 255–74.

—— 'Makedonia: eden pogled odnavor' ('Macedonia: an outsider's view'), *Puls (Skopje)* 11 (552): 22–4.

2000

Wiberg, Håkan and Biljana Vankovska, 'Civil–military relations in Macedonia', COPRI Working Papers 16/2000.

—— and Biljana Vankovska, 'Civil–military relations in the third Yugoslavia', COPRI Working Papers 19/2000.

—— 'Demokratijata i vojskata: za eden kompleksen odnos' ('Democracy and the army: a complex relationship'), *Sovremena Makedonska Odbrana* 2: 11–22.

—— 'East-Central Europe – where and how?', in Wojciech Kostecki, Katarzyna Żukrowska and Bogdan Goralczyk (eds), *Transformations of Post-Communist States*, London: Macmillan: 23–40.

—— 'Former Yugoslavia: nations above all', ibid.: 202–22.

—— 'Emmanuel Adler, Michael Barnett and anomalous northerners', *Cooperation and Conflict* 35 (3): 289–98.

—— 'Heroische "non-oorlogen" in Noord-Europa' ('Heroic "Non-Wars" in Norden'), in André W.M. Gerrits and Jaap H. de Wilde (eds), *Aan het slagveld ontsnapt. Over oorlogen die niet plaatsvonden*, Zutphen: Walburg Pers: 117–31.

—— 'The Nordic security community: past, present, future', in Bertel Heurlin and Hans Mouritzen (eds), *Danish Foreign Policy Yearbook 2000*, Copenhagen: DUPI (Danish Institute of International Affairs): 121–37.

—— 'Patterns of war and peace – how much can we trust?', in Young Seek Choue (ed.), *Will World Peace be Achievable in the 21st Century?*, Seoul: Institute of International Peace Studies, Kyung Hee University: 387–413.

—— 'Review of Carl-Ulrik Schierup (ed.), *Scramble for the Balkans. Nationalism, Globalism and the Political Economy of Reconstruction*', *European Societies* 2 (2): 230–3.

1999

Wiberg, Håkan and Christian P. Scherrer (eds), *Ethnicity and Intra-State Conflict: Types, Causes and Peace Strategies*, Aldershot: Ashgate.

—— 'Introduction', ibid.: 1–12.

—— 'Conversion and peace – past and future perspectives', *Peace Forum (Seoul)* 15 (27): 23–39.

—— 'Koga slonovite se borat trevata strada' ('When the elephants fight, the grass suffers'), *PULS (Skopje)* 9 (436): 20–2.

—— 'Kosovo/a: Fortid, nutid og fremtid' ('Kosovo/a past, present, future'), *COPRI Nyhedsbrev* 3: 8–14.

—— 'Roles of civil society – the case of Kosovo', in Kristof Tamas and Malin Hansson (eds), *Conference Report – International Migration, Development and Integration*, Stockholm: Ministry of Foreign Affairs: 85–98.

1998

Wiberg, Håkan, 'Identifying conflict and solutions', *Review of International Affairs (Belgrade)* (1070–1): 27–32 (also published in Serbian and in *Romanian Journal of International Affairs* (1): 175–87).

1997

Wiberg, Håkan, Ib M.C. Nielsen and Jens Rudbeck, 'Intra state conflict: causes and peace strategies. Report from a COPRI symposium', COPRI Working Paper 16/1997.

—— and Jens Rudbeck, 'Research on internal conflicts and conflict resolution at Danish research institutions – A COPRI survey', COPRI Working Paper 14/1997.

—— 'Kriegsursachenforschung – wie dürftig ist sie?' ('How poor is research on causes of war?'), *Ethik und Sozialwissenschaften* 8 (3): 308–12.

1996

Wiberg, Håkan and Jaap de Wilde (eds), *Organized Anarchy in Europe: The Role of States and IGOs*, London: I.B. Tauris.

—— 'Third party intervention in Yugoslavia: problems and lessons', ibid.: 203–26.

——, Hans Mouritzen and Ole Wæver, with Anjo Harryvan, Jan van der Harst, Kornelija Jurgaitiene, Wojciech Kostecki and Lars Poulsen-Hansen, *European Integration and National Adaptation: A Theoretical Enquiry*, New York, NY: Nova.

—— and Wojciech Kostecki, 'Poland', ibid.: 157–84.

——, Anjo Harryvan and Jan van der Harst, 'The Netherlands', ibid.: 101–28.

—— 'The EU, would-be insiders and outsiders', ibid.: 43–64.

—— and Pertti Joenniemi, 'Konfliktläkning: Kontext, särart, motiv, problem' ('Conflict mitigation: context, peculiarities, motive, problems'), in Jan Øberg (ed.), *Att läka konflikter: Engagemang, möjligheter, problem*, Lund: Transnational Foundation for Peace and Futures Studies: 17–31.

—— 'Förhållandet mellan massmedia och politik' ('The relationship between mass media and politics'), ibid.: 77–82.

—— 'Conversion and transition', in Martin Grundmann (ed.), *Arms Conversion in the Baltic Sea Area and in Russia*, Münster: Lit Verlag: 13–27.

—— 'De jugoslaviska konflikternas dynamik' ('The dynamics of the Yugoslav conflicts'), in Neven Milivojević, Jens Stilhoff Sørensen, Joakim Thomasson and Erik Windmar (eds), *Bortom kriget*, Stockholm: Carlssons: 113–29.

—— 'Divided nations and divided states', in Jan-Mient Faber (ed.), *The Balkans: A Religious Backyard of Europe*, Ravenna: Longo Editore: 25–51.

—— 'Für und gegen militärische Intervention: Am Beispiel des ehemaligen

Jugoslawien' ('For and against military intervention: the example of former Yugoslavia'), in Hajo Schmidt (ed.), *Friedenspolitik und Interventionspraxis*, Hagen: FernUniversität – Gesamthochschule: 33–53.

—— 'Identitet, Etnicitet, Konflikt. En Essä' ('Identity, ethnicity, conflict: an essay'), in Kristian Gerner, Rune Johansson, Klas-Göran Karlsson, Kerstin Nyström and Kim Salomon (eds), *Stat, Nation, Konflikt. En Festskrift tillägnad Sven Tägil*, Helsingborg: Bra Böcker: 317–42.

—— 'Identity, ethnicity, conflict', in Simon Bekker and David Carlton (eds), *Racism, Xenophobia, and Ethnic Conflict*, Durban, South Africa: Indicator Press: 1–29.

—— 'Identity, ethnicity, conflict', in Stefano Bianchini and Dušan Janjić (eds), *Ethnicity in Postcommunism*, Belgrade: Institute for Social Sciences & Forum for Ethnic Relations & Europe and the Balkans: 51–66.

—— 'Krigen i Bosnien en sag mellem tre parter' ('The Bosnian War is a three party conflict'), *Udenrigs* 51 (2): 58–65.

—— 'The Norden going European: how much and what kind?', in Susanna Perko (ed.), *The Nordic–Baltic Region in Transition: New Actors, New Issues, New Trends*, Research Report No. 75, Tampere: TAPRI: 66–84.

—— 'Relating to the EU: who does what?', *Romanian Journal of International Affairs* 2 (1–2): 28–49.

—— 'Security problems of small nations', in Werner Bauwens, Armand Clesse and Olav F. Knudsen (eds), *Small States and the Security Challenge in the New Europe*, London: Brassey's: 21–41.

—— 'Ustanovlyeniye Mira v Byvshey Yugoslavii: Problemy i Uroki' ('Making peace in former Yugoslavia: problems and lessons'), in Georgij G. Pocheptsov (ed.), *Natsional'naya Bezopastnost' Stran Perechodnogo Perioda*, Kiev: Defence Ministry: 126–33.

1995

Wiberg, Håkan and Judit Balázs (eds), *Changes, Chances, Challenges: Europe 2000*, Budapest: Akadémiai Kiadó.

—— 'Introduction: peace research, the old, new and post-new agendas', ibid.: 1–24.

—— and Ole Wæver, 'Baltic Sea/Black Sea: regionalization on the fringes of the new Europe', in Ioan Maxim and Olav Fagelund Knudsen (eds), *Regionalisation. Concepts and Approaches at the Turn of the Century*, Bucharest: Romanian Institute of International Studies and Norwegian Institute of International Affairs: 202–28.

—— 'FN og det muliges kunst' ('The UN and the art of the possible'), in Lene Bartelsen and Bolette Bisp Andersen (eds), *Retten til en bedre verden: FN og menneskerettighederne*, Copenhagen: FN-forbundet: 86–98.

—— 'Former Yugoslavia: nations above all', in Wojciech Kostecki, Bogdan Goralczyk and Katarzyna Żukrowska (eds), *In Pursuit of Europe*, Warsaw: Institute for Political Studies: 93–106.

—— 'Identity, ethnicity, conflict', in *Neprievarta ir Tolerancija Kintančioje Rytų Virurio Eurupoje*, Vilnius: Lietuvos Neprievartinio Veiksmo Centras: 32–55.

—— (ed.), *Peace and War: Social and Cultural Aspects*, Warsaw: BEL CORP (for UNESCO and COPRI).

—— 'Introduction', ibid.: 1–8.

—— 'La Jugoslavia e la Soluzione dei Conflitti: Problemi e Lezioni', in Antonino Drago and Matteo Soccio (eds), *Per un Modello di Difesa Nonviolento: Che Cosa ci Insegna il Conflitto nella Ex-Jugoslavia?*, Venice: Editoria Universitaria: 36–52.

—— 'Peace research and Eastern Europe: how much need for reappraisal?', in Pierre Allan and Kjell Goldmann (eds), *The End of the Cold War: Evaluating Theories of International Relations*, Amsterdam: Kluwer Law International: 147–78.

—— 'Security and identity in Former Yugoslavia', in Stefano Bianchini and Paul Shoup (eds), *The Yugoslav War, Europe and the Balkans: How to Achieve Security?*, Ravenna: Longo Editore: 117–28.

—— 'Social and cultural origins of violence: non-military aspects of international security', in UNESCO, *Non-Military Aspects of International Security: Peace and Conflict Issues*, Paris: UNESCO: 229–58.

—— 'The Yugoslav conflict formation', in Sefa Martin Yürükel (ed.), *Krigen på Balkan/The Balkan War*, Moesgård: Aarhus Universitet, Afdeling for Etnografi og Socialantropologi: 93–100.

1994

Wiberg, Håkan and Erik André Andersen (eds), *Storm over Balkan* ('Storm over the Balkans'), Copenhagen: Reitzel.

—— 'Den lange historiske baggrund' ('The long historical background'), ibid.: 8–21.

—— 'Krisernes dynamik' ('The dynamics of the crises'), ibid.: 22–41.

—— and Jan Øberg, 'Fremtidsscenarier' ('Future scenarios'), ibid.: 42–67.

——, Salvino Busuttil and James Calleja (eds), *The Search for Peace in the Mediterranean Region. Problems and Prospects*, Valletta: Mireva.

—— and James Calleja, 'Introduction: The Mediterranean, the Middle East and Europe', ibid.: 1–15.

—— 'Making peace in Former Yugoslavia: problems and lessons', ibid.: 231–55.

—— and Bjørn Møller (eds), *Non-Offensive Defence for the 21st Century*, Boulder, CO: Westview.

—— and Bjørn Møller, 'Introduction', ibid.: 1–7.

—— 'Neutral and non-aligned states in Europe and NOD', ibid.: 176–94.

—— 'Europe. The Western project and the hesitant north', *Research Paper No. 7*, Athens: Research Institute for European Studies.

—— 'Internationale Konflikte: Auf dem Weg zu friedlicheren Konzepten und Lösungen?' ('International conflicts: towards more peaceful concepts and solutions?'), in Wolfgang Hofkirchner (ed.), *Weltbild – Weltordnung. Perspektiven für eine zerbrechliche und endliche Erde*, Münster: Agenda: 81–94. (Also published in Bulgarian.)

—— 'Jugoslavien: upplösning skapar upplösning' ('Yugoslavia: dissolution creates dissolution'), in Erik Windmar (ed.), *I stället for en ny världsordning – fallet Jugoslavien*, Stockholm: Fredshögskolan: 16–31.

—— 'Making peace in former Yugoslavia: problems and lessons', *Eurobalkans/EYPΩ BAλKANIA* 17: 22–33.

—— 'The peace research movement', in Karlheinz Koppe and Wolfgang Reichardt (eds), *Geschichte der Friedensforschung: Einführung und ausgewählte Texte*, Hagen: Fernuniversität: 275–88.

—— 'Religion and conflict resolution', in *The Contribution of Religions to the Culture of Peace*, Barcelona: Centro Unesco de Catalunya: 225–9.

—— 'Societal security and the explosion of Yugoslavia', *Balkan Forum* 3 (2): 51–72.

—— 'Yugoslavia and conflict resolution: problems and lessons', in Dušan Janjić (ed.), *Religion and War*, Belgrade: European Movement in Serbia: 104–24.

1993

Wiberg, Håkan and Judit Balázs (eds), *Peace Research for the 1990s*, Budapest: Akademiai Kiadó.

—— 'European peace research in the 1990s', ibid.: 9–25.

—— 'The dynamics of disarmament in the Middle East', ibid.: 191–5.

——, Ib Damgaard Petersen and Paul Smoker (eds), *Inadvertent Nuclear War: Implications of the Changing Global Order*, Oxford: Pergamon.

—— 'Accidental nuclear war: the problematique', ibid.: 3–30.

—— 'The dissolution of Yugoslavia: a study of interaction', in Frank D. Pfetsch (ed.), *International Relations and Pan-Europe*, Münster: Lit Verlag: 361–87.

—— 'Jugoslavien som grekisk tragedi' ('Yugoslavia as a Greek tragedy'), *Internasional politikk* 51 (3): 291–308.

—— 'Many roads to peace', in Jose Palau and Radha Kumar (eds), *Ex-Yugoslavia: From War to Peace*, Madrid: Ecosimposio: 135–43.

—— 'Proliferation and deployment issues in recent years: the implications for inadvertent nuclear war', in Carin Atterling Wedar, Peeter Vares and Michael D. Intriligator (eds), *Implications of the Dissolution of the Soviet Union for Accidental/Inadvertent Use of Weapons of Mass Destruction*, Tallinn: Estonian Academy of Sciences: 140–53.

—— '(Re)conceptualizing security', *Arms Control* 13 (3): 487–92.

—— 'Scandinavia', in Richard D. Burns (ed.), *Encyclopedia of Arms Control and Disarmament*, vol. 1, New York, NY: Scribner: 209–26.

—— 'Societal security and the explosion of Yugoslavia', in Ole Wæver, Barry Buzan, Morten Kelstrup and Pierre Lemaitre (eds), *Identity, Migration and the New Security Agenda in Europe*, London: Pinter: 93–109.

1992

Wiberg, Håkan, Nils Petter Gleditsch and Dan Smith, 'The Nordic countries: peace dividend or security dilemma?', *Cooperation and Conflict* 27 (4): 323–48.

——, Björn Hettne, Jyrki Käkönen, Sverre Lodgaard and Peter Wallensteen (eds), *Norden ved skillevejen* (The Nordic Region at the Crossroads), Copenhagen: Fremad.

—— (ed.), *Omstilling – fra militær til civil* (*Conversion from Military to Civilian*). Copenhagen: Arbejderbevægelsens Internationale Forum.

—— and Keld Jensen, 'Military defence in Denmark: expenditures and conversion problems', *Cooperation and Conflict* 27 (4): 349–76.

—— and Ole Wæver, 'Norden in the Cold War realities', in Jan Øberg (ed.), *Nordic Security in the 1990s: Options in the Changing Europe*, London: Pinter: 13–34.

—— 'An alternative scenario: dissolution of Norden', ibid.: 243–54.

—— and Ole Wæver, 'Peace research in the Baltic region: identifying joint projects', in Christian Wellmann (ed.), *Strengthening Peace Research in the Baltic Sea*

Region: Agendas Ideas, Institutes, (PFK-texte Nr. 21), Kiel: Projektverbund Friedenswissemschaften Kiel an der Christian-Albrechts-Universität: 31–57.

—— 'Conversion: context and problematique', in *The Rose–Roth Initiative Seminar on Defence Conversion,* Copenhagen: Folketinget, February.

—— 'Democracy, change and conflict in Eastern Europe', in Jörg Calliess and Bernhard Moltmann (eds), *Aufbruch in eine Neue Weltordnung,* Rehburg-Loccum: Evangelische Akademie Loccum: 255–72.

—— 'Divided nations and divided states', in Jörg Calliess and Bernhard Moltmann (eds), *Weltsystem und Weltpolitik jenseits der Bipolarität II,* Rehburg-Loccum: Evangelische Akademie Loccum: 457–77.

—— 'Divided states and divided nations as a security problem: the case of Yugoslavia', COPRI Working Paper 14/1992.

—— 'FN's rolle' ('The role of the United Nations'), in Rolf C.-Dupont, Søren Eliasen and Keld Jensen (eds), *Krigen mod Irak,* Roskilde University: GeoRuc: 29–44.

—— 'Jugoslavien: Konfliktmønstre og løsningsmuligheder' ('Yugoslavia: conflict patterns and possible solutions'), in Erik André Andersen (ed.), *Jugoslavien i omvandling,* Copenhagen University: Informationskontor om Østeuropa: 3–36.

—— 'Jugoslavien: Låsningar och lösningar' ('Yugoslavia: deadlocks and solutions'), *Internationella Studier* 1: 15–40.

—— *Jugoslaviens sönderspränging* ('The implosion of Yugoslavia'). Lund: Den Transnationella Stiftelsen för Freds-och Framtidsstudier.

—— 'New perspectives on non-offensive defence', in *Peace and Conflict Issues after the Cold War* (UNESCO Studies on Peace and Conflict), Paris: UNESCO: 45–77.

—— 'Nordisk sikkerhed – i går, i dag, i morgen' ('Nordic security – yesterday, today, tomorrow'), *Frit Norden* 203: 8–12.

—— 'Peace research and Eastern Europe: how much need for reappraisal?', in Pierre Allan and Kjell Goldmann (eds), *The End of the Cold War,* second edn, Amsterdam: Kluwer: 147–78.

—— 'Politisk katastrof: Jugoslavien och EG' ('Yugoslavia and EU: a political catastrophe'), *Clarté* 65 (2): 42–53.

—— 'Post-1989 challenges for peace research', in Günther Bächler (ed.), *Perspektiven. Friedens- und Konfliktforschung in Zeiten des Umbruchs,* Zürich: Rüegger: 39–54.

—— 'Problems of conversion', *Peace and the Sciences*: 42–50.

1991

Wiberg, Håkan, Barry Buzan and Ole Wæver, 'Four papers on Norden in a changing Europe', *Arbejdspapirer*/Center for Freds- og Konfliktforskning 7/1991.

——, Björn Hettne, Jyrki Käkönen, Sverre Lodgaard and Peter Wallensteen, *Norden, Europe and the Near Future,* Report No. 3, Oslo: PRIO.

—— 'Bundan minjok wa bundan kukka' ('Divided nations and divided states'), *Pyeonghwa yeonku* (Peace Studies) (Seoul) 1 (1): 129–55.

—— 'Divided nations and divided states, *Arbejdspapirer*/Center for Freds- og Konfliktforskning 11/1991.

—— 'The dynamics of disarmament in the Middle East', *Arbejdspapirer*/Center for Freds- og Konfliktforskning 10/1991.

—— 'Du må ikke kræve mere, end du kan få' (Article on economic sanctions), *Vandkunsten* 5: 11–22.

—— 'Eastern Europe in transition – a chance or a threat to peace?', in Wojciech Kostecki (ed.), *Eastern Europe in transition – a chance or a threat to peace?*, Warsaw: Polish Institute of International Affairs: 7–28.

—— 'Focus on: states and nations as challenges for peace research', *Journal of Peace Research* 28 (4): 337–43.

—— 'Friedensforschung und die Golfkrise: Einige Bemerkungen' ('Peace research and the Gulf Crisis: some remarks'), in Reiner Steinweg *et al.* (eds), *Die Welt im Umbruch. Friedensbericht 1991*, Wien: VWGS-Verlag: 236–55.

—— 'Golfkrigen som gåde' ('The Gulf War as a riddle'), *Dansk Sociologi* 2 (2): 76–81.

—— 'Jugoslaviens brokiga historia' ('The complex history of Yugoslavia'), *Nyheter från Psykologer mot Kärnvapen* 2: 3–9.

—— 'Reflections on major armed conflicts', in Karin Lindgren (ed.), *States in Armed Conflict 1989*, Uppsala: Department of Peace and Conflict Research: 18–27.

—— 'Security and arms control policies of the Nordic countries', *Arbejdspapirer*/Center for Freds- og Konfliktforskning 6/1991.

1990

Wiberg, Håkan, Klaus Benjowski, Bertel Heurlin and Gregor Putensen (eds), *Endzeit für Deutschlands Zweistaatlichkeit – Konsequenzen für Europa* (*The Final Hours of the Two Germanies – Consequences for Europe*), Berlin: Akademie der Wissenschaften der DDR.

——, Nils Petter Gleditsch, Bjørn Møller and Ole Wæver, *Svaner på vildveje? Nordisk sikkerhed mellem supermagtsflåder og europæisk opbrud* (*Swans Astray? Norden between Superpower Navies and European Restructuring*), Copenhagen: Vindrose.

—— and Bjørn Møller, 'Nicht-offensive Verteidigung as Vertrauensbildende Massnahme? Probleme und Konzepte' ('Non-offensive defence as a CBM? Problems and concepts'), in Schweizerische Friedensstiftung (ed.), *Blocküberwindende Vertrauensbildung nach dem europäischen Herbst*, Bern: Swiss Peace Foundation: 39–82.

——, Peter Wallensteen, Sverre Lodgaard and Allan Rosas, *Evaluation of Peace Research in Finland*, Helsinki: VAPK-Publishing (The Publications of the Academy of Finland 2/90).

—— 'Arms races, formal models, and quantitative tests', in Nils Petter Gleditsch and Olav Njølstad (eds), *Arms Races: Technological and Political Dynamics*, London: Sage: 31–57.

—— 'Arms races – why worry?', ibid.: 352–75.

—— 'Can non-offensive defence improve arms reductions?', *Disarmament* 1: 83–100.

—— 'Hotbilder i Norden sedan 1945' ('Threat images in Norden since 1945'), in Nikolaj Petersen and Carin Lindgren (eds), *Trussel eller tillid: Nordiske omverdensbilleder under forandring*, Stockholm: NORDSAM: 97–117.

—— 'Ikke-offensivt forsvar som konfliktløsning og som konfliktobjekt' ('Non-offensive defence as conflict resolution and as an object of conflict'), in Sørensen, Henning (ed.), *Ikke-offensivt Forsvar: En introduktion*, Copenhagen: Samfundslitteratur: 71–85; and (rejoinder to comment by H.C. Bjerg): 88–91.

—— (ed.), *Konfliktteori och fredsforskning* (*Conflict Theory and Peace Research*), second rev. edn, Stockholm: Scandinavian University Books.

—— 'Gidslerne i de magtpolitiske spil' ('Hostages in power political games'), *Forskning og Samfund* 16 (8): 14–19.

—— 'Nonoffensive defense and the Korean Peninsula', in UNIDIR (ed.), *Nonoffensive Defense: A Global Perspective*, New York, NY: Taylor & Francis: 132–42.

1989

Wiberg, Håkan, 'Alternatives to deterrence?', in Radmila Nakarada and Jan Øberg (eds), *Surviving Together: The Olof Palme Lectures on Common Security 1988*, London: Gower: 59–70.

—— (ed.), *Farväl till avskräckningen?* ('Good-bye to deterrence?'), Lund: Lund University Press.

—— 'Inledning: Kaiser Wilhelms misstag' ('Introduction: the mistake of Kaiser Wilhelm'), ibid.: 5–25.

—— 'Avskräckningens grundproblem' ('The basic problems of deterrence'), ibid.: 27–53.

—— 'Tillitsskapande åtgärder, gemensam säkerhet, en ny världsordning: Realism hos alternativ som en fråga om logik och som en fråga om makt' ('Confidence building measures, common security, a New World Order: realism of alternatives as a question of logic and a question of power'), ibid.: 187–209.

—— 'Danmark mellem Norden og Europa' ('Denmark between Norden and Europe'), in Bertel Heurlin and Christian Thune (eds), *Danmark og det internationale system: Festskrift til Ole Karup Pedersen*, København: Politiske Studier: 135–50.

—— 'Epistemologiske aspekter på Hans Mouritzen: Finlandization' ('Epistemological aspects on Hans Mouritzen: Finlandization'), *Politica* 21 (2): 189–96.

—— *Maritime tillidsskabende foranstaltninger* (*Maritime Confidence Building Measures*), Copenhagen: SNU.

—— 'The nukes are ill', in Niels Barfoed, Thomas Bredsdorff, Leif Christensen and Ove Nathan (eds), *The Challenge of an Open World: Essays Dedicated to Niels Bohr*, København: Munksgaard: 157–65.

—— 'Väst och Sovjet' ('The West and USSR'), *Internationella Studier* 2: 27–39.

—— 'Wissenschaftsbegriff der Friedensforschung' ('The concept of science in peace research'), in Wilfried Graf, Ina Horn and Thomas Macho (eds), *Zum Wissenschaftsbegriff der Friedensforschung. Ergebnisse einer Umfrage* (*On the Concepts of Science in Peace Research: Results of a Survey*), Vienna: Verband der Wissenschaftlichen Gesellschaften Österreichs: 350–9.

1988

Wiberg, Håkan, 'Concepts of security: a logical and analytical framework', in Narindar Singh (ed.), *Peace and Development*, New Delhi: Indian Council and Social Science Research: 31–53.

—— 'The peace research movement', in Peter Wallensteen (ed.), *Peace Research: Achievements and Challenges*, Boulder, CO: Westview Press: 30–53.

—— 'What is the use of conflict theory?', ibid.: 105–18.

—— 'Realism of alternatives as a question of logic and as a question of power', *Peace and the Sciences* 4: 1–20.

1987

Wiberg, Håkan, 'Small nations' strategies', in Sakamoto Yoshikazu (ed.), *Strategic Doctrines and their Alternatives*, New York, NY: Gordon & Breach: 199–225 (also *World Futures* 24: 199–224).

—— 'Security of small nations: challenges and defences', *Journal of Peace Research* 24 (4): 339–63.

—— 'Atomvintern och kärnvapenmakternas strategier' ('Nuclear winter and the strategies of nuclear powers'), in Jan Øberg (ed.), *Atomvintern*, Stockholm: Myrdalsstiftelsen: 80–90.

—— 'Violence and war – the state of the art', *Rauhantutkimus* 3: 3–16.

—— 'Koreanska paradoxer'('Korean paradoxes'), *Internationella Studier* 2: 2–7.

1986

Wiberg, Håkan, 'Nuclear weapon free zones as a process – the Nordic case', in Torben Størner *et al.* (eds), *Peace and the Future*, Århus: Aarhus University Press: 191–208.

—— 'The Nordic countries: a special kind of system?', *Current Research on Peace and Violence* 18 (1/2): 2–12.

—— 'Medaljens baksida – en annan bild av Sverige' ('The other side of the coin – a different picture of Sweden'), in Mats Friberg and Johan Galtung (eds), *Alternativen*, Stockholm: Akademilitteratur: 63–82.

—— 'The peace philosophy of Alva Myrdal and Olof Palme' (in Japanese), *Heiwa no Toride* 4: 1–10.

—— 'Stjärnornas krig – vad handlar det egentligen om?' ('What is Star Wars really about?'), *Internationella Studier* 4: 24–33.

1985

Wiberg, Håkan, 'National security of small states: problems and options', in Anselm Skuhra and Hannes Wimmer (eds), *Friedensforschung und Friedensbewegung*, Wien: VWGÖ: 63–90.

—— 'Bortom avskräckningen: vägar och hinder' ('Beyond deterrence: roads and obstacles'), in *Fred, konflikt och samhällsutvecklingen*, Linköping: Stifts- och landsbiblioteket: 30–50.

—— *Balance of Power and Nuclear Deterrence.* Report to the Swedish Ministry of International Affairs.

—— *Confidence-Building Measures.* Report to the Swedish Ministry of International Affairs.

1984

Wiberg, Håkan, 'Överlever Storebror 1984?' ('Will Big Brother survive 1984?'), in *Tankar kring NITTONHUNDRAÅTTIOFYRA*, Lund: Kursverksamhetens förlag: 78–89.

—— 'The Peace research movement', in Gernot Heiss and Heinrich Lutz (eds), *Friedensbewegungen: Bedingungen und Wirkungen*, Wiener Beiträge zur Geschichte der Neuzeit: Band 11: 165–85.

—— 'The development of peace research in the universities of the Europe region', *Higher Education in Europe* 9 (2): 15–25.

—— 'Review of Miriam Spielmann: *If peace comes. . .*', *Current Research on Peace and Violence* 17: 188–91.

1983

Wiberg, Håkan, Margareta Bertilsson, Kristian Gerner and Andrzej Kutylowski (eds), *Konflikt och Solidaritet i Polen* (*Conflict and Solidarity in Poland*), Stockholm: Prisma.

—— 'Inledning', ibid.: 9–34.

—— 'The other side of the coin: dialogues on development', *Scandinavian Journal of Development Alternatives* 2 (2): 64–87.

—— 'Terrorbalansen och det offensiva försvaret' ('Balance of terror and offensive defence'), in Jan Øberg (ed.), *Försvar för en kärnvapenfri värld*, Stockholm: Wahlström & Widstrand: 21–33.

—— 'Nuclear weapon free zones as a process: the Nordic case', in Kari Möttölä (ed.), *Nuclear Weapons and Northern Europe*, Helsinki: The Finnish Institute of International Affairs: 14–24.

—— 'Measuring military expenditures: purposes, measures, sources', *Cooperation and Conflict* 8 (3): 161–77.

—— with Jeanne Naur and Michele Naur, *Forhandlinger og frygt* (*Negotiations and Fear*), Copenhagen: Samtid.

—— and Felisa Tibbitts, 'On the relevance of theories of aggression for the study of Macro Conflicts', in Hylke Tromp (ed.), *Course on Political Violence*, Groningen: Rijksuniversiteit, Polemologisch instituut.

1982

Wiberg, Håkan, *Krig, rustningar, säkerhetspolitik* (*War, Armaments, Security Policy*), Lund: Zenit.

—— 'Social scientists and men of practice: the case of confidence-building', *Current Research on Peace and Violence* 14: 176–87.

—— 'Conflicts in the Middle East – the Lund seminar', *International Peace Research Newsletter* 20 (1): 29–34.

—— 'Review essay on Rudolph J. Rummel: *Understanding conflict and war*, vols. 1–5', *Journal of Peace Research* 9 (4): 369–86.

—— and Andrzej Kutylowski (eds), *Journal of Peace Research* 19 (2) (Special issue on Poland): 97–203.

—— 'Self-determination as an international issue', in Ioan M. Lewis (ed.), *Nationalism and Self Determination in the Horn of Africa*, London: Ithaca Press: 43–65.

—— *Konfliktinteoriat ja rauhantutkimus* (*Theories of Conflict and Peace Research*), Helsinki: Tammi.

—— 'Vad skall vi med sociologi till?' ('What's the use of sociology?'), in Bodil Jönsson (ed.), *Erövra högskolan*, Stockholm: Tidens förlag: 170–94.

—— 'Ett israeliskt dilemma: har PLO stärkts eller krossats? (An Israeli dilemma: was PLO strengthened or crushed?)', *Internationella studier* 5: 3–7.

1981

Wiberg, Håkan (ed.), *Journal of Peace Research* 18 (2) (Special issue on peace): 109–220.

—— 'JPR 1964–80 – What have we learnt about peace?', ibid.: 111–48.

—— 'Detente in Europe?', in Egbert Jahn and Yoshikazu Sakamoto (eds), *Elements of World Instability: Armaments, Communication, Food, International Division of Labour*, Frankfurt: Campus: 303–12.

—— and Pierre Deleu, 'Peace action, peace education and peace research: some reflections', in W. Branders (ed.), *Vredesopvoeding, een probleem?*, Antwerp: Instituut voor conflictstudie: 10–27.

—— 'Forskning, underrättelse och rätt' ('Research, intelligence and law), in *Dommen over Gleditsch og Wilkes. Fire kritiske innlegg*, Oslo: PRIO (P-28/81): 39–56.

—— 'Review essay on Mary Kaldor: *The Disintegrating West*', *Journal of Peace Research* 8 (4): 363–8.

—— 'Dilemmas of disarmament education', in Magnus Haavelsrud (ed.), *Approaching Disarmament Education*, Guildford: Westbury House: 129–44.

1980

Wiberg, Håkan, Nils Petter Gleditsch, Odvar Leine, Hans Henrik Holm, Tord Høivik, Arne Martin Klausen and Erik Rudeng, *Johan Galtung: A Bibliography of his Scholarly and Popular Writings, 1951–80*, Oslo: PRIO.

—— and Wilhelm Agrell, *Säkerhet och nedrustning* (*Security and Disarmament*), special issue of *Försvar i nutid* (4–5).

—— Wiberg, Håkan (ed.), 'Building confidence in Europe. An analytical and action-oriented study', *Bulletin of Peace Proposals* 1 (2): 150–66 (also in Finnish, French, German).

—— 'Disarmament education: issues and perspectives', *Bulletin of Peace Proposals* 71 (3): 221–8.

—— 'Justification of social science', in Hans-Henrik Holm and Erik Rudeng (eds), *Social Science – For What? Festschrift for Johan Galtung*, Oslo: Universitetsforlaget: 116–21.

—— 'Kapplöpningen mellan upprustning och nedrustning' ('The race between armament and disarmament'), in Ulrich Herz (ed.), *Nedrustning under debatt, 1978–82*, Stockholm: Arbetsgruppen för svensk folkriksdag för nedrustning: 287–304.

—— 'Ändrade regler för supermakternas spel?' ('Changed rules for the superpower games?'), *TIDEN* 1980: 99–107.

—— 'Waroom bewapent een natie zich' ('Why do nations arm?'), Antwerp: Europees Studie en Informatiecentrum.

1979

Wiberg, Håkan (ed.), *Dragkampen på Afrikas Horn* (*Competing Forces in the Horn of Africa*), Uppsala: Scandinavian Institute for African Studies.

—— 'Introduktion', ibid.: 9–18.

—— 'Världsbilder och säkerhetspolitik' ('World images and security policy'), in *Elva åsikter om svensk säkerhetspolitik*, Stockholm: Folk och Försvar: 180–218.

—— 'Europas framtid och den svenska neutraliteten' ('The future of Europe and Swedish neutrality'), in *Rusta för fred – rädda livet*, Stockholm: Gidlunds: 119–40.

—— 'Konfliktlösning och fredsforskning' ('Conflict resolution and peace research'), in *Rapport fra 21. Nordisk Forskerseminar på Lillehammer*, Oslo: Nordisk samarbejdsråd for kriminologi: 69–89.

—— 'Detente in Europe', *Current Research on Peace and Violence* 11: 104–13.

—— 'Focus on: the horn of Africa', *Journal of Peace Research* 16 (3): 189–96.

—— and Jan Øberg, 'Rustningar, ekonomi, militarism' ('Armaments, economy, militarism'), *Bokcaféts månadsbulletin* 40: 4–12.

1978

Wiberg, Håkan, *Neutronbomben* (*The Neutron Bomb*), Copenhagen: Samarbejdskomiten for fred og sikkerhed.

—— 'Swedish national security: a review and a critique', *Bulletin of Peace Proposals* 9 (4): 308–16.

—— and Jan Øberg, 'Totalförsvar – långt mer än militär' ('Total defence – far more than the military'), in Bo Wirmark (ed.), *Fredens spiral*, Stockholm: Gummessons: 90–111.

—— and Pierre Deleu, 'A rejoinder to Gernot Köhler: structure-dynamic arms control', *Journal of Peace Research* 5 (4): 345–9.

—— 'A significance test for matching', in Gunnar Windahl (ed.), *Experimental Research in Psychoanalysis*, Lund: AV-Centralen: 135–7.

—— 'Current trends in peace research', *Rauhaan tutkien* 5/6: 64–6.

—— and Carl-Einar Stålvant (eds), *Armament, Tensions and War*. Stockholm: NORDSAM.

1977

Wiberg, Håkan, *Visions of the Future: A Cross-National Survey*, Lund: Lund University, Department of Sociology.

—— 'Images of the world in the year 2000', in Alexander Szalai and Riccardo Petrella (eds), *Cross-National Survey Research: Theory and Practice*, Oxford: Pergamon Press: 279–343.

—— 'The conditions of non-violent action', in Gustaaf Geeraerts (ed.), *Possibilities of Civilian Defence in Western Europe*: 103–20.

—— 'How is it possible to evaluate propositions about the future?', in Stephan Schwarz (ed.), *Knowledge and Concepts in Futures Studies*, Boulder, CO: Westview: 121–61.

—— 'Säkerhetspolitiken i framtiden' ('Security politics in the future'), *TIDEN* 1976 (8): 495–505.

242   *Selected bibliography*

1976

Wiberg, Håkan, *Konfliktteori och fredsforskning* ('Conflict theory and peace research'), Stockholm: Scandinavian University Books.

——, Helmut Ornauer, Andrzej Sicinski and Johan Galtung (eds), *Images of the World in the Year 2000: A Comparative Ten Nation Study*, The Hague: Mouton.

—'Replication on a youth group: the students', ibid.: 185–216.

—— with Aleksander Lutyk, Dorota Mycielska and Andrej Siciński, 'Age groups and the future', ibid.: 279–316.

——, Johan Galtung and Helmut Ornauer, 'The future: forgotten, and to be discovered', ibid.: 561–85.

—— and Helmut Ornauer, 'History and organisation of the year 2000 project', ibid.: 589–600.

—— 'Do we get disarmament by negotiations?', *Peace and the Sciences:* 139–47. (Also in German.)

—— and Jan Øberg, 'Kapprustningar och rustningsdynamik' ('Arms races and armament dynamics'), *Internationella Studier* 1: 18–29.

1975

Wiberg, Håkan, 'Dependence and global inequalities', in *Theories of Dependence and Dominance Structures*, vol. 2, Oslo: PRIO: 158–75.

—— 'The prospects of peace', in *Proceedings of the International Peace Research Association Fifth Conference*, Oslo: IPRA: 19–41.

1974

Wiberg, Håkan, 'Are urban guerillas possible?', in Johan Niezing (ed.), *Urban Guerilla*, Rotterdam: Rotterdam University Press: 11–21.

—— 'Peace research and peace education: a pessimistic note', in Christoph Wulf (ed.), *Handbook on Peace Education*, Oslo: IPRA: 137–49.

1972

Wiberg, Håkan and Lars Dencik, 'Strategic thinking as a function of social attitudes', in Bengt Höglund and Jørgen Wilian Ulrich (eds), *Conflict Control and Conflict Resolution*, Copenhagen: Munksgaard: 39–71.

—— *Examinationsformer och studieresultat* (Examination forms and study achievements), Lund: Lunds Universitet, Pedagogiska Utvecklingsenheten, Report no. 5.

—— 'Rational and Non-Rational Models of Man', in Joachim Israel and Henri Tajfel (eds), *The Context of Social Psychology*, London: Academic Press: 297–369.

1969

Wiberg, Håkan, 'On the relationships between science and values', in Lars Dencik (ed.), *Scientific Research and Politics*, Lund: Studentlitteratur: 25–36.

1968

Wiberg, Håkan, 'Some comments on the meaning and functions of game theory', *Cooperation and Conflict* 3 (4): 247–53.

—— 'Social position and peace philosophy', *Journal of Peace Research* 5 (3): 277–91.

—— 'Recent trends in the theory of race conflict', in *Proceedings from the International Peace Research Association Second Conference*, vol. 2, Assen: van Gorcum: 205–23.

—— 'Descartes som matematiker' ('Descartes as mathematician'), in Rolf Lindborg, *René Descartes*, Stockholm: Natur och kultur: 76–86.

—— 'Notes on the efficiency of economic sanctions', in Peter Wallensteen (ed.), *International Sanctions: Theory and Practice*, Uppsala: Avdelningen för fredsforskning: 13–50.

—— *Sociologiska aspekter på freds- och konfliktforskning* ('Sociological aspects of peace and conflict research'), Report to '1967 års kommitté för internationell politik'.

—— (ed.), *Proceedings from the Third Nordic Conference on Peace Research*, Lund: Avdelningen för freds- och konfliktforskning.

1967

Wiberg, Håkan and Lars Dencik, 'Strategic thinking as a function of social attitudes', in George Fisk (ed.), *The Psychology of Management Decision*, Lund: Gleerups: 209–30.

1966

Wiberg, Håkan, *Inledning till spelteorin* ('Introduction to game theory'), Lund: Studietexter och kompendier utgivna av filosofiska institutionen, no. 22.

Index

eBooks – at www.eBookstore.tandf.co.uk

A library at your fingertips!

eBooks are electronic versions of printed books. You can store them on your PC/laptop or browse them online.

They have advantages for anyone needing rapid access to a wide variety of published, copyright information.

eBooks can help your research by enabling you to bookmark chapters, annotate text and use instant searches to find specific words or phrases. Several eBook files would fit on even a small laptop or PDA.

NEW: Save money by eSubscribing: cheap, online access to any eBook for as long as you need it.

Annual subscription packages

We now offer special low-cost bulk subscriptions to packages of eBooks in certain subject areas. These are available to libraries or to individuals.

For more information please contact webmaster.ebooks@tandf.co.uk

We're continually developing the eBook concept, so keep up to date by visiting the website.

www.eBookstore.tandf.co.uk